The business of time

Manchester University Press

general editors
ELIZABETH CURRIE,
SALLY-ANNE HUXTABLE
AND JAMES RYAN

founding editor
PAUL GREENHALGH

To buy or to find out more about the books currently available in this series, please go to: https://manchesteruniversitypress.co.uk/series/studies-in-design-and-material-culture/

The business of time

A global history of the watch industry

Pierre-Yves Donzé

Manchester University Press

Copyright © Pierre-Yves Donzé 2022

The right of Pierre-Yves Donzé to be identified as the author of this work has been asserted by him in accordance with the Copyright, Designs and Patents Act 1988.

Published by Manchester University Press
Oxford Road, Manchester M13 9PL

www.manchesteruniversitypress.co.uk

This book was originally published as *Des nations, des firmes et des montres: Histoire globale de l'industrie horlogère de 1850 à nos jours* (Neuchâtel: Editions Alphil, 2020)

British Library Cataloguing-in-Publication Data
A catalogue record for this book is available from the British Library

ISBN 978 1 5261 6257 1 hardback
ISBN 978 1 5261 7625 7 paperback

First published 2022

The publisher has no responsibility for the persistence or accuracy of URLs for any external or third-party internet websites referred to in this book, and does not guarantee that any content on such websites is, or will remain, accurate or appropriate.

Typeset
by R. J. Footring Ltd, Derby, UK

Contents

List of figures	vi
List of tables	ix
List of boxes	x
Acknowledgements	xi
List of abbreviations	xiii

	Introduction	1
1	The situation in the mid-nineteenth century	8
2	Responding to the American challenge, 1870–1890	26
3	The first phase of technological and industrial diffusion, 1890–1914	47
4	The transformation of the watch industry, 1914–1945	65
5	The first wave of foreign direct investment, 1945–1970	87
6	The impact of electronics, 1970–1985	118
7	Reorganisation of global value chains after 1985	138
8	Epilogue: the world watch industry in 2017	168
	Conclusion	176

Appendix. Estimates of world watch production	180
Bibliography	183
Index	194

Figures

1.1 Silver watch made by George Graham, watchmaker in London, circa 1695–1750. © Metropolitan Museum of Art, CC0, via Wikimedia Commons — 11

1.2 Fritz Zuber-Bühler, *The watchmaker and his family*, second half of the nineteenth century. © Musée International d'Horlogerie, La Chaux-de-Fonds — 13

1.3 A Swiss pocket watch, 1863. © Compagnie des Montres Longines, Francillon SA — 14

1.4 'The Proletarian Watch', Georges-Frédéric Roskopf, La Chaux-de-Fonds, 1867. © Musée International d'Horlogerie, La Chaux-de-Fonds — 15

1.5 Silver watch with two movements, Sylvain Mairet, Le Locle, circa 1860. © Musée International d'Horlogerie, La Chaux-de-Fonds — 17

1.6 Works of the American Watch Company, between 1859 and 1872. Hatch & Co. Public domain, via Wikimedia Commons — 20

2.1 Imports and exports of watches by the United States, 1870–1890 — 29

2.2 Centennial Exhibition, Philadelphia, Machinery Hall, 1876. Centennial Photographic Co. Public domain, via Wikimedia Commons — 30

2.3 La Chaux-de-Fonds, 1870–1890. © Bibliothèque de la Ville de La Chaux-de-Fonds, Audiovisual department, photograph by Albert Schönbucher — 32

2.4 Complication watch, known as 'La Merveilleuse', Ami LeCoultre Piguet, Le Brassus, circa 1878. © Musée International d'Horlogerie, La Chaux-de-Fonds — 33

2.5 Advertisement for Omega, 1913. *Indicateur Davoine*, La Chaux-de-Fonds, 1913, p. 469 — 37

2.6 The factory of the watch manufacturer Bloch-Geismar, Besançon, undated (early twentieth century). Unknown photographer. Public domain, via Wikimedia Commons — 41

3.1 Workers leaving the Longines factory, Saint-Imier, Switzerland, 1911. © Compagnie des Montres Longines, Francillon SA — 49

3.2 The Tavannes Watch factory, circa 1920. © Mémoires d'Ici, Centre de recherche et de documentation du Jura bernois, Collection Rémy Prêtre — 51

3.3 Advertisement for Hamilton Watch, 1920. Internet Archive Book Images, via Wikimedia Commons — 54

3.4	US imports of French and German watches and watch movements, 1890–1914	56
3.5	Japy Frères works, Beaucourt, circa 1910. Unknown photographer, via Wikimedia Commons	57
3.6	Pocket-watch workshop, Gebrüder Junghans, 1925. Unknown photographer, via Wikimedia Commons	59
3.7	Workers leaving Hattori main factory, 1937. © The Seiko Museum Ginza, Tokyo	60
3.8	Registration of the brand Citizen by Rodolphe Schmid in Switzerland, 1918. *Archives de l'horlogerie*, Berne	61
4.1	Swiss wristwatch exports, 1920–1940	68
4.2	Catalogue of the Swiss watch company Numa Jeanin, 1931. Photograph by the author	68
4.3	Advertisement for the manufacturer of watch movements O. Kessler SA, Grenchen, Switzerland, 1928. *La Fédération horlogère Suisse*, 12 December 1928	70
4.4	Organisation of the Swiss watchmaking cartel, 1934	73
4.5	French exports and imports of complete watches, 1920–1937	74
4.6	Advertisement for Montres Lip, 1918. *L'Illustration*, 12 January 1918	75
4.7	Woman working on a drilling machine at Hamilton Watch, circa 1936–1937. National Archives and Records Administration, via Wikimedia Commons	78
4.8	Exports and imports of watches and watch movements by the United States, 1914–1940	79
4.9	Seikosha, watch assembly workshop, circa 1930. © The Seiko Museum Ginza, Tokyo	81
5.1	Advertisement for Movado, 1951. *Europa Star: Asia*, 1951, vol. 6, p. 182. © Archives Europa Star	90
5.2	Advertisement for Ernest Borel, 1953. *Europa Star: Asia*, 1953, vol. 15, p. 13. © Archives Europa Star	93
5.3	Advertisement for Timex, 1956. *Europa Star: Asia*, 1956, vol. 38, p. 99. © Archives Europa Star	96
5.4	Kelton–Timex employee numbers and production volume, 1960–1981	98
5.5	Acquisition of Durowe by Ebauches SA, 1968. *Europa Star: Asia*, 1968, vol. 104, p. 38. © Archives Europa Star	100
5.6	Dial fitting work through a conveyor belt system at Seiko, circa 1960. © The Seiko Museum Ginza, Tokyo	103
5.7	Advertisement for Rolex in Hong Kong, 1951. *Europa Star: Asia*, 1951, vol. 5, p. 40. © Archives Europa Star	105
5.8	Watch and clock production in the Soviet Union and Russia, 1945–2008	110
5.9	Chinese watch production volume, 1957–1981	112
6.1	Clock and watch production in the United States, Switzerland, and Japan, 1960–1990	120

6.2	Advertisement for Seiko, 1977. © The Seiko Museum Ginza, Tokyo	123
6.3	Demonstration in support of the strikers occupying the Bulova factory, 1976, Neuchâtel. © Bibliothèque de la Ville de La Chaux-de-Fonds, Audiovisual department	126
6.4	Roskopf watches in the catalogue of Bader-Hafner, Switzerland, circa 1940. © Musée International d'Horlogerie, La Chaux-de-Fonds	127
6.5	Swiss exports of Roskopf watches, volume and share of total exports, 1945–2000	128
6.6	Digital watch developed by Texas Instruments, Ébauches and Longines, 1972. © Compagnie des Montres Longines, Francillon SA	131
6.7	The French watch market, 1970–1979	133
6.8	Charles Piaget, leader of the Lip workers, speaking in Besançon, August 1973. © Bibliothèque Municipale de Besançon, Photographie de L'Est Républicain (Bernard Faille), PH 49341	134
7.1	Value of watch exports by Switzerland, Japan, and Hong Kong, 1970–2010	140
7.2	Number of companies and employees in the Swiss watch industry, 1970–2013	142
7.3	Proportion of Swiss watches fitted with foreign cases, five-year average, 1950–2014	143
7.4	Nicolas G. Hayek, 1994. *Europa Star*, 1994, vol. 208, p. 55. © Archives Europa Star	144
7.5	Value of Swiss exports of non-metallic watches, 1980–2009	146
7.6	The Swatch summer collection, 1986. *Europa Star*, 1986, vol. 158, p. 124. © Archives Europa Star	147
7.7	Advertisement for Omega, 1999. *Europa Star*, 1999, vol. 234, p. 25. © Archives Europa Star	150
7.8	Global production of Japanese watch companies and proportion of production outside Japan, 1995–2010	153
7.9	Shipments of Japanese mechanical watches in Japan, 1992–2010	154
7.10	Advertisement for Seiko, 2019. © The Seiko Museum Ginza, Tokyo	155
7.11	Composition of Hong Kong's watch exports, 1960–2010	157
7.12	Fossil's turnover and share of foreign sales, 1987–2018	161
7.13	Titan workshop, 1996: design department and tool room. *Europa Star*, 1996, vol. 218, p. 4. © Archives Europa Star	164
8.1	ETA (Thailand) factory in Bangkok, December 2020. © Google Street View	171
8.2	Advertisement for Rolex, 2021	173
8.3	Apple Watch. © Apple	174
C.4	Advertisement for Audemars Piguet, 2015. © Audemars Piguet	179

Tables

1.1	Volume of world watch production, 1790 and 1870	9
2.1	World watch production, 1870 and 1890	27
2.2	The 10 main markets of the Swiss watch industry, 1890	38
3.1	World watch production, 1890 and 1914	48
3.2	The 10 main markets of the Swiss watch industry, 1920	50
4.1	World watch production, 1914 and 1937	66
4.2	The 10 main markets of the Swiss watch industry, 1938	67
4.3	Watch companies in Besançon employing more than 20 people, 1930	76
4.4	The six largest German watch companies, 1927	76
5.1	World watch production, 1937–1970	88
5.2	Main world watch companies in 1970	88
5.3	Main concentrations in the Swiss watch industry, 1971	91
5.4	The 10 main markets of the Swiss watch industry, 1970	94
5.5	The largest watch companies in West Germany, 1970	101
5.6	Hong Kong watch industry, 1960–1990	106
5.7	Watch exports from Hong Kong, Japan, and Switzerland, 1960–2010	108
6.1	World watch production, 1970 and 1984	119
6.2	Hong Kong watch companies with foreign capital, 1974–1978	124
7.1	Swiss watch exports, 1980–2010	148
7.2	Main outlets for Chinese exports of complete watches, 2000 and 2015	158
8.1	Top 10 exporters of complete watches in terms of value, 2017	169
8.2	Top 10 exporters of watch cases in terms of value, 2017	170
8.3	Top 10 exporters of movement components in terms of value, 2017	170
8.4	The 25 largest watch companies in the world, 2017	172

Boxes

2.1 Extract from the catalogue for the Centennial Exhibition, Philadelphia, Machinery Hall, 1876 — 30

2.2 The Omega calibre according to Frédéric Bessire, head of Louis Brandt & Frère's exports, 1896 — 37

3.1 Waltham and Elgin manufacturers attempt to limit Hamilton Watch expansion: letter from American Watch to Ball & Co. (1904) — 55

Acknowledgements

This book is the result of some 15 years of research devoted to the Swiss and world watch industry. It is the English version of a work originally published in French in 2020 by Editions Alphil, in Neuchâtel (Switzerland), under the title *Des nations, des firmes et des montres: histoire globale de l'industrie horlogère de 1850 à nos jours*. My interests and questions have evolved over the course of my academic career and have fed my reflections on the history of the watch industry. Readings, meetings, debates, and work on other subjects of business history (mainly in the fields of medical technology and the luxury and fashion industry) have enabled me to renew my perspectives on watchmaking. It is not possible to mention here all the people who have supported me and the institutions that have welcomed me over these years. However, I would like to express my sincere thanks to the International Museum of Horology in La Chaux-de-Fonds and the Federation of the Swiss Watch Industry in Biel, which have always responded favourably to my requests and thus greatly facilitated the progress of my work. A friendly thank you also to the Seiko Museum, in Tokyo, for its availability. In addition, the many colleagues and friends with whom I have had the pleasure of exchanging information and debating issues during these years have contributed to my intellectual development and made me aware of the importance of approaching the history of watchmaking from a global perspective. I warmly thank Jean-Philippe Arm, Johann Boillat, Bram Bouwens, Alain Cortat, Olivier Crevoisier, Thomas David, Estelle Fallet, Patrick Fridenson, Rika Fujioka, Stéphanie Ginalski, Valère Gogniat, Sachio Imakubo, Hugues Jeannerat, Joël Jornod, Walter von Känel, Matthias Kipping, Christophe Koller, Takafumi Kurosawa, Stéphanie Lachat, Patrick Linder, Laurence Marti, Hervé Munz, Hélène Pasquier, Jean-Michel Piguet, Sabine Pitteloud, Véronique Pouillard, Minoru Sawai, Thierry Theurillat, Laurent Tissot, Ilan Vardi, Béatrice Veyrassat, and Ben Wubs.

Academic research has led me to publish numerous articles on specific topics in international academic journals. The material of these works is brought together in this book, which offers a general analysis of the evolution and transformation of the world watch industry from the mid-nineteenth century to the present day, intended for a wide audience. It is not an encyclopaedia of all the 'great watchmakers' and 'major brands' that have been active in watchmaking from its origins to the present day, but a narrative explaining the global changes in watch production and distribution. Instead of an exhaustive treatise, I preferred the clarity of the narrative. I would like to thank very sincerely my friend Alain Cortat, CEO of Editions Alphil, for his critical reading of a first version of the manuscript and his many suggestions. However, the author remains solely responsible for any factual errors and interpretations proposed in the following pages.

Finally, I would like to express a special thought for Hiroko and my daughters Yuki and Natsu, who give me every day the love and energy necessary to carry out so many projects.

Osaka, August 2021

Abbreviations

AFHS   Archives of the Federation of the Swiss Watch Industry
AG   Aktiengesellschaft (public limited company)
ASUAG   Allgemeine Schweizerische Uhrenindustrie Aktiengesellschaft (General Swiss Watch Industry Co. Ltd), also known as the Société Générale de l'Industrie Horlogère Suisse
BFG   Baumgartner Frères Granges
DFEP   Département Fédéral de l'Economie Publique (Federal Department of Public Economy)
EEC   European Economic Community
FH   Swiss Federation of Watch Manufacturers' Associations
GWC   General Watch Co.
HMT   Hindustan Machine Tools
IWC   International Watch Company
JETRO   Japan External Trade Organization
LMH   Les Manufactures Horlogères
MIH   Musée International d'Horlogerie
R&D   research and development
SA   Société Anonyme (public limited company)
SGT   Société des Garde-Temps
SII   Seiko Instruments Inc.
SIIJ   Société Intercantonale des Industries du Jura
SMEs   small and medium-sized enterprises
SMH   Société Suisse de Microélectronique et d'Horlogerie
SSIH   Société Suisse pour l'Industrie Horlogère SA
UBAH   Union des Branches Annexes de l'Horlogerie

Introduction

The starting point of this book is the fact that, today, the *Swiss* watch industry does not exist – or, put more precisely, it no longer exists. Certainly, there are many watch companies established on Swiss territory and Switzerland is the main producer of watches (in value). However, at the beginning of the twentieth century, a national character for this business is difficult to discern.

First of all, the nationality of the companies should be discussed, since companies are the basic units of industries. The composition of the shareholding makes it possible to distinguish various models, including companies controlled by Swiss capital and headquartered in Switzerland (such as Swatch Group and Rolex), companies with foreign capital and headquarters but which control Swiss watch manufacturers (LVMH or Citizen, for example), and companies established in Switzerland and controlled by foreign capital (Richemont) – clearly, a long way from a homogeneous national industry. Moreover, all these companies, regardless of their ownership structure, are integrated into production systems organised on a global scale. Some of them have subsidiaries in Europe and Asia for the manufacture of components. Others are supplied by independent subcontractors, mostly based in China and Thailand. Under these conditions, it is difficult to define exactly the *Swiss* character of the watch industry present in Switzerland.

This preliminary remark does not apply exclusively to Switzerland. A similar observation can be made today for other countries with watch industries, particularly Japan, Germany, and China. Watchmaking is now a globally organised industry, although some activities are concentrated in particular territories, such as Switzerland for luxury watches or China for other watches.

However, until the middle of the twentieth century, the nation was the scale on which various watch industries were organised and competed on world markets. The Swiss watch industry was made up of companies with their headquarters in Switzerland, controlled by Swiss capital, and producing all their components in Switzerland. The model was similar in Germany, France, Japan, the Soviet Union, and, to some extent, the United States. Global competition was based on companies deeply rooted in national territories, sometimes supported and protected by states. This led to situations in which the Swiss watch industry was competing, for example, with American watchmaking (particularly in the last third of the nineteenth century) or Japanese watchmaking (in the 1960s through to the 1980s).

The globalisation of watch companies during the second half of the twentieth century thus appears to be a fundamental paradigm shift. From then on, globalised firms, whose territorial anchorage was much weaker, competed on world markets. This transformation can be observed in most industries. In the automobile industry, for example, General Motors (GM), Toyota, and Volkswagen, which dominate this industry, are all largely globalised firms, although they were initially organised in national territories (GM in the United States at the beginning of the twentieth century, Toyota in Japan in the early 1930s, and Volkswagen in Germany in 1937). Each industry, however, has its own dynamics. Swiss chocolate manufacturers relocated their factories abroad in the interwar years (1919–1938), and Lindt & Sprüngli now has production centres in five European countries and the United States. Why and under what conditions has this transformation in the global watch industry taken place? These are the questions this book aims to answer.

The notion of competition in the global economy has given rise to countless studies and publications since the end of the eighteenth century in the fields of economics, history, and management. Authors from classical economics are primarily interested in the specificities of firms to explain their competitiveness and development on a global scale. In a free market regulated by supply and demand, companies must adopt innovative models to deliver goods and services under better conditions than their competitors. In this context, the competitiveness of firms has given rise to two main types of theories. First, some researchers, such as Michael Porter, argue that it is the position and strategy of firms that allow them to develop.[1] Among business historians, Alfred D. Chandler has shown that large American companies have grown strongly because their internal organisation is based on their strategic objective.[2] In watchmaking, Swatch Group has established itself as the world's largest watch manufacturer because Nicolas Hayek had a well-defined strategy when he founded the company (to rationalise production and the brand portfolio). Second, other management researchers claim that it is, rather, the specific resources of companies that make their competitiveness possible.[3] This approach focuses notably on Japanese companies in the 1970s and 1980s, whose success on the world market was based on their ability to implement innovative production systems through the internalisation of know-how and technology.[4] This type of research can thus explain the success of Swiss watch companies since the 1990s by their access to a specific resource: the luxury watch made in Switzerland.

However, the laws of the free market are insufficient to explain the rise, transformation, and global expansion of firms on their own. In some situations, firms resort to the support of the state in which they are established, and the protected national market offers opportunities for growth.[5] This approach does not stem from classical economics but, rather, from the German historical school, in the tradition inaugurated by Friedrich List and Alexander Hamilton.

As Alexander Gerschenkron demonstrated, late industrialising countries such as Germany or Japan needed protectionist state intervention to support the growth of their companies during the early industrialisation phase.[6] Industrial policies, particularly in Japan and other Asian countries, emphasised the crucial role of the state in the development of competitive industries.[7] In the case of the global watch industry, states have been key players, with customs protectionism having ensured the growth of watch production in France, the United States, and Japan, while the governments of the Soviet Union, China, and India have intervened through state-owned enterprises to establish a watch industry on their soil. Switzerland itself saw the federal authorities regulate the industry from the 1930s to the 1960s. However, the ability of states to support the development of their companies was fundamentally challenged in the 1980s and 1990s, in the context of neo-liberal policies introduced notably under pressure from international financial organisations such as the International Monetary Fund (IMF) and the World Bank (the so-called Washington Consensus policy).[8] In conclusion, the literature on industrial policies shows that, in particular situations, companies benefit from state support – it has facilitated their growth, or at least delayed their disappearance. On the other hand, apart from the special case of socialist regimes, the state has not replaced private enterprises.

In order to discuss the conditions under which the globalisation of the world watch industry is taking place, the main characteristics of this sector should be presented. Each industry has its own specificities, in terms of products and organisation, which have a major impact on its evolution and on the conditions of global competition.[9] To understand the context in which the watch sector has developed on a global scale and the causes of the transformation of competitive conditions, it is necessary therefore to identify the characteristics of the industry. This book focuses in particular on four factors that have had a decisive influence on the dynamics of the watch industry.

First, it is about the primacy of the Swiss model. Since the beginning of the nineteenth century, Swiss watchmakers have held a dominant position on the world market, while watch manufacturers in other countries have developed on the basis of their home markets. For the former, who had an extremely limited domestic market, the challenge was to have access to all the countries of the world and to adapt their products to the tastes of local consumers. For the latter, the reduction of foreign competition on the national market was perceived as a favourable factor during the first phase of industrial development. The coexistence of these two development models, and their evolution over time, has had a major impact on the dynamics of world watchmaking.

Second, it is about the nature of the product that has conditioned the globalisation process. Until the 1960s, the watch was a relatively expensive object, but one that was easy to transport. It is a precision instrument, comprising many components, for which the mechanisation of production is a complex process. The cost of labour played an essential role. This is why Swiss watchmaking developed in the Jura mountains, a rural region with a surplus of labour ready to work for low wages. In the United States, high wages led American entrepreneurs in the 1860s and 1870s to invest in production technologies such as machine tools. Japanese companies in the 1960s and 1970s benefited from both modern production technologies and low labour wages, both of which supported their international expansion. Generally speaking, while transport costs were extremely low, the control of labour costs was a major factor in the competitiveness of companies. Watch manufacturers therefore initially concentrated on organising production. The manufacture of watches comprises three main distinct phases: the manufacture of the blanks (the watch movement without the regulating parts, the mainspring, the dial, and the hands), the manufacture of the complete movement, and the final assembly. Each of these stages has been subject to a specific industrialisation process which has strengthened the competitive advantage of the firms that have been able to adopt it: Swiss watch manufacturers who benefited from the industrial production of blanks in the nineteenth century and the first part of the twentieth century; American manufacturers who managed to mass-produce watch movements (1860–1930s); the Japanese watchmaker Seiko, which was the first major company to introduce the gradual automation of assembly, during the 1960s and 1970s. This mastery of the production processes made it possible to relocate certain activities to low-wage countries when production volumes were sufficient – and being able to mass-produce made it possible to globalise an industrialised production system.

Third, it is about changes in watch consumption habits and social uses over time.[10] A luxury object under the *ancien régime* of France, the watch became a necessary instrument for daily life in the context of urbanisation and industrialisation. The globalisation of time-measurement systems between the end of the nineteenth century and the interwar period made the watch a useful object on a global scale. However, at the end of the twentieth century, the multiplication of electronic goods that display time, particularly mobile phones, considerably reduced the usefulness of watches. Watches became essentially fashion accessories. The recent launch of connected watches, notably the Apple Watch, appears in this context as a major innovation, one which once again makes the watch a useful object.

Fourth, and finally, it is about technical change, which is a major factor in industrial dynamics. Improvements in watch precision, the ability to mass-produce simple and inexpensive watches, and the integration of electronic technologies have not only upset the competitiveness of firms but also contributed to their expansion beyond the borders of their domestic market. Over the last two centuries, it is undoubtedly the arrival of quartz technology in the 1970s that has had the most profound impact on the evolution of global competition in watchmaking. This technical breakthrough was rapid and brutal. Between 1975 and 1980, the share of quartz watches in total Japanese watch production rose from 8.5% to 62.5%.

This book is therefore a history of the world watch industry from the early nineteenth century to the present day. Despite the existence of numerous works on watchmaking, only a very small number of authors have so far approached this topic from a truly global perspective.[11] Moreover, they have favoured an approach based on competition between nations. They present the evolution of the world watch industry as a succession of national models, which in turn dominate the world market (British craftsmanship, the Swiss industrial district, American manufacturing, the large Japanese company). The multinational company and the globalisation of production systems are only superficially mentioned. This is no doubt due to the sources used – generally statistics produced by national organisations and publications by other authors who were interested in particular national watch industries. A few consultant and investor studies do adopt a truly global perspective, but only for the last 20 years, and the analysis is not comprehensive.[12]

This book proposes to go beyond this paradigm of succession between national models and to observe the emergence and growth of transnational and global organisations. It has three main features. First, it is organised chronologically, with eight chapters running from the early nineteenth century to the present day. Second, it offers a global panorama of watch production, based as much as possible on original sources. Third, statistical estimates of world watch production are presented in the first table in each of chapters 1–6, the more historical chapters, while chapters 7 and 8 give a more general consideration of production in more recent times. The methodology used to produce these estimates is set out in the appendix.

Providing the reader with statistics regarding world watch production was necessary, if difficult, to identify the major manufacturing countries and the dynamics of national rankings over time. Although Switzerland has dominated the world watch industry since the early nineteenth century, it had been challenged by several other nations. Based on the tables given at the beginning of each chapter, I explore the evolution of watchmaking activity both at the global level and in each of the major countries. I have used as much as possible the recent research published by scholars on the various national cases and companies – including the articles and books I have published over the past 15 years. I have also used archival material to supplement the information, from archives in Switzerland, France, and the United States, as well as newspapers, directories, and other documents published in various countries (France, Germany, India, Japan, Hong Kong, Switzerland, the United States, and the Soviet Union). Thus, a wide range of material has been gathered in order to write a truly global history of watchmaking.

The classical approach to business history followed by this book will no doubt seem old-fashioned in the eyes of historians working in Western universities today. In these institutions, the dominant focus is no longer on industry, technology, and finance, but on gender, culture, and consumer issues. Writing a global history of the watch industry from this perspective would of course be possible, as some historians have done for specific countries or companies.[13] Watchmaking has the image of a male-dominated profession and industry. This is largely true regarding management – although there are always a few exceptions, from Marie Tissot, who ran the family business in Le Locle, Switzerland, from the 1930s to the early 1970s, to Nayla Hayek, chairwoman of Swatch Group, the world's largest watch company, since 2010. However, as far as the workforce is concerned, women played a major role and accounted for about half of the jobs during the first part of the twentieth century in the Swiss watch industry.[14] In the United States and Japan, the industrialisation of watchmaking also relied on female labour. Beyond production, the question of masculinity and femininity would be relevant to discuss issues related to the design, wearing, and consumption of watches. Gender is, for example, an important dimension of the shift from pocket watches to wristwatches, because it was based, among other factors, on the invention of a new market: fashion watches for ladies (see chapter 4, pp. 67–69). Yet to analyse the detailed transformations in the social uses of watch consumption around the world since the early nineteenth century was beyond the scope of this book and would lead to a different narrative.

My objective is to discuss the dynamics of an industry, to understand how it emerged in the world, and to shed light on a specific process of globalisation of production. The British historian David Edgerton has brilliantly argued that Western academics have ceased to be interested in the productive and technological dimensions of historical development and that this happened precisely at the moment when factories physically left their horizons.[15] As if they had disappeared. But even if they have been relocated elsewhere in the world, mainly to Asia, factories – and what constitutes their resources: capital, technology, materials, and labour – remain essential to a proper understanding of the present world. Through the example of the watch industry, this book helps to highlight the contributions and the need for a global business history.

Notes

1 Michael E. Porter, *Competitive Strategy: Techniques for Analyzing Industries and Competitors* (New York: Free Press, 1980).
2 Alfred D. Chandler, *Strategy and Structure: Chapters in the History of the Industrial Enterprise* (Cambridge: MIT Press, 1962).
3 Edith Penrose, *The Theory of the Growth of the Firm* (New York: John Wiley and Sons, 1959).
4 Ikujio Nonada and Hirotaka Takeuchi Nonaka, *The Knowledge-Creating Company: How Japanese Companies Create the Dynamics of Innovation* (Oxford: Oxford University Press, 1995).
5 Mehdi Shafaeddin, *How Did Developed Countries Industrialize? The History of Trade and Industrial Policy: The Cases of Great Britain and the USA* (Geneva: United Nations Conference on Trade and Development, 1998).
6 Alexander Gerschenkron, *Economic Backwardness in Historical Perspective: A Book of Essays* (Cambridge: Belknap Press, 1962).
7 Chalmers Johnson, *MITI and the Japanese Miracle: The Growth of Industrial Policy, 1925–1975* (Stanford: Stanford University Press, 1982).
8 Mario Cimoli, Giovanni Dosi, and Joseph E. Stiglitz, eds, *Industrial Policy and*

Development: The Political Economy of Capabilities Accumulation (New York: Oxford University Press, 2009).

9. Takafumi Kurosawa, 'Industry history: its concepts and methods', in *Industries and Global Competition: A History of Business beyond Borders,* eds Bram Bouwens, Pierre-Yves Donzé and Takafumi Kurosawa (New York: Routledge, 2017), 1–24; Matthias Kipping, Takafumi Kurosawa, and Eleanor Westney, eds, *Oxford Handbook of Industry Dynamics* (New York: Oxford University Press, forthcoming).

10. Vanessa Ogle, *The Global Transformation of Time, 1870–1950* (Cambridge: Harvard University Press, 2015); Alexis McCrossen, *Marking Modern Times: A History of Clocks, Watches, and Other Timekeepers in American Life* (Chicago: University of Chicago Press, 2013).

11. Davis S. Landes, *Revolution in Time: Clocks and the Making of the Modern World* (Cambridge: Belknap Press of Harvard University Press, 2nd edn 2000, 1st edn 1983); Amy K. Glasmeier, *Manufacturing Time: Global Competition in the Watch Industry, 1795–2000* (New York: Guilford Press); Cyril Bouquet, 'Swatch and the global watch industry', in *Cases in the Environment of Business: International Perspectives*, ed. David W. Conklin (Thousand Oaks: Sage Publications, 2006), 50–69.

12. See, for example, Credit Suisse Global Research, *Watch Industry: Prospects and Challenges* (Zurich: Credit Suisse, 2013).

13. See for example Angel Kwolek-Folland, *Incorporating Women: A History of Women and Business in the United States* (New York: Twayne Publishers, 1998).

14. Stéphanie Lachat, *Les pionnières du temps: vies professionnelles et familiales des ouvrières de l'industrie horlogère suisse (1870–1970)* (Neuchâtel: Alphil, 2014).

15. David Edgerton, *The Shock of the Old: Technology and Global History Since 1900* (London: Profile Books, 2006).

1

The situation in the mid-nineteenth century

In 1818, the young Édouard Bovet, a watch merchant from Val-de-Travers (canton of Neuchâtel, Switzerland), arrived in Guangzhou (China) on a ship belonging to the British East India Company. With two of his brothers, he had settled in London three years earlier and set up a watch-trading business. The Bovets sold watches on the English market that they had had made in Switzerland, where a fourth brother had stayed. Their presence in the British capital had given them the opportunity to enter into contact with the powerful trading house Magniac & Co. (which in 1832 became the famous trading company Jardine, Matheson & Co.). The company specialised in trade with China and in 1818 entrusted the sale of watches in China to the Bovet brothers. Édouard worked for some time for the Magniac company, then in 1822 founded a company with his brothers in London and Switzerland. The Bovets adapted the watch to the tastes of the Chinese consumer (engraving of the movement, Chinese characters on the dial, etc.) and business experienced a tremendous boom. Their company exerted a real domination of the watch trade with China until the second half of the nineteenth century. In 1830, Édouard Bovet returned to the Val-de-Travers a hero, accompanied by a Chinese servant and a son born of his relationship with a Chinese woman. The triumph was short-lived, however – he had to go into exile in Besançon (France) the following year after taking part in an attempted republican revolution in his homeland. He continued to produce watches there until his return to Val-de-Travers in 1848, a year before his death.[1]

Édouard Bovet's trajectory is highly representative of the ability of Swiss watch merchants in the first part of the nineteenth century to establish themselves in distant markets, thanks to their commercial dynamism and the adaptability of their products. Dozens of similar examples could be cited for all continents. However, what makes the case of the Bovet brothers interesting is the fact that they were established in London, precisely in the heart of the British Empire, where there were also many watchmaking craftsmen who were characterised by the excellence of their manufacture. However, it was not this London watchmaking elite that seized the opportunities offered by the commercial infrastructure set up within the empire, but Swiss traders, who were distinguished by their flexibility and business acumen. The Bovets embodied the expression of a commercial capitalism that enabled Switzerland to establish itself as the leading watchmaking nation during the first part of the nineteenth century, to the detriment of Britain.

Although there were watchmakers in most European countries and North America in the mid-nineteenth century, watch production was then concentrated mainly in four nations: Switzerland, Britain, France, and the United States. There was, however, no multinational enterprise as such in this industry, and the transnational networks of the watch-merchant families served mainly to distribute watches across national borders, not to establish an international division of labour in manufacturing. Thus, national production figures reflected the realities of the manufacturers at that time.

The 1850s and 1860s belong to the pre-statistical era for which no precise figures on the production and trade of industrial goods exist for all of these countries. However, various reports and surveys provide a rough estimate of the volume of watch manufacture for these four nations around 1790 and around 1870. These estimates are presented in table 1.1.

The evolution of world watch production between 1790 and 1870 calls for three comments. First, the strong growth in the general volume of production should be highlighted. The number of watches produced rose from around 400,000 to around 3 million, a 7.5-fold increase. This increase was the result of both supply factors and demand-related causes. On the supply side, organisational models were varied and responded to conditions in each country, but they made it possible, both in continental Europe and in the United States, to manufacture an ever-increasing volume of watches. As for demand, it was largely stimulated by the rise of modern industrial societies. Factories, railways, schools, and the army are all institutions based on a strict discipline of time.[2]

Second, Britain, which accounted for half of world production at the end of the eighteenth century, faced a collapse of its competitiveness. The level of production did not show a strong decline – about 10% – but the relative position of the country experienced a significant decrease. In 1870, Britain still ranked third in the world, but it was far behind Switzerland and had been overtaken by France.

Table 1.1 Volume of world watch production (approximate number of pieces), 1790 and 1870

Country	1790		1870		1790–1870
	Volume	%	Volume	%	Growth in %
Switzerland	150,000	38	2,100,000	70	1,300
Britain	200,000	50	180,000	6	−10
France	30,000	8	420,000	14	1,300
United States	10,000	3	150,000	5	1,400
Others	10,000	3	60,000	5	500
Total	400,000	100	2,910,000	100	650

Source: See appendix.

Third, this growth was based primarily in Switzerland, which in 1870 produced more than 2 million watches and accounted for 70% of world production. Its market share had almost doubled since 1790 and it had no real competitor nation. France and the United States also showed considerably high growth rates (more than 1,000%), but the starting level was relatively low. Finally, no significant nation had managed to enter the watch industry, with the exception of Germany, the relative share of which was still low.

The dynamics of the watch industry between 1790 and 1870 thus revealed highly contrasting developments throughout the world. These can be explained essentially by distinct organisational models and national specificities.

Britain's relative decline

Britain was the world's leading watchmaking nation in the eighteenth century, a dominance that can be explained by the economic and political importance of this country. London was then one of the largest and richest cities in the West. It represented a major outlet for the producers of manufactured goods such as watches and clocks. This explains the presence of several Swiss watchmakers and merchants in the British capital since the eighteenth century. For example, Moïse DuBois (1699–1774), a textile and clock merchant domiciled in Le Locle, sent two of his sons to settle in London, while a third began making watches. This transnational family network between Switzerland and Britain continued over the following generations and made it possible to sell watches in London.[3]

In addition, London was the capital of an empire that stretched from North America to East Asia. International trade was not liberalised until the beginning of the nineteenth century, and companies with monopolies in certain markets, such as the famous British East India Company for trade with China, were essential intermediaries for Swiss watchmakers.[4] Another consequence of British imperialism was the importance of marine chronometry as a navigational instrument. In 1714, the English authorities thus set up the Board of Longitude, an organisation charged with supporting research to define the longitude of a ship at sea. John Harrison (1693–1776) was one of the beneficiaries for his development of marine chronometers.[5]

This economic and geopolitical context gave rise to a watch industry that experienced a major boom in the second half of the eighteenth century.[6] Production was mainly concentrated in three regions: the city of London, where watchmaking craftsmen organised themselves into a corporation in 1631 called the Clockmakers' Company; Lancashire, north of Liverpool, which had a tradition of metalworking; and the city of Coventry, east of Birmingham. The mode of production was characterised by a division of labour between small, home-based workshops in Lancashire and Coventry, and artisanal work by London watchmakers. A few attempts were made to set up factories in Coventry in the mid-nineteenth century, following the example of Rotherham & Sons, but they did not become competitive industrial enterprises in the long term.

Figure 1.1 Silver watch made by George Graham, watchmaker in London, circa 1695–1750.

Then, during the first two-thirds of the nineteenth century, British watchmaking declined. The volume of production did not itself reveal a state of crisis. It remained stable during this period, amounting to around 200,000 watches per year. But it is in relative terms that the collapse of British domination is expressed: while at the end of the eighteenth century it had accounted for half of world production, by 1870 its share only amounted to around 6%. Britain was thus unable to adapt its watch industry to the new needs of the market, and watchmakers from other countries (mainly Swiss but also American) emerged as new competitors, ultimately imposing themselves on the world market. Why did British watchmakers experience such difficulties?

Alun C. Davies has perfectly highlighted the technological factor and the inability, if not unwillingness, of British watchmakers to adopt modern production technologies at the beginning of the nineteenth century.[7] In London, watchmaking production flourished in the eighteenth century within a corporate framework – that is, an organisation controlled by master watchmakers who pursued artisanal methods to produce unique, high-quality pieces. Liliane Hilaire-Pérez has clearly shown, through the example of the London manufacturers Vulliamy & Son, the continuity of this model of work organisation between the second half of the eighteenth century and the beginning of the nineteenth century. She speaks of 'multi-purpose companies without concentration', which coordinated a vast network of suppliers and subcontractors in order to respond to a multitude of specific requests from a wealthy local clientele.[8]

During the first part of the nineteenth century, more and more imported watches appeared on the British market. The number of Swiss watches alone is estimated to have been 42,000 in 1853 and to have reached around 160,000 by the early 1860s, a volume almost equivalent to domestic production.[9] Low Swiss wages made it possible to produce watch movements cheaply, export them to London, and assemble them there with gold or silver cases bearing the British hallmark. The final product was sold as a cheap English watch.[10] The growth of this market offered business opportunities. A new generation of Swiss watch traders established a long-term presence in England, following the example of the Baume brothers. The Baume brothers had works in Les Bois (now canton of Jura) and had specialised in the manufacture of watches for the English market. In the mid-1840s, they opened a branch in London under the name Baume Bros.[11] This company established itself as one of the major importers of Swiss watches in Britain. American companies also entered England. American Watch Company, from Waltham, opened an office in London in 1874. The aim was not only to gain access to the local market, but also to make this branch office the gateway to the British Empire and the world market. Its sales amounted to more than 50,000 pounds in 1877.[12]

The reaction of British entrepreneurs to this competition was elitist and conservative. During the first third of the nineteenth century, in London, the watchmakers' guild unsuccessfully demanded the adoption of a protectionist policy and rejected the position of the authorities, who advised mechanisation of production in order to increase the volume of output and lower manufacturing costs.[13] The promoters of liberalism ran the country and vehemently opposed any intervention that would go against the sacrosanct free trade values. In 1887, however, they accepted, through the Merchandise Marks Act, the principle that imported foreign products had to indicate their origin in order to inform the British consumer.[14] The first watches with an indication of Swiss origin were products intended for the English market.

As for London's watchmakers, they failed to grasp the importance and opportunity represented by the emergence of a new demand from the middle classes for simple and inexpensive watches. Their objective was to maintain and strengthen their position of excellence on the world market, as they perceived the mechanised production of watches would see the loss of their status as master watchmakers. This technical conservatism is perfectly illustrated by the famous failure of the Swiss watchmaker Pierre Frédéric Ingold, who attempted to introduce mechanised watch production in London in the 1830s and 1840s.[15] Furthermore, in 1858, the London watchmakers set up a new organisation, the British Horological Institute, to defend their interests as craftsmen.

A new world's leading watchmaking nation: Switzerland

The relative decline of Britain in the first two-thirds of the nineteenth century mainly benefited Switzerland, which established itself as the world's leading watchmaking nation. Admittedly, watchmaking in Switzerland was a much older activity, dating back to the seventeenth century, and one that experienced an initial phase of strong expansion in the second half of the eighteenth century.[16] In 1790, Swiss watch production, concentrated in the city of Geneva and in the mountains of the Jura, already represented more than a third of the world market. Swiss watchmakers were thus able to compete with the British. Their competitiveness was essentially based on two factors.

First, the production system enabled them to achieve low manufacturing costs, which gave Swiss watches a price advantage. On the one hand, wages were low. In 1800, the real wages of craftsmen in the city of Zurich were among the lowest in Western Europe – in London they were more than twice as high.[17] The figures are not known for Geneva, but the trend is clearly similar. On the other hand, production in the mountains of the Jura (mainly Vallée de Joux, Le

Figure 1.2 Fritz Zuber-Bühler, *The watchmaker and his family*, second half of the nineteenth century.

Figure 1.3 A Swiss pocket watch, 1863.

Locle, La Chaux-de-Fonds, and Saint-Imier) could be freely organised, as there were no corporations in this region. It took the form of a proto-industrial system characterised by a strong division of labour between numerous homeworkers. In the case of the Swiss watch industry, this mode of production is known as *établissage*, but very similar forms were widespread throughout the world before the Industrial Revolution.[18] The trader, called *établisseur* or *watch manufacturer*, was at the heart of this system, which he coordinated with his capital and his knowledge of markets. He distributed work to the homeworkers, who were legally independent, and then marketed the finished watches. Product inspection, and final assembly in some cases, was carried out in a workshop controlled by the trader (*comptoir*). This production system made it possible to limit production costs because investments were extremely limited – and labour costs very low.

Second, Swiss watch merchants showed an extremely developed commercial dynamism, which is explained by the narrowness of the domestic market. Unlike their English, French, and American competitors, Swiss watchmakers were forced to export their products and adapt them to varied local demands in terms of design and quality. They faced the need to 'get out of watchmaking mountains', as historian Béatrice Veyrassat writes.[19] At the end of the eighteenth century, Swiss watch traders were established in the world's main markets: Europe, the Middle East, the United States, and Latin America. However, it should be noted that the sale of watches was not their only occupation. They traded many other goods, including textiles, colonial goods (coffee, sugar, tobacco), alcohol, and slaves. In addition, these traders set up extensive networks of agencies worldwide, usually based on family ties. For example, Louis Courvoisier

(1758–1832), a watchmaker in La Chaux-de-Fonds, had a brother-in-law in Trieste and a second in Livorno, as well as a distant relative in Moscow.[20]

The productive and commercial factors that underpinned the success of Swiss watchmaking in the eighteenth century remained the main reasons for the strong growth of the following decades. In 1870, Swiss watchmakers produced more than 2 million watches, more than 10 times the volume of 1790 and about 70% of world production. How can such a substantial development be explained?

First of all, the production system did not undergo any fundamental transformation and remained organised in the form of the *établissage*, although *établissage* itself underwent tremendous development, including in urban areas such as La Chaux-de-Fonds, Le Locle, and Saint-Imier. Although machines were introduced in some operations, there was no actual revolution in Swiss watchmaking until the 1870s. At that time, watch factories (places in which salaried workers were concentrated and worked under the orders of a superintendent) were still virtually non-existent. The Longines factory, opened in Saint-Imier in 1867 by Ernest Francillon, is commonly regarded as one of the first industrial watch factories in Switzerland. In 1875, it employed only 120 people.[21] However,

Figure 1.4 'The Proletarian Watch', Georges-Frédéric Roskopf, La Chaux-de-Fonds, 1867.

during its first years, the mode of production remained traditional, with a division of labour between workers and essentially manual work, the main difference with the *établissage* being the concentration of workers under the same roof and the end of their status as independent workers. It is in a second stage that mechanisation and product standardisation appeared.[22] The lack of transformation of the production system was the consequence of low worker wages. Until the 1880s, Switzerland was a country of emigration. Its economy was unable to feed a population that had grown by more than 1 million since the beginning of the century (1.7 million in 1798 and 2.8 million in 1880). The presence of cheap labour therefore did not encourage entrepreneurs to invest in new production technologies.

However, although Swiss watchmaking remained traditionally organised, the manufacture of movement blanks (*ébauches*) had been the subject of industrialised production since the end of the eighteenth century. This basic part of the watch movement, including the plate and bridges, but not the regulating parts, was difficult to produce within a worker's own home because it involved brass or steel working technologies based on the use of machines. In this case, it was not the high wages but the technical characteristics of the work that led to industrialisation. At the end of the eighteenth century, two large movement-blank factories were founded.

The first was opened in 1777 in Beaucourt (France), in the Montbéliard countryside, by Frédéric Japy. After an apprenticeship with Abraham Louis Perrelet in Le Locle, Japy set up a production workshop in France, just a few kilometres from the border with Switzerland. He brought with him watchmaking machines, developed by Jean-Jacques Jeanneret-Gris, from Le Locle, and was therefore able to embark on the mechanised manufacture of movement blanks. Production boomed, from around 100,000 movements in 1800 to almost 500,000 in 1854.[23] Japy's clientele was essentially Swiss. Between 1815 and 1817, he opened sales depots in La Chaux-de-Fonds, Geneva, and Le Locle. In terms of volume, 91% of sales of movement blanks was made to Swiss clients in 1806 and 75% in 1854.

The second factory was Benguerel & Humbert, founded in Fontainemelon (now canton of Neuchâtel) by watch merchants from La Chaux-de-Fonds in 1793. It expanded its activities with the takeover in 1838 of a small movement-blank factory opened four years earlier by the Eguet brothers in Corgémont (Saint-Imier, canton of Bern).[24] It was Japy's main competitor on the Swiss watch-blank market.

The Japy and Fontainemelon factories supplied Swiss watch manufacturers with inexpensive blanks and thus supported the competitiveness of this industry. However, the mechanisation of production did not lead to product standardisation. These factories met the various needs of a multitude of watchmakers. For example, between 1825 and 1870, Fontainemelon offered its customers around a thousand different models of movement blanks.[25]

Swiss watchmakers benefited from a second factor that contributed to their success: their commercial dynamism and their adaptability to changes in demand. During the years 1800–1870, the United States represented an extraordinary opportunity for growth, with a population that increased from 5.3 million in 1800 (six times less than France) to 38.6 million in 1870 (equivalent to France). For the most part, Neuchâtel merchants and bankers seized this opportunity. Established in Philadelphia and New York, they represented many Swiss watchmakers, such as Auguste Mayor, son of a Neuchâtel banker, who moved to New York in 1836 at the age of 21 and made his fortune there.[26] Watch exports to the New World were booming, supported by the Treaty of Friendship and Trade (concluded in 1850 and ratified in 1855), which granted Switzerland low customs duties. The total value of Swiss exports to the New World amounted to more than 8 million francs in 1864 and grew to a peak of more than 18 million francs in 1872.[27] At that time, the New World accounted for between a third and a half of all Swiss watch exports.[28]

Figure 1.5 Silver watch with two movements, Sylvain Mairet, Le Locle, circa 1860.

A newcomer: France

France was one of the leading watchmaking nations under the *ancien régime*, with a large production of clocks and pocket watches in Blois and Paris.[29] It had followed a development model similar to that of London, based on the demand of the local aristocracy. This explains why Paris attracted many talented watchmakers in the second half of the eighteenth century, such as Ferdinand Berthoud and Abraham-Louis Breguet (both born in Neuchâtel, Switzerland), who pursued brilliant careers in Versailles and Paris. However, watch production collapsed in the mid-nineteenth century, despite a rapidly growing market, driven by the triumph of the bourgeoisie during the Second Empire.

The Parisian watch industry faced an inability to move to the industrial production stage. Despite several attempts to set up watch factories during the 1780s and 1790s, no one remained in the capital, forcing Parisian craftsmen to depend on external supplies. During the first part of the nineteenth century, they gradually disappeared in the face of Swiss competition and the emergence of a watch industry in Franche-Comté.[30]

The watch industry in Besançon originated at the end of the eighteenth century as the result of a transfer of technology from Switzerland. Since the 1770s, Franco-Swiss exchanges in watch business were attested. For example, young men from Franche-Comté stayed in Neuchâtel to train in watchmaking.[31] The best-known example is undoubtedly Frédéric Japy, cited above. In 1793, a national watch factory was founded in Besançon, with the support of the state. This was a political act by the revolutionary authorities, who wanted to develop their own watch industry so that France would no longer have to depend on Switzerland for its supplies. It was mainly Swiss watchmakers who set up this factory. Its director, Laurent Mégevand, came from Geneva. He was accompanied by an important Swiss colony, mainly from Neuchâtel, which provided him with his first workers. This company produced between 15,000 and 20,000 watches a year during the Revolution and the Empire, but it ended in bankruptcy.[32]

After the failure of this state-owned company, a few private bankers and business people invested in the watch industry in Besançon. The first factories appeared in the first part of the nineteenth century, but the industrial organisation remained based on the fragmentation of production and home-based work, with a strong presence of Swiss watchmakers. Among the 32 watch companies registered in Besançon between 1827 and 1857, 12 belonged to Swiss nationals.[33] Édouard Bovet was one of them, exiled in the city of Franche-Comté between 1831 and 1848. During the 1850s, many small workshops were opened in the rural areas near the Swiss border. In particular, they developed subcontracting activities for watchmakers in Besançon using Swiss parts.[34]

This first generation of manufacturers was supported by the state. The Doubs Chamber of Commerce and Industry, created in 1819, was involved in the political debate to obtain protection for its watch industry. The Swiss manufacturers, who made use of labour established in the countryside, had low production costs and flooded the French market with cheap watches, most of which were smuggled in. The French customs authorities therefore prohibited the import of watches and opposed the establishment of watch workshops in villages close to the Swiss border, in an attempt to eliminate the smuggling activities.[35] Hallmarking watches was also introduced in 1819 but was ineffective because it was copied by Swiss watchmakers. Finally, in 1834, the ineffective ban on importing watches was lifted and replaced by an import tax of 4%, later increased to 10%.[36]

State protection therefore had no significant impact on the development of a watch industry in Besançon. It was the action of entrepreneurs and industrialists that enabled the city to establish itself during the Second Empire as the national watch capital of France. The total number of hallmarked watches (gold and silver) manufactured annually in this city, which amounted to around 50,000 in the 1840s, rose from 100,000 pieces in 1854 and 200,000 in 1860, to more than 350,000 by the end of the 1860s.[37] Besançon no longer had any competitors on the national market. In 1866, it supplied 98.3% of all watches manufactured in France. While Haute-Savoie, particularly the town of Cluse, also saw a development of the watch industry during the nineteenth century, this region specialised in subcontracting operations for Geneva watchmakers and was unable to engage in the manufacture of finished watches.[38] Besançon therefore became the foundation for the tremendous growth in the French watch industry. In 1870, France was, with a share of 14% of world production, the world's second-largest watchmaking nation, well behind Switzerland but ahead of Britain (see table 1.1, p. 9).

This success was to the detriment of Swiss watchmakers, whose share of the French market fell from 57% in 1850 to 8% in 1866.[39] However, the watch industry in Besançon was not autonomous: it did not produce its blanks (acquired from Japy or in Switzerland) and did not master watch decoration (it sent its cases to Switzerland to be engine-turned and engraved). Hence, the Besançon case expresses an industrial development based on basic technologies that the region did not control. Technological and industrial dependence on Switzerland increased over the following decades.

The beginnings of the American watch industry

Until the mid-nineteenth century, the production of pocket watches in the United States was the business of immigrant craftsmen and small workshops. The American market was dominated by watches imported from Switzerland and Britain.[40] American entrepreneurs, confronted with the high cost of labour in their country, had to adopt innovative measures in order to build a competitive industry – hence, they invested in production technologies. The 'American system' – characterised by the concentration of workers in factories, product standardisation, interchangeability of parts, and division of labour – was born in this context. This system of mass production appeared in arsenals and gun factories, before being adopted by various consumer goods industries, such as clocks and sewing machines.[41]

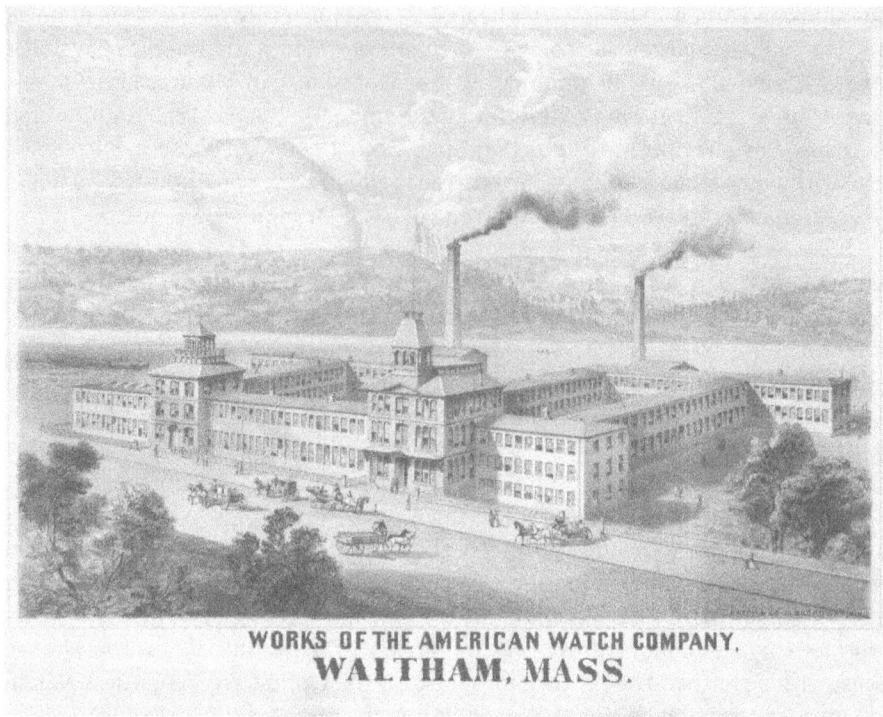

Figure 1.6 Works of the American Watch Company, between 1859 and 1872.

The first and main company was the American Watch Company in Waltham, Massachusetts, a suburb of Boston. Founded by a group of businessmen, including a New York watch retailer, its origins date back to the early 1850s.⁴² One of its founders was Aaron L. Dennison, a 30-year-old mechanic, who spent the first half of the 1850s in Switzerland acquiring technical knowledge and purchasing watch parts. These capitalists invested considerable sums of money. The capital of their company was 200,000 dollars in 1858 and 1.5 million dollars in 1873. This money was used to acquire land, build a factory and buy machine tools. In 1870, the company employed around a thousand workers. The production volume rose from 12,000 watch movements in 1860 to 55,000 in 1870, a growth largely sustained by the strong demand for watches during the Civil War (1861–1865). The company was extremely profitable. For the years 1860–1869, the total turnover amounted to nearly 6 million dollars, with a gross profit of 40%.⁴³

In 1864, a second industrial watch factory was established, in Elgin (Illinois), some 20 miles from Chicago, under the name National Watch Company (more commonly known as the Elgin National Watch Company).⁴⁴ Although slightly smaller in size than the American Watch Company, with a capital of 500,000 dollars in 1865, it was based on a similar organisational model. In fact, several watchmakers, mechanics, and technicians were lured away from Waltham in the early years. Its production was around 30,000 pieces per year in 1867–68.[45]

Finally, a dozen other, less important watch factories were founded during this period.[46] However, none of them managed to challenge the duopoly exercised by the two major manufacturers of Waltham and Elgin, which controlled nearly 80% of American watch production at the time.[47] The value of this production amounted to 2.8 million dollars in 1869.[48]

However, despite its impressive growth, the American watch industry was largely absent from foreign markets. American watch exports amounted to only 4,000 dollars in 1870,[49] and the Waltham and Elgin factories concentrated on their domestic market, which was also the world's largest watch market. They soon became formidable competitors for Swiss watchmakers, who had made the United States one of the main bases for their growth since the end of the eighteenth century.

The birth of a watch industry in Germany

The last European country to see the emergence of a watch industry on its territory during the first two-thirds of the nineteenth century was Germany. This country had a long tradition of clock and watch production, particularly in the Black Forest, as well as in the cities of Dresden, Leipzig, and Nuremberg. According to classical historiography, it was even a Nuremberg clockmaker, Peter Henlein (1479–1542), who invented the world's first watch.[50] In particular, there is evidence of a watchmakers' guild in Dresden from 1668.[51]

However, the contemporary watch industry was born on the fringes of this tradition. Saxony, in the east of the country, is the main region in which a watch industry emerged in the 1840s.[52] Until then, attempts by watchmakers to develop production beyond the artisanal scale had proved unsuccessful, despite financial support from the King of Saxony. The action of entrepreneur Ferdinand Adolph Lange proved decisive. Trained at the Technical College in Dresden and benefiting from an apprenticeship as a watchmaker, as well as a training period in Switzerland and France, Lange founded his own company in the town of Glashütte in 1845 with a particular aim: to mass-produce quality watches in order to compete with the Swiss watchmakers who were then dominating the German market, and to offer products cheaper than British watches.[53]

Lange's idea was to import the Swiss model of the division of labour between self-employed homeworkers. He established himself in Saxony precisely because of the low wages in this region, which would allow him to keep manufacturing costs as low as possible. In addition, the municipality of Glashütte agreed to take charge of the training of the first generation of apprentices. Some of them left Lange after a few years to set up their own business, but only Lange's company managed to develop over the long term, particularly through its exports to the American market, where it had been since 1853. However, the company remained somewhat small: it employed only a few dozen people and produced only a few hundred watches until the 1880s. In 1875, it was taken over by the second generation under the name A. Lange & Söhne, but it was not until the turn of the century that the company began to move towards industrialisation.

The Black Forest presents a different case of development, characterised by the transition from clocks to watches.[54] During the 1830s and 1840s, imports of American clocks, mass-produced on the other side of the Atlantic, endangered local production because these imports were too inexpensive. The local clock and cuckoo clock industry, organised on the basis of home-based work in the countryside, had to adapt. The local elites decided to reposition themselves, in watchmaking. The Furtwangen Watchmaking School set up courses to support local apprentices, who brought out their first watches in 1852. A teacher was sent to Glashütte and then to La Chaux-de-Fonds to acquire the necessary technical knowledge. In 1853, a limited company for the manufacture of pocket watches was founded, with the aim of adopting American methods of mass production. Despite these efforts, the watch industry in the Black Forest failed to develop, mainly for technical reasons (such as the inability to adopt the interchangeability of parts, which was necessary for the adoption of the American system) and economic reasons (for example, low wages for homeworkers did not encourage investment in production technology).[55] In 1864, however, the company Grebrüder Junghans was founded in Schramberg in the Black Forest and soon became the largest watch manufacturer in Germany. Initially, it concentrated on the production of clocks and cases using production methods inspired by the American system (25,000 cases were produced in 1864).[56] Over the next two decades, the company developed into a large industrial company.

Conclusion

During the first two-thirds of the nineteenth century, watchmaking around the world underwent a profound upheaval. The strong increase in demand mainly benefited Swiss watch traders. They profited from cheap labour and a flexible production system that allowed the manufacture of a wide variety of watches to meet the tastes of consumers around the world. During this period, Switzerland established itself as the undisputed leader in the watch industry, whereas Britain had been facing stagnation since the end of the eighteenth century.

A watch industry emerged also in other countries, such as France, Germany, and the United States. The production technologies there were largely identical to those used in Switzerland. A new organisational model can be observed especially in the United States: industrial manufacturing and mass production of standardised movements. The final assembly of American watches was still largely carried out by independent craftsmen or small companies. The latter, specialising in packaging and distribution, were close to the market. They adapted the design of the watches to the desires of the consumers, while benefiting from cheap movements because they were mass-produced. Admittedly, in terms of volume, the United States still accounted for only 5% of world watch production in 1870 and was only the fourth-largest watchmaking nation, behind Switzerland, France, and Britain. However, the technological model adopted by the Waltham and Elgin factories enabled the American watch industry to grow rapidly in the following decades. European manufacturers had no choice but to adapt to this new competitor or disappear.

Notes

1 Robert Silvia, 'Édouard Bovet-dit-de-Chine, négociant en horlogerie (1797–1849)', in *Biographies Neuchâteloises,* ed. Michel Schlup (Hauterive: G. Attinger, 1998), vol. 2, 48–55.
2 Nigel Thrift, 'The making of a capitalist time consciousness', in *The Sociology of Time,* ed. J. Hassard (London: Palgrave Macmillan, 1990), 105–129.
3 Pierre-Yves Donzé, 'Les industriels horlogers du Locle (1850–1920), un cas représentatif de la diversité du patronat de l'Arc jurassien', in *Les systèmes productifs dans l'Arc jurassien: Acteurs, pratiques et territoires (XIXE–XXE siècles),* ed. Jean-Claude Daumas (Besançon: Maison des Sciences de l'Homme, 2005), 61–82.
4 This company lost its monopoly in 1813 but remained a major player in the trade between China and Britain until the Opium War (1839–1842).
5 M. Diane Burton and Tom Nicholas, 'Prizes, patents and the search for longitude', *Explorations in Economic History,* vol. 64 (2017): 21–36.
6 Glasmeier, *Manufacturing Time,* ch. 4.
7 Alun C. Davies, 'Time for a change? Technological persistence in the British watch industry', *Material Culture Review/Revue de la culture matérielle,* vol. 36, no. 1 (1992): 57–64.
8 Liliane Hilaire-Pérez, *La pièce et le geste: artisans, marchands et savoir technique à Londres au XVIIIe siècle* (Paris: Albin Michel, 2013), 340.
9 Glasmeier, *Manufacturing Time,* 82.
10 David M. Higgins, *Brands, Geographical Origin, and the Global Economy: A History from the Nineteenth Century to the Present* (Cambridge: Cambridge University Press, 2018), 52–55.
11 *Journal suisse d'horlogerie* (1930): 102–104.
12 Charles W. Moore, *Timing a Century: History of the Waltham Watch Company* (Cambridge: Harvard University Press, 1945), 54–56.
13 Roy A. Church, 'Nineteenth-century clock technology in Britain, the United States, and Switzerland', *Economic History Review,* vol. 28, no. 4 (1975): 618.
14 Higgins, *Brands, Geographical Origin, and the Global Economy,* 19, 26, 54–55.
15 Church, 'Nineteenth-century clock technology', 624; Glasmeier, *Manufacturing Time,* 102.
16 Pierre-Yves Donzé, *Histoire de l'industrie horlogère suisse de Jacques David à Nicolas Hayek (1850–2000)* (Neuchâtel: Alphil, 2009), 13–16.
17 Roman Studer, 'When did the Swiss get so rich? Comparing living standards in Switzerland and Europe, 1800–1913', *Journal of European Economic History,* vol. 37, no. 2 (2008): 448.
18 Donzé, *Histoire de l'industrie horlogère suisse,* 16–25; Philippe Blanchard, *L'établissage: étude historique d'un système de production horloger en Suisse (1750–1950)* (Chézard-Saint-Martin: La Chatière, 2011).
19 Béatrice Veyrassat, 'Sortir des montagnes horlogères: les faiseurs de globalisation (1750-years 1830/1840)', in *Unternehmen, Handelshäuser und Wirtschaftsmigration im*

neuzeutlichen Alpenraum, eds Marie-Claude Schöpfer, Markus Stoffel, and Françoise Vannotti (Brig: Rotten Verlag, 2014), 257–279.
20 Pierre-Yves Donzé, *Les patrons horlogers de La Chaux-de-Fonds: dynamique sociale d'une élite industrielle (1840–1920)* (Neuchâtel: Alphil, 2007), 27.
21 Pierre-Yves Donzé, *Du comptoir familial à la marque globale: Longines* (Saint-Imier: Éditions des Longines, 2012).
22 Patrick Linder, *De l'atelier à l'usine: l'horlogerie à Saint-Imier (1865–1918). Histoire d'un district industriel. Organisation et technologie: un système en mutation* (Neuchâtel: Alphil, 2008); Donzé, *Du comptoir familial à la marque globale*.
23 Pierre Lamard, *Histoire d'un capital familial au XIXe siècle: le capital Japy (1777–1910)* (Montbéliard: Société Belfortaine d'Émulation, 1988), 61 and 144.
24 Bernard Romy, *Le meunier, l'horloger et l'électricien: les usiniers de la Suze, 1750–1950* (Biel: Intervalles, 2008), 99–107.
25 Béatrice Veyrassat, 'Manufacturing flexibility in nineteenth-century Switzerland: social and institutional foundations of decline and revival in calico-printing and watchmaking', in *World of Possibilities: Flexibility and Mass Production in Western Industrialization*, eds Charles Sabel and Jonathan Zeitlin (Cambridge: Cambridge University Press, 1997), 190.
26 'Mayor Auguste', *Actes de la Société Helvétique des Sciences Naturelles*, vol. 87 (1904): 61–69.
27 Christophe Koller, *'De la lime à la machine'. L'industrialisation et l'État au pays de l'horlogerie: Contribution à l'histoire économique et sociale d'une région suisse* (Courrendlin: CSE, 2003), 114.
28 Jean-François Bergier estimates that the value of Swiss watch exports rose from 17 million francs in 1840 to 60 million in 1879. He gives no indication of the growth trend between these two dates. See Jean-François Bergier, *Histoire économique de la Suisse* (Lausanne: Payot, 1983) 241.
29 Marie-Agnès Dequidt, *Horlogers des Lumières: Temps et société à Paris au XVIIIe siècle* (Paris: CTHS, 2014).
30 Ibid., 264–275.
31 Jean-Luc Mayaud and Joëlle Mauerhan, *Besançon horloger, 1793–1914* (Besançon: Musée du Temps, 1994); Natalie Petiteau, *L'horlogerie des Bourgeois conquérants: histoire des établissements Bourgeois de Damprichard, Doubs: 1780–1939* (Besançon: Les Belles Lettres, Université de Besançon, 1994).
32 Mayaud and Mauerhan, *Besançon horloger*, 32.
33 Ibid., 43.
34 Petiteau, *L'horlogerie des Bourgeois conquérants*, 26.
35 Ibid., 25–26.
36 Mayaud and Mauerhan, *Besançon horloger*, 38; Philippe Gern and Silvia Arlettaz, *Relations franco-suisses: la confrontation de deux politiques économiques* (Geneva: Georg, 1992), 32 and 73–74.
37 Mayaud and Mauerhan, *Besançon horloger*, 64.
38 Pierre Judet, *Horlogeries et horlogers du Faucigny (1849–1934): Les métamorphoses d'une identité sociale et politique* (Grenoble: Presses Universitaires de Grenoble, 2004).
39 Mayaud and Mauerhan, *Besançon horloger*, 68. The authors point out that these figures do not take smuggling into account.
40 Michael C. Harrold, *American Watchmaking: A Technical History of the American Watch Industry, 1850–1930* (Columbia: NAWCC, 1984).
41 David A. Hounshell, *From the American System to Mass Production 1800–1932: The Development of Manufacturing Technology in the United States* (Baltimore: Johns Hopkins

University Press, 1985); Donald R. Hoke, *Ingenious Yankees: The Rise of the American System of Manufactures in the Private Sector* (New York: Columbia University Press, 1990).
42 Moore, *Timing a Century*.
43 Ibid.; Baker Library, Harvard University, Boston, MSS 598, American Waltham Watch, ZA-1.
44 E. C. Alft and William H. Biska, *Elgin Time: A History of the Elgin National Watch Company, 1864–1968* (Elgin: Elgin Historical Society, 2003).
45 Koller, *'De la lime à la machine'*, 105.
46 Harrold, *American Watchmaking*.
47 Ibid.
48 Bureau of the Census, *Biennial Census of Manufactures* (Washington, DC: US Department of Commerce, 1905).
49 Bureau of Foreign and Domestic Commerce, *Foreign Commerce and Navigation of the United States* (Washington: US Department of Commerce, 1870).
50 Gustav Speckhart, *Peter Henlein der Erfinder der Taschenuhr: fachgeschichtliche Abhandlung* (Nuremberg: Verl. J. L. Engraving, 1890).
51 Peter Plassmeyer and Sibylle Gluch (eds), *Einfach – Vollkommen: Sachsens Weg in die internationale Uhrenwelt – Ferdinand Adolph Lange zum 200. Geburtstag*(Dresden: Deutscher Kunstverlag, 2015), 85.
52 Ibid.
53 Hans-Heinrich Schmid, *Lexikon der Deutschen Uhrenindustrie 1850–1980* (Nuremberg: German Society for Chronometrie, 2017), vol. 2, 386–387.
54 Ryoji Morri, *19 seiki doitsu no chiiki sangyo fukko: kindaika no naka no byutenberuku shoeigyo* (Kyoto: Kyoto University Press, 2013).
55 Ibid., chs 3 and 4.
56 Schmid, *Lexikon der Deutschen Uhrenindustrie*, 306–308.

2

Responding to the American challenge, 1870–1890

In September 1876, Jacques David, technical director of Longines in Saint-Imier (Switzerland), visited three American watch factories, including that of Waltham. He then urgently wrote a letter to Ernest Francillon, the head of Longines, who had remained in Switzerland:

> We absolutely must follow in the footsteps of these people if we do not want to be chased away by them from all markets. The sums to be spent are enormous in order to be able to produce, but we will only be able to produce by these means. It is necessary to adopt a system which combines the advantages of Swiss labour with the advantages of the American machine, but the first thing to obtain is consciousness among our workers.[1]

This correspondence highlights the double challenge facing Old World watchmakers: investing in new production technologies (mechanisation) as well as transforming working relationships (concentration of workers in factories). In short, it was a question of industrialising the manufacture of watches. The stakes were high for all European watchmakers. The American model of mass production of watch movements imposed a reaction. Industrial production allowed productivity gains and a lowering of selling prices, which made a strong increase in supply possible and which called into question the very existence of old models. The responses to the American challenge were varied and led to a re-composition of the hierarchy between watchmaking nations (see table 2.1).

The world market experienced a strong rise, supported by the launch of simple and inexpensive watches that met growing demand in the context of urbanising and industrialising societies – the watch becoming a useful and necessary object. The volume of world production thus rose from just under 3 million watches in 1870 to almost 10 million 20 years later. Switzerland maintained its leading position and continued to dominate the world market, with a share of more than 50%. The industrial development of watch manufacturing in other countries, however, threatened its former position as a quasi-monopoly. In 1890, three nations had a similar share, at 13–16% (i.e. around 1.5 million watches), but with distinct dynamics: while French production increased threefold during these two decades, that of the United States increased tenfold and Germany grew from a production that was limited to a few thousand pieces in 1870 to 1,300,000. Finally, Britain continued its relative decline, despite a slight increase in absolute terms. These various national dynamics essentially express the nature of the responses to the American challenge in terms of industrial organisation, production technology, and state interventionism.

Table 2.1 World watch production, 1870 and 1890

Country	1870		1890		1870–1890
	Volume	%	Volume	%	Growth in %
Switzerland	2,100,000	70	5,000,000	52	138
Britain	180,000	6	250,000	3	39
France	420,000	14	1,320,000	14	214
United States	150,000	5	1,500,000	16	900
Germany	–	–	1,300,000	13	–
Others	60,000	5	230,000	2	283
Total	2,910,000	100	9,600,000	100	230

Sources: See appendix.

The success of the American system

The American watch industry showed tremendous development between 1870 and 1890, with a growth rate of 900%. Although it fell short of its Swiss rival, it managed to establish itself as the world's second-largest watchmaking nation, with 16% of production in 1890.

This success was mainly due to the Waltham and Elgin factories, which continued to mass-produce watches. The American Watch Company, whose capital increased to 2 million dollars in 1885 and to 3 million four years later, saw its production reach 413,000 movements in 1890. The company also improved its productivity. In 1883, it took only 2.2 days, on average, for a worker to make a watch, compared with 4 days in 1859, while the average Swiss worker took 7.5 days to make a watch in 1876.[2] Finally, profits declined somewhat but remained at very high levels: gross profit was 33.9% of sales for the years 1870–1884.[3] As for the National Watch Company, it followed a similar development and reached a production level of nearly 500,000 movements in 1890, thus surpassing its rival in Waltham.[4]

In addition, many other watch companies were established in the United States during the 1870s and 1880s. Some 20 factories opened across the country during these two decades.[5] However, the presence of the two industrial giants made it difficult for the new entrants to survive. The level of investment required to achieve competitive production costs was such that most of these new watch companies disappeared after a few years of activity. The duopoly exercised by Waltham and Elgin gave them an almost uncontested dominant position.

It should also be pointed out that these two factories came closer together in the mid-1880s and cooperated in order to strengthen their power. They specialised in the production and sale of watch movements, not finished watches.

Because the final assembly and decoration were operations that were difficult to automate and were not standardised, the companies in Waltham and Elgin concentrated on the manufacture of movements, which they delivered to wholesalers, who then distributed them to independent assemblers throughout the United States, known as jobbers. This division of labour was based on standardised watch movements, allowing the emergence of industrial watch-case factories. However, the recession of 1882–1885 brought these various players closer together, ensuring lower prices. The National Association of Jobbers in American Watches was founded in 1885 and remained in operation until 1892, when the Sherman Antitrust Act of 1890, a law banning agreements aimed at reducing competition, put an end to the Association.[6] However, after the dissolution of the Association, discussions and agreements between the Waltham and Elgin manufacturers continued until the 1920s, despite the legal ban.

American Watch's expansion outside the United States also began during this period. In 1874, it opened an office in London, which was responsible for sales to all foreign markets. The American company adapted the design of its products to its end market, a flexibility made possible by the fact that it concentrated on the mass production of movements rather than complete watches.[7] In particular, it cooperated with a watch-case factory opened by Dennison in Britain, in Birmingham, around 1874–1876. According to Édouard Favre-Perret, in a contemporary account, sales of American watches on the British market in the mid-1870s amounted to around 20,000–30,000 pieces per year.[8] This volume, which represented almost a third of Waltham's production, was clearly overestimated, especially since Favre-Perret was then engaged in making Swiss manufacturers aware of the American threat. Birmingham, however, remained the only foreign subsidiary of Waltham's factory. It re-exported throughout the British Empire, to Latin America, China, and Japan. Between 1870 and 1890 it brought in several tens of thousands of pounds a year.

However, despite a real expansion of business outside the United States, it is indeed the American market that constituted the basis for the growth of the factories in this country. In 1889, American watch exports accounted for only 3.4% of national production.[9] Moreover, the balance of trade in watches remained largely negative, although the value of exports was certainly rising (see figure 2.1). However, the fall in watch imports was the main feature of the development of the US watch trade during the 1870s. After reaching a peak of 3.5 million dollars in 1872, imports fell to 772,000 dollars in 1877. They remained below the 1 million mark for the next two years. This collapse in foreign watch purchases was a direct result of the rise of the Waltham and Elgin factories. The main victims of this fall were Swiss watchmakers, who had dominated the American market in the mid-nineteenth century.

The 1876 Centennial Exhibition, held in Philadelphia to celebrate the centenary of the Declaration of Independence of the United States, was an opportunity for European manufacturers to become aware of this new competition.[10] The event, which attracted nearly 10 million visitors, was a gigantic communication

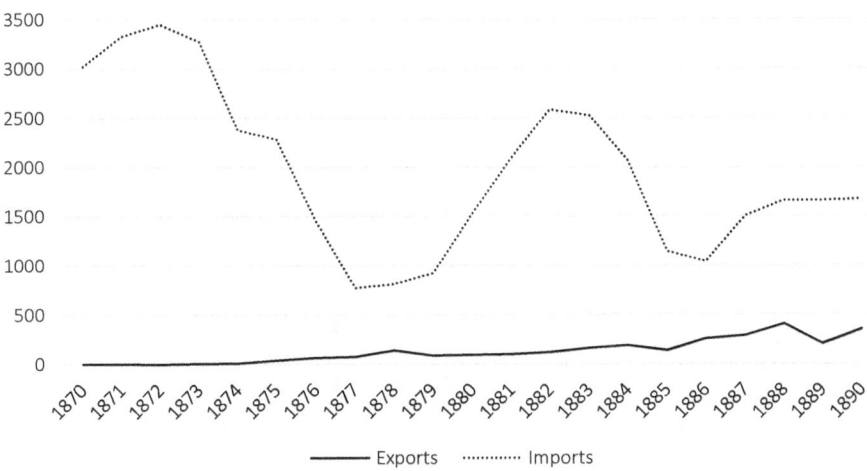

Figure 2.1 Imports and exports of watches by the United States (contemporary value in $1,000s), 1870–1890.

Source: Bureau of Foreign and Domestic Commerce, *Foreign Commerce and Navigation of the United States*, 1870–1890.
Note: These figures include the value of complete watches, movements, and parts.

operation set up by the American authorities and major American companies to establish the reputation of the United States as the world's leading industrial nation.[11] Machinery Hall, at the heart of the exhibition, was dedicated to the American system of mass production. It was a monumental building of steel and glass, in which the main American factories were staged (figure 2.2). Among the steam engines, textile machines, locomotives, and printing machines were Waltham's watches, manufactured on a series of machine tools in front of the public (box 2.1). In comparison, the Swiss exhibitors, which included several watchmakers, were concentrated in the small Swiss pavilion among the St Gallen embroidery and other products illustrating domestic industry. The contrast with the watches in Machinery Hall was striking.

The major Swiss watch manufacturers sent two delegates to Philadelphia, whose mission was to bring back detailed information on American competitors. They were Jacques David, an engineer at the Longines factory, and Théodore Gribi, an employee of Borel & Courvoisier in Neuchâtel. The setting up of this technical delegation in Philadelphia was one of the reasons for the creation of the Société Intercantonale des Industries du Jura (SIIJ), a trade association that, after 1876, brought together representatives of the watchmaking cantons. In June 1876, Ernest Francillon, director of Longines, spoke of the 'absolute necessity'[12] of taking advantage of the World's Fair 'to carry out a serious and in-depth investigation into the organisation, tools, financial situation and in general everything concerning American watch factories'.[13]

David and Gribi were fascinated by what they observed in the United States and returned from Philadelphia with a strong desire to transform and

Figure 2.2 Centennial Exhibition, Philadelphia, Machinery Hall, 1876.

Box 2.1 Extract from the catalogue for the Centennial Exhibition, Philadelphia, Machinery Hall, 1876

Waltham Watch in Philadelphia's Machinery Hall, 1876
Next below is one of the most interesting exhibits in the hall. The American Watch Company, of Waltham, Massachusetts, have a work-shop, in which a number of their most experienced and skilful workers are engaged in the manufacture of watches by machinery. Every part of the process is illustrated by the work done here. The machines used are of the most delicate and perfect character, and the operations are marked by an accuracy and skill which elicit the warm praise of the interested spectators who surround the workshop. The Waltham watches have long been regarded as the best of American manufacture, and the universal testimony of all who have used them is that they are unexcelled by any in the world.

Source: Philadelphia City Archives, 231.7, James D. McCabe, *The Illustrated History of the Centennial Exhibition* (Philadelphia: The National Publishing Co., n.d. 1877?), 417–418.

modernise the Swiss watch industry. David brought back several examples of American watches in his suitcases, which he made available to manufacturers and watchmaking schools in Switzerland so that they could observe American machine-made goods. But if the engineer from Saint-Imier has remained in the collective memory, it is above all for his famous report to the SIIJ on watchmaking in the United States, written in collaboration with Gribi.[14] Having visited the three main watch companies in the United States, Waltham Watch (900 workers), Elgin Watch (650 workers), and Springfield Watch (300 workers), David revealed the existence of extremely modern factories, financed by capitalists and run by salaried managers, in which machines were omnipresent. He showed that the mechanisation and interchangeability of parts allowed Americans to mass-produce cheap watches for a large public. In a long technical part of the report, he presented the tools and manufacturing techniques adopted in these companies, the principle of which can be summed up as follows: 'do by machine everything that can be done this way'.[15] The conclusion of his report presents as a plea for the modernisation of Swiss watchmaking, through the generalisation of the use of machines, the standardisation of watch calibres, the hiring of American mechanics, and the development of watchmaking schools. In the end, he declared that 'these new factories must be founded in Switzerland, and if they are not created here, they will be created in the United States and there will be nothing left for us after a few years, because the Americans are already selling their watches in all our markets, in Russia, England, South America, Australia and Japan'.[16]

Jules Borel, Gribi's employer, went further. In October 1876 he presented the SIIJ with a concrete proposal to hire an American engineer who had worked for Waltham for some 20 years: 'This man would come to Switzerland and would make himself available to watch and watch tool manufacturers to direct them in the reorganisation or transformation of their manufacturing system [...]'.[17] However, the SIIJ committee decided to tone down these remarks. David and Gribi's report had indeed set the Swiss watchmaking world in turmoil. Many manufacturers continued to defend the artisanal production system and were firmly opposed to the widespread use of machines in watchmaking. Attached to an idealised image of the watchmaker's work, based on the independence of the homeworker and the excellence of craftsmanship, they refused to industrialise their industry and preferred to support it by strengthening product quality. The mixed reactions to the report led the SIIJ committee to refrain from publishing it. Although the SIIJ continued to play an important role in the collective defence of the interests of the watch industry, the modernisation of production was essentially carried out at company level.

The limited modernisation of the Swiss watch industry

Two figures highlight the fundamental difference between the American and Swiss watch industries. First, the difference in productivity is obvious.

Figure 2.3 La Chaux-de-Fonds, 1870–1890.

On average, a Swiss worker produced 40 watches per year around 1876–1877, compared with 150 for an American worker.[18] This difference gave American watches a definite advantage in terms of manufacturing costs and came as the result of massive investment in the means of production (machine tools and factories), as well as product development focused on the standardisation of calibres. In Switzerland, low labour costs discouraged entrepreneurs from investing in production technologies.

Second, the production volume of the largest companies in both countries illustrates the confrontation of two distinct industrial worlds. While the Longines factory, one of the largest in Switzerland, produced 20,000 watches in 1885, Waltham and Elgin each produced more than 400,000 watches during the same period.[19] The difference in productivity, therefore, was not only apparent in the industry of the two countries, but also in their largest firms. In this context, it became very difficult for Swiss manufacturers to remain competitive.

During the 1870s, Swiss watch exports to the United States collapsed. In value, after reaching a peak of 18 million francs in 1872, they only amounted to 4 million in 1877.[20] In volume, exports fell to fewer than 200,000 watches in 1874.[21] The crisis was particularly severe because Switzerland was heavily dependent on the American market. It called into question the very existence of a watch industry in Switzerland. As mentioned above, on their return from Philadelphia, David and Gribi called on their colleagues to change the production method. However, they met with a variety of reactions.

Figure 2.4 Complication watch, known as 'La Merveilleuse', Ami LeCoultre Piguet, Le Brassus, circa 1878.

In the former watchmaking regions, particularly Geneva, Le Locle, and La Chaux-de-Fonds, many voices were raised in opposition to the attempts at modernisation proposed by Jacques David and a few major industrialists. They preferred to fight against American competition with high-quality products. In a reaction that was not unlike that of English watchmakers against Swiss competition at the end of the eighteenth century, certain craftsmen and merchants opted for top-of-the-range production. They chose to produce high-precision watches for a niche market and reformed various institutions to support this strategic choice. In Geneva, for example, the Observatory had been organising a chronometry competition since 1872 to encourage the production of quality watches.[22] Similarly, the directors of several watchmaking schools were opposed to the introduction of utilitarian teaching, with the director of a school in La Chaux-de-Fonds declaring in 1877 that it was thanks to 'good watchmaking' that the Swiss would succeed in fighting American competition.[23] This position can largely be explained by the lack of financial means to start industrial production and the desire to perpetuate small family businesses.[24]

However, the position remained a minority one. The Swiss watch industry as a whole was gradually but irreversibly moving towards a modernisation of its structures, characterised by the emergence of industrial manufacturing and the mechanisation of work as new organisational modes. Several large factories developed on the basis of the American model, namely the concentration of workers, division of labour, mechanisation, and product standardisation. This is the case of Longines in particular, but also of several other companies that established themselves as leading players in the Swiss watch industry. The company Louis Brandt & Fils is emblematic of this change. Founded in La Chaux-de-Fonds in 1848 and organised along the lines of an establishment, it left the Neuchâtel mountains in 1880 and opened a watch factory in the city of Biel. The opposition of the watchmakers and workers of La Chaux-de-Fonds to such industrial projects explains the relocation of the Brandt family's company to a town with no great watchmaking tradition. In 1889, the company employed 600 people and produced 100,000 watches a year. Five years later, it launched the Omega calibre, which met with phenomenal success.[25] It was also during this period that the companies Georges Favre-Jacot & Cie (later Zenith), International Watch Company (IWC), and Tavannes Watch organised themselves on the American model. They produced their own movements and most of their components. These companies then entered a phase of tremendous growth. Several other, smaller factories also emerged under a similar model. In La Chaux-de-Fonds, Jewish merchants adopted this new mode of production and opened, after 1880, many medium-sized factories, contributing to the transformation of the local industrial structures.[26]

In parallel to these few factories, which remain exceptions, new producers of movement blanks founded companies and also adopted the principle of mass production. At the end of the 1880s, there were around 20 of these, mainly in the new watchmaking regions, where the workforce accepted factory work (Biel and Jura, Grenchen, Solothurn).[27] Competition between them was fierce, so much so that the factories in Fontainemelon and Japy lost their monopoly position. The manufacturers of components also followed this industrial transformation.[28]

This industrialisation of the production of blanks and components benefited assembly-makers – that is, manufacturers of complete watches who do not produce their own movements and parts. They benefited from cheap and high-quality components, as these enabled them to produce a wide variety of watches and meet the tastes of consumers around the world. Around 1890, the Swiss watch industry thus managed to combine the advantages of the American system (mass production of blanks and components) with the flexibility of *établissage* (ability to launch a wide variety of products on the market). This is exactly what Jacques David had recommended on his return from Philadelphia.[29] And it was on this new industrial organisation that the Swiss watch industry based its growth until the 1960s.

The limited modernisation of production structures led to the formation of an industrial district – that is, an industry concentrated geographically in the Jura mountains and made up of numerous interdependent small and medium-sized enterprises (SMEs).[30] The coordination of certain activities and the defence of industrial interests led to the emergence of several associations which illustrate the transition to a form of organised capitalism. The SIIJ played an essential role in this context. In particular, it lobbied the federal authorities intensively, advocating free trade (a lack of customs duties), taxation limitation, and state interventionism in favour of the industry. For example, it was involved in supporting the limitation of postal tax increases (1876, 1878), the introduction of federal legislation on the (non-tax) control of precious metals (1877), the adoption of a liberal customs convention with Romania (1877), and the promotion of a patent law (1882). This political activity was relayed via several watch manufacturers who were deputies in the Federal Assembly, generally in the ranks of the Radical Party. In the 1880s and 1890s, when federal customs policy evolved towards greater protectionism, the SIIJ became an ardent defender of the 'free trade dogma'.[31] Finally, the lobbyist policy organised by the SIIJ enabled the watch industry to be integrated into the country's other industrial and export sectors, united within the Swiss Federation of Commerce and Industry (Vorort; today Economiesuisse), which has functioned since its creation in 1870 as an advocate for the watch industry.

The SIIJ also operated internally. It deployed an intense rationalisation policy, with the aim of better coordinating the watch industry's productive and commercial activities. At the production level, its interventions were aimed at the adoption of certain standardisation measures. The introduction of machines and the quest for interchangeability of parts called for the adoption of common standards, particularly in terms of units of measurement, and therefore collaboration between manufacturers at the technical level. The SIIJ took charge of this. From the very first meetings of its management board, Ernest Francillon thus had a new measuring device based on the metric system adopted by the entire industry (1876). In 1877, this rationalisation function was entrusted to a technical subcommittee chaired by Jacques David. This subcommittee adopted numerous concrete measures, one of the first of which was the unification of screw sizes (1879). At the commercial level, the SIIJ also played an important role in organising the representation of Swiss watch companies at international exhibitions in order to control the image disseminated by the industry to the outside world. It was also responsible for gathering information on competition, with the appointment in 1877 of a permanent subcommittee for the United States, Britain, and France. In particular, it was responsible for collecting the calibres of watches produced by these countries – mainly those of the American Waltham – and circulating them among its members. In 1887, this subcommittee became a commercial information bureau which, among other things, informed its members about the solvency of various Swiss and foreign customers. This activity gave rise in 1913 to an *ad hoc* institution, l'Information horlogère, established in La Chaux-de-Fonds.

However, the industrialisation of the Swiss watch industry presented a major barrier: it necessitated very significant financial investments. Investing in new production technologies was extremely expensive for small family businesses. It was often necessary to resort to external capital, either through bank loans or by opening up capital to new investors. Moreover, it was difficult to make the investments profitable. The Longines factory thus experienced great financial difficulties during the 1870s, only escaping bankruptcy thanks to the relations of its owner, Ernest Francillon, with private bankers.[32] The same was true of the Brandt brothers' factory (Omega), whose growth was not only due to the construction of a modern factory and the mass production of watches, but also to the constant support of the private bank Rieckel in La Chaux-de-Fonds since the 1890s.[33] As for Tavannes Watch, it was financially supported by the Jewish watch merchants Schwob, from La Chaux-de-Fonds.[34] Finally, in Geneva, wealthy private bankers considered watchmaking too risky and did not invest their fortunes in it. The company J. M. Badollet & Cie, which was the most modern watchmaking factory in Geneva in the mid-1870s, did not get any financial support from banks and went bankrupt in 1891. As for the many smaller factories, they had to resort to self-financing, as well as to credit from the many local banks that flourished in the villages of the Jura mountains during the last third of the nineteenth century.

What was the effect of this limited modernisation on the international competitiveness of the Swiss watch industry? To answer this question, two distinct markets need to be considered. First, let us look at the American market, which remains the largest in the world. The large Swiss manufacturers, which were heavily dependent on it, adopted a particular strategy: the development of watch movements of the same size as those of the Waltham and Elgin companies (i.e. the 19-line and 21-line Swiss calibres, which corresponded to the 16-size and 18-size American ones).[35] This made it possible to export movements to the United States and to carry out final assembly on site, using American cases. The share of movements in the volume of exports to the United States reached 35.5% in 1890, whereas it was only 5.9% for the world as a whole in the same year.[36] This strategy both reduced manufacturing costs and provided American consumers with products that were suitable for them. Longines designed numerous 19-line calibres for the American market, while in 1894 the Brandt brothers launched their famous Omega calibre, a 19-line calibre specially developed for export across the Atlantic (box 2.2, figure 2.5).[37] This product adaptation enabled Swiss watchmakers to see their exports to the United States grow once again. The volume of watches and movements surpassed the 200,000 mark in 1886 and reached 625,000 pieces in 1890.[38] Seen from the United States, these exports represented approximately half of national production in 1890. However, since

Box 2.2 The Omega calibre according to Frédéric Bessire, head of Louis Brandt & Frère's exports, 1896

The Omega movement was combined from the outset in order to be able to fight advantageously against the American factories, and for this, two things had to be considered in the first place:

1. The perfect similarity of the dimensions of the movements and the mobiles to allow the use of the American cases without any trouble or retouching;
2. The next concern was to obtain a winding mechanism that was as simple, solid and safe as possible, allowing direct setting of the time by the winding stem without the need for special accessories such as buttons, pushchairs, pulls, etc.

The thing, especially the time setting, presented real difficulties in order to avoid falling into the systems already used and patented in America. A special arrangement was finally combined, with excellent results. The patent was taken out in Switzerland and in different countries, in order to protect the house from harmful counterfeiting. [...]

Source: Document quoted by Marco Richon, *Omega Saga* (Biel: Fondation Adrien Brandt Pour le Patrimoine Omega, 1998), 203.

Figure 2.5 Advertisement for Omega, 1913.

Swiss manufacturers exported a large share of movements, they accounted for only a small share of the market in terms of value. In 1890, the United States imported watches and movements worth 1.7 million dollars, while sales from the Waltham factory alone amounted to 4.1 million dollars.[39]

Second, it is necessary to look beyond the United States (see table 2.2). Global demand for watches was growing strongly, and it was mainly Swiss traders who were capturing these developing markets. Dependence on the US market was therefore declining. In 1890, the American market accounted for only 13.3% of the volume of Swiss watch exports and only 8.8% in market share by value. Germany had become the main outlet for Swiss watchmakers, absorbing more than a quarter of exports in 1890. This country had an unprecedented economic and demographic dynamism. The federal authorities succeeded in improving the conditions of access to the German market at the end of the 1880s by revising the trade treaty between the two countries.[40] In addition, the United Kingdom, and its huge empire, as well as Austria-Hungary, were also ahead of the United States. Finally, three other countries (Russia, France, and Italy) had a market share of more than 5%. The boom in European markets was thus enabling Swiss watchmakers to reduce their dependence on the United States. However, the geographical diversification of outlets was limited: the first three markets alone accounted for more than half of exports.

Table 2.2 The 10 main markets of the Swiss watch industry, 1890

Country	Exports (million francs)	Market share (%)
Germany	27.9	26.8
United Kingdom	16.5	15.9
Austria-Hungary	10.5	10.1
United States	9.1	8.8
Russia	7.7	7.4
Italy	6.6	6.3
France	5.7	5.4
Belgium-Luxembourg	2.6	2.5
Spain	1.8	1.7
The Netherlands	1.4	1.4
Others	14	14
Total	104.1	100

Source: Federation of the Swiss Watch Industry (personal communication with author).

The industrial failure of British watchmakers

The American success story had particularly violent repercussions in Britain. It dealt a fatal blow to a sector that had been unable to respond to the loss of its competitiveness against Swiss watchmakers in the mid-nineteenth century. The opening of a subsidiary of American Watch in London contributed to the boom in imports of cheap watches. The British Horological Institute (BHI) pursued an elitist strategy. English watchmakers debated American competition in the columns of the *Horological Journal*, published by the Institute, during the years 1876 to 1877, but did not realise the importance of the issue, remaining convinced of the superiority of their products. The Institute also worked to maintain a traditional production method. For example, in the mid-1880s, it opposed the introduction of courses on the use of machine tools for apprentice watchmakers.[41]

However, there were some attempts to move to mechanised watchmaking in Lancashire, particularly in Prescot, as well as in Birmingham. The English Watch Company was the brainchild of American entrepreneur Aaron Dennison, co-founder of the Waltham factory. In the early 1870s, he founded the Anglo-American Watch Company in Birmingham, which quickly specialised in the production of cases on English territory to assemble movements imported from the United States. Watch production was sold to British investors, who founded English Watch Company. However, this company was unable to remain competitive with imported watches and was liquidated in 1895.[42]

The second attempt to provide an industrial response to foreign competition was the founding of the Lancashire Watch Company in Prescot in 1889. It was organised on the model of the National Watch Company factory in Elgin, which the director of the Lancashire factory, T. P. Hewitt, visited during a stay in the United States. However, this company also failed to launch competitive watches on the market. Hewitt's strategy of mass production of entry-level watches was hampered by problems of work organisation and product development. It was indeed complicated, if not impossible, to set up factory production by employing former independent watchmakers and home-based workers. Their work culture was unsuited to the industrial factory. Furthermore, the Lancashire Watch Company launched too many different models and products on the market. It was impossible to standardise production and achieve low manufacturing costs. The company was closed down in 1910.[43]

The industrial census organised in Great Britain in 1907 perfectly illustrates the existential difficulties of its watch industry. While domestic production was estimated at 75,000 watches, the volume of imports amounted to 2.5 million watches.[44] The maintenance of a traditional and artisanal production system in the context of a market open to foreign competition thus led to the disappearance of the British watch industry.

The French watch industry focused on its national market

The weak commitment of French watchmakers to foreign markets, particularly in the United States, meant that American competition did not lead to a debate as existential as in Switzerland. The 1870s therefore did not correspond to a decade of crisis for French watchmakers. On the contrary, the upward trend in the number of watches hallmarked in Besançon which began in the early 1850s continued through to 1883, when it reached a peak of 500,000 pieces. Afterwards, there was a real collapse in production until 1888 (fewer than 300,000 pieces), followed by a new phase of growth.[45] However, the difficulties of the 1880s were not linked to the development of American watchmaking but to the import of Swiss watches. The terms of the debate on the future of the watch industry were therefore specific to the French market.

The transformation of the production system was not a major issue. A few large factories were set up in Besançon during this period, particularly in the field of component production. This is the case, for example, of the Société Générale des Monteurs de Boîte Or, founded in 1880, which at the end of the century employed around 250 people in the production of cases.[46] However, the French watch industry remained a sector comprising SMEs. They gradually introduced machines into their workshops and modernised production, but there was no upheaval in industrial organisation.

Some entrepreneurs and local politicians in Besançon explained the crisis of the 1880s by the focus on the domestic market and therefore the need to strengthen local competitiveness. Victor Dreyfus, a member of the administrative commission of the Besançon Watchmaking School, published a small booklet in 1890 in which he explained the French difficulties with regard to the development of the Swiss watch industry.[47] In particular, he stated that:

the obvious cause of the stagnation of the production in Besançon is that it is deprived of the resources that exports could provide for its activity; not only to ensure its future, but if its existence is not to be called into question, it is important that our manufacturers, alongside Swiss manufacturers, take an honourable place on foreign markets as quickly as possible.[48]

Improving the competitiveness of French watches depended not only on their price, but also, and above all, on their quality. With this in mind, Dreyfus and Besançon watch manufacturers committed to the development of collective institutions to improve the precision of their watches. In 1885, a chronometric service was opened at the Besançon Observatory, followed three years later by the launch of a competition.[49] Similarly, in 1890, the French state recognised and subsidised the Besançon Watchmaking School, which thus became national; it had previously been municipal. In 1896, a certificate in chronometry was even launched by the Faculty of Sciences of the University of Besançon.[50]

The strengthening of the customs barrier was a second response to trade difficulties. The Franco-Swiss treaty of 1882 imposed high customs duties on Swiss watches. The introduction of specific, not *ad valorem*, taxes disadvantaged low-value watches and thus helped to maintain this market for Besançon watchmakers. New rates adopted in 1892 further reinforced customs protectionism.[51] However, this policy was the subject of debate among French watchmakers. Their great dependence on Switzerland for the supply of blanks and components made some of them favour free trade between the two countries. The Besançon Chamber of Commerce was therefore opposed to the new tariffs of 1892.[52]

In this context of a strong focus on a national market, the Japy family was among the rare entrepreneurs to propose a reform of the industrial organisation

Figure 2.6 The factory of the watch manufacturer Bloch-Geismar, Besançon, undated (early twentieth century).

of the French watch industry. In March 1877, on the occasion of the awarding of prizes to the apprentices and workers of the Chambre syndicale d'horlogerie, Émile Japy, director of the Parisian subsidiary of the family business, took the floor and defended the idea of modernising production structures.[53] He encouraged the introduction of machines and the mass production of watches in order to lower manufacturing costs and target a mass market. This was exactly the new strategy of his company in Beaucourt. The emergence of several blank factories on Swiss territory caused him to lose the traditional domination he had exercised until then. The company diversified and looked for new markets. In the watch business, Japy began in 1869 to produce and sell complete watches.[54] However, it was difficult to compete with American watches. Although Japy's management stated in the annual report of 1876–1877 that 'it is essential to adopt automatic machines'[55] for the manufacture of watches, the conservative management of the company, which preferred self-financing to bank loans, led to a technological backwardness. Watch production became loss-making in 1880.[56] The great variety of products also made the introduction of American mass-production methods problematic. It was only in 1888 that Japy decided to radically transform his organisation. He then enlisted the services of a Swiss engineer, Auguste Sandoz, who 'undertook to make a good mechanical watch with interchangeable parts that would not advance more than the watches we make today, i.e. three minutes a day [...]'.[57] He was sent to America on a study trip and continued his work in 1890–1891. The following year, Sandoz resigned, mainly because of the difficulties in implementing the new organisation of work in the Japy workshops. He settled on the other side of the border, in the village of Chézard (canton of Neuchâtel), where he founded a watch factory under the name Sandoz & Cie. The inability of Japy's managers to transform the organisation of their firm is a perfect illustration of the limited impact of American competition on an industry that confined itself to its national market.

A new watchmaking giant: Germany

Germany experienced tremendous development of its watch industry in the context of widespread economic and demographic growth. The production of watches rose from a maximum of several tens of thousands of pieces in 1870 to more than a million in 1890. This sharp rise was based on the adoption of American production methods by a handful of companies. However, the watches manufactured by these companies were not enough to meet the growing domestic demand – Germany became the leading market for Swiss watches in 1890.

The two original watch production centres in Germany show contrasting developments. On the one hand, in Glashütte, A. Lange & Söhne continued on the path of technical excellence. Although the company grew from 100 to 250 employees between 1870 and 1900, its production remained limited: in 1891 it amounted to around 1,500 pocket watches.[58] It thus had little impact on industrial development. On the other hand, the Gebrüder Junghans company in the Black Forest experienced unprecedented growth, initially based on the production of alarm clocks. In 1872, one of its directors, Arthur Junghans, travelled to the United States, where he visited clock factories in Connecticut. Adopting product standardisation and mass-production methods, he made his company the world's leading alarm clock manufacturer in the 1880s, with a workforce of about 850 workers in 1889. Building on this success, Junghans began to develop simple and inexpensive watches, working with Swiss technicians, but did not become a major watch producer until after 1900.[59]

Therefore, industrialised watch production in Germany appeared essentially outside these two centres. Various companies managed to set up mechanised production of simple and inexpensive watches, often employing Swiss watchmakers. One example is Gebrüder Thiel, a company founded in Thuringia in 1862, which produced about 1 million pocket watches in 1897.[60] At the same time, the Bavarian Thomas Haller AG, founded in 1842, produced around 200,000 pocket watches.[61]

Conclusion

The rise of the American factories in Waltham and Elgin had a considerable impact on the world watch industry. The challenge was both technological and commercial. These two companies adapted new production techniques to manufacture watch movements, enabling final assemblers to offer a wide variety of watches at an extremely low cost. The watches were therefore not produced entirely by machine, as the final operations were carried out by hand. In addition, the Waltham and Elgin factories were established in the United States, the world's largest market, and exported, particularly to the British Empire, through their subsidiary in London. The European responses to the American challenge were fourfold.

First, Swiss watchmakers embarked on a partial modernisation of their production system. Basically, the manufacture of movement blanks and components had the highest degree of concentration and mechanisation – a model relatively close to that implemented in the United States. This rationalisation made it possible to remain competitive in terms of price, a major challenge due to the size of the American market. However, the final assembly of the watch and its decoration and design remained operations little affected by the industrial transformation process. The Swiss watch industry managed to retain its comparative advantage based on its ability to offer a wide variety of products to customers in all countries of the world. Productive modernity and commercial flexibility strengthened Switzerland's dominant position in the world watch market.

Second, there was some opposition to the introduction of the US production system and the idea of mass-producing standardised products. Indeed, the promotion of high-quality craft production was considered as a way to fight American competition. This position was particularly that of the London watchmakers, but can also be observed in old watchmaking centres in Switzerland such as Geneva or Le Locle. Ultimately, this path to survival through product excellence was often problematic. The British watch industry disappeared towards the end of the nineteenth century and Geneva watchmakers largely abandoned their elitist position. In certain rarer cases, such as those of the Geneva companies Patek, Philippe & Cie, and Vacheron & Constantin, small artisanal structures that concentrated on the manufacture of products of excellence managed to survive, gradually mechanising their production system and maintaining, or even strengthening, their competitiveness.

Third, in France, customs protectionism was a means of maintaining a large internal market for companies that were not very competitive on the world market. State intervention targeted particularly American and Swiss companies. In Britain, on the other hand, the absence of protectionism can be considered to have been detrimental to attempts at industrialised watch production – high production costs in the early years of operation being an unfavourable development factor in the context of a liberalised market.

Fourth, and finally, it must be emphasised that the American challenge did not call into question the basis of competition in the watch industry. It remained largely based on national foundations. The desire to keep national markets to domestic producers (United States and France), the shared ambition to achieve production excellence (Britain), and the need for collective action to strengthen the presence of the country's industry on world markets (Switzerland) led to national situations in which the common interests of watch companies outweighed their competition. Furthermore, it should be noted that there was virtually no direct foreign investment in the world watch industry before the 1890s. The American Watch subsidiary which opened in London in 1874 is a notable exception. Even so, the subsidiary transferred only a minimal part of its manufacturing activities to Britain. Similarly, although early German watch factories often poached Swiss watchmakers, there was no Swiss direct investment in German watchmaking. The watch is a product with a high added value, it can be easily transported, and it can therefore be easily exported. Moreover, industrialisation involved major investments and required large volumes of production. Under these conditions, Swiss watchmakers preferred to export to Germany rather than open new factories there. In 1890, the world watch industry was not very globalised and was still organised on national grounds.

Notes

1. Quoted in Donzé, *Du comptoir familial à la marque globale*, 46.
2. Moore, *Timing a Century*, 232.
3. Calculated on the basis of Moore, *Timing a Century*. Profit is unknown for the years 1885–1890.
4. E. C. Alft and William H. Biska, *Elgin Time: A History of the Elgin National Watch Company, 1864–1968* (Elgin: Elgin Historical Society, 2003), 24.
5. Harrold, *American Watchmaking*.
6. Moore, *Timing a Century*.
7. Ibid., 55.
8. Cited by James C. Watson, *American Watches: An Extract from the Report on Horology at the International Exhibition at Philadelphia in 1876* (New York: Robbins & Appleton, 1877), 33.
9. Bureau of the Census, *Biennial Census of Manufactures*, 1905; Bureau of Foreign and Domestic Commerce, *Foreign Commerce and Navigation of the United States*, 1889.
10. Laurence Bodenmann, ed., *Philadelphia 1876: le défi américain en horlogerie* (La Chaux-de-Fonds: Musée International d'Horlogerie, 2011).
11. Bruno Gilberti, *Designing the Centennial: A History of the 1876 International Exhibition in Philadelphia* (Lexington: University Press of Kentucky, 2015).
12. Musée International d'Horlogerie (MIH), La Chaux-de-Fonds, Minutes of the meetings of the SIIJ, 30 June 1876.
13. Ibid.
14. Jacques David, *Rapport à la Société intercantonale des industries du Jura sur la fabrication de l'horlogerie aux États-Unis* [Report to the SIIJ on the manufacture of watches in the United States], 1876; the report was unpublished at the time, but a facsimile was published by Longines, Saint-Imier, 1992.
15. Ibid., 48.
16. Ibid., 99.
17. MIH, minutes of the SIIJ, 3 October 1876.
18. Quoted by Watson, *American Watches*, 34.

19 Jacqueline Henry-Bédat, *Une région, une passion: l'horlogerie: une entreprise: Longines* (Saint-Imier: Compagnie des Montres Longines, 1992), 213.
20 Koller, *'De la lime à la machine'*, 114.
21 Watson, *American Watches*, 33.
22 Pierre-Yves Donzé, *L'invention du luxe: histoire de l'horlogerie à Genève de 1815 à nos jours* (Neuchâtel: Alphil, 2017), 57.
23 Mémoires d'Ici, Saint-Imier (MDI), *Fonds de l'Ecole d'horlogerie de Saint-Imier*, Report of the Meeting of the Directors of the Watchmaking Schools of French-Speaking Switzerland (17 May 1877).
24 Donzé, *Les patrons horlogers de La Chaux-de-Fonds*.
25 Marco Richon, *Omega Saga* (Biel: Fondation Adrien Brandt Pour le Patrimoine Omega, 1998), 18–19.
26 Donzé, *Les patrons horlogers de La Chaux-de-Fonds*.
27 Philippe de Coulon, *Les ébauches: deux siècles d'histoire horlogère* (Neuchâtel: La Baconnière, 1951).
28 Johann Boillat, *Les véritables maîtres du temps: le cartel horloger suisse (1919–1941)* (Neuchâtel: Alphil, 2013).
29 Donzé, *Du comptoir familial à la marque globale*, 49.
30 Linder, *De l'atelier à l'usine*.
31 Cédric Humair, *Développement économique et État central (1815–1914): un siècle de politique douanière suisse au service des élites* (Berne: Lang, 2004), 352.
32 Laurence Marti, *Une région au rythme du temps: Histoire socio-économique du Vallon de Saint-Imier et environs, 1700–2007* (Saint-Imier: Édition des Longines, 2007), 126–127.
33 Joëlle Knobel, 'Une manufacture d'horlogerie biennoise: la Société Louis Brandt & Frère (Omega), 1895–1935' (Master diss., University of Neuchâtel, 1997).
34 Christine Gagnebin-Diacon, *La fabrique et le village: la Tavannes Watch Co (1890–1918)* (Porrentruy: Cercle d'Études Historiques de la Société Jurassienne d'Émulation, 1996).
35 See the journal *La Fédération horlogère suisse*, 24 September 1893.
36 *Statistique annuelle du commerce extérieur de la Suisse* (Berne: Direction Générale des Douanes, 1890).
37 Patrick Linder, *Au cœur d'une vocation industrielle: les mouvements de montre de la maison Longines: (1832–2007): tradition, savoir-faire, innovation* (Saint-Imier: Édition des Longines, 2007), 98–151; Richon, *Omega Saga*, 203.
38 *Statistique annuelle du commerce extérieur de la Suisse*, 1886 and 1890.
39 Moore, *Timing a Century*, 81; Bureau of Foreign and Domestic Commerce, *Foreign Commerce and Navigation of the United States*, 1890.
40 Humair, *Développement économique et État Central*, 539–540.
41 Davies, 'Time for a change?', 61.
42 Moore, *Timing a Century*.
43 Davies, 'Time for a change?'; John G. Platt, *Lancashire Watch Company History and Watches* (Chester: Inbeat Publications, 2016).
44 Davies, 'Time for a change?', 63.
45 Mayaud and Mauerhan, *Besançon horloger*, 64.
46 Ibid., 73.
47 V. Dreyfus, *La défense d'une industrie nationale: la fabrique d'horlogerie de Besançon* (Besançon: Imprimerie Millot Frères et Cie, 1890).
48 Ibid., 13.
49 Mayaud and Mauerhan, *Besançon horloger*, 82.
50 Ibid., 87.
51 Gern and Arlettaz, *Relations franco-suisses*, 112–113, 300.

52 Ibid., 188.
53 'Distribution solennelle des récompenses aux ouvriers et apprentis', *Revue Chronométrique*, vol. 9 (1876–1877): 221–232.
54 Lamard, *Histoire d'un capital familial*, 184.
55 Ibid., 219.
56 Ibid., 223.
57 Ibid., 286.
58 Schmid, *Lexikon der Deutschen Uhrenindustrie*, 386–387.
59 Ibid., 310–312.
60 Ibid., 598–599.
61 Ibid., 217.

3

The first phase of technological and industrial diffusion, 1890–1914

In September 1910, the management of the Longines factory, one of the largest in Switzerland with more than 900 workers, dismissed all its staff. The company had earlier suffered a violent strike, organised by the workers' unions, which had demanded the compulsory affiliation of the heads of workshops (called 'visitors') to their organisation. Faced with the intransigence of the employers, nearly 400 workers had presented their resignations, and this led to the lockout. The conflict was settled in the following days thanks to the intervention of the local authorities. The management of Longines reintegrated the dismissed workers and agreed no longer to refuse to unionise its professional and managerial staff, while the union undertook to leave the latter free to join or not the union.[1] This social conflict, which was one of the most important that the Swiss watch industry had ever experienced, marked the end of an era: it was now the company directors who decided on the organisation of work in their factories. From then on, the workers' unions concentrated on defending workers' working conditions (wages, social insurance, paid holidays) and no longer on the principle of factory work. Conflicts related to the introduction of machines into the manufacturing process also gradually disappeared during the 1900s.

Thus, at the beginning of the 1890s, the industrialisation of watchmaking – that is, the concentration of workers in factories and the use of machines – was widely accepted and no longer the subject of much debate among company directors. American watch manufacturers had not succeeded in establishing themselves as the new dominant players in the global watch industry, although they exercised strong dominance in their home market. They introduced, however, a new mode of production which European competitors had to adopt, at least partially, including in protectionist countries such as France.

The quarter century between 1890 and the outbreak of World War I was a period of strong growth, marked by the expansion of international trade and the development of companies on a global scale. Urbanisation, the development of railways and communications, and the rise of factory work provided favourable conditions for the large-scale consumption of timepieces. The clock and watch became useful and necessary instruments in modern societies.[2] Furthermore, the unification of time on a national scale, the worldwide dissemination of the Gregorian calendar, as well as the adoption of Greenwich Mean Team (GMT) as the universal reference time were leading to a globalisation of the Western time-measurement system.[3]

World demand for watches thus entered a phase of strong growth, reflected in the increase in global production, which rose from around 10 million pieces in 1890 to more than 26 million in 1914 (see table 3.1). This development benefited above all Swiss and American companies, which continued to dominate the world market. Between them, these two nations even saw their market share increase during this period from 67.7% to 72.8%. However, they presented a distinct profile. Although Switzerland's production doubled, its relative importance declined. This was mainly due to the small size of the Swiss market. Swiss watchmakers sold most of their production on world markets and did not benefit from the development of a large and protected domestic market, unlike the United States. American watchmaking showed indeed very high growth, but this was essentially based on the domestic market. The rise in demand also enabled some entrepreneurs to set up new organisational models that would soon compete with existing manufacturers. This was particularly the case in the United States, where a jewellery merchant based in New York City, Joseph Bulova, developed his business on a transnational scale, between Switzerland and the United States (see p. 55).

Table 3.1 World watch production, 1890 and 1914

Country	1890		1914		1890–1914
	Volume	%	Volume	%	Growth (%)
Switzerland	5,000,000	52.1	10,500,000	40.2	110
United States	1,500,000	15.6	8,500,000	32.6	466.7
France	1,320,000	13.8	2,000,000	7.7	51.5
Germany	1,300,000	13.5	4,300,000	16.5	230.8
Britain	250,000	2.6	100,000	0.4	−60
Japan	–	–	100,000	0.4	–
Others	230,000	2.4	600,000	2.3	160.9
Total	9,600,000	100	26,100,000	100	171.9

Sources: See appendix.

The other European nations followed varied trajectories, ranging from the strong development of Germany to the decline of Britain and the stagnation of France. Finally, a newcomer appeared: Japan. Japanese production amounted to less than 1% of world production in 1914, but for the first time watchmaking factories were beginning to operate outside Western countries. The transfer of technology and the transplantation of production were phenomena that affected the whole of the manufacturing industry during this period of initial globalisation.[4]

The development of knockdown production in the Swiss watch industry

Between 1890 and 1914, the Swiss watch industry underwent an unprecedented phase of development and retained its position as the undisputed world market leader. Annual watch production doubled between these two dates, from 5 to 10 million pieces. This strong expansion was based on the generalisation of manufacturing work and the maintenance of the organisational form of an industrial district which, thanks to the division of labour between numerous small specialised workshops, made it possible to produce a wide variety of products. The comparative advantage of the Swiss watch industry was based on both productive and commercial elements.

The transformation of the production system gave rise to a few large watch companies (IWC, Longines, Omega, Tavannes Watch, Zenith) and several firms producing blanks that employed hundreds of workers. It also led to the emergence of a machine tool industry, which developed the equipment necessary for the industrial production of watches. Moreover, this upheaval of the productive structures led workers to join together in trade unions. In 1911, workers came together in the Federation of Workers in the Watch Industry, which had more than 17,000 members in 1914 and fought for the improvement of working conditions in factories. The power of this union led to the creation of several employers' organisations, the Bernese Cantonal Association of Watch Manufacturers, founded in 1916, being one of the most important.[5] Alongside

Figure 3.1 Workers leaving the Longines factory, Saint-Imier, Switzerland, 1911.

these large companies, hundreds of small specialised workshops emerged and developed. They were active in the manufacture of special components, in the assembly of watches or movements, as well as in watch decoration, all these operations being difficult to standardise and to carry out on production lines, for technical or commercial reasons. In 1911, the Swiss watch industry included 858 companies employing a total of almost 35,000 people, an average of 40.8 people per firm.[6]

As for the commercial aspects, they were characterised by the extension and diversification of outlets (see table 3.2). In 1920, the United States once again became the leading market for Swiss watches, accounting for 22.2% of exports. However, with the exception of that country, there was a strong diversification, which had two major aspects compared with 1890 (see table 2.2, p. 38). First, Switzerland was less dependent on a few large outlets. While the top three markets had accounted for more than 50% of exports in 1890 and the top 10 markets for a total of 86%, these proportions fell to less than 40% and 70%, respectively, in 1920. Second, the presence of Asian and Latin American countries among the 10 largest markets was remarkable. India, Japan, and China together then represented a market equivalent to that of Britain and France combined. Argentina was as important an outlet as France alone. Thus, between 1890 and 1920, the Swiss watch industry freed itself from its historically strong dependence on European and North American markets.

Table 3.2 The 10 main markets of the Swiss watch industry, 1920

Country	Value of exports (millions of francs)	Market share (%)
United States	72.2	22,2
United Kingdom	35.8	11.0
India	21.5	6.6
Spain	19.5	6.0
Japan	19.2	5.9
France	15.0	4.6
Argentina	14.2	4.4
China	11.9	3.7
Canada	9.2	2.8
Germany	8.9	2.7
Others	99	30
Total	325.8	100

Source: Federation of the Swiss Watch Industry (personal communication with author).

Moreover, this context of worldwide expansion of watch exports led some entrepreneurs to adopt a new practice aimed at strengthening their foothold in certain markets: knockdown production. This involved exporting the watch in disassembled form (movements or parts of movements) and assembling it in the country where it was sold.[7] The generalisation of mechanised production at

Figure 3.2 The Tavannes Watch factory, circa 1920.

the beginning of the twentieth century ensured the interchangeability of parts and facilitated the export of disassembled watches, since their assembly no longer required any particular adjustment work. This practice was not unique to watchmaking. It could be observed in most mechanical industries, but it was generally large multinational companies that used this method to organise themselves globally, such as the sewing machine manufacturer Singer or the electrical equipment company General Electric, and not small firms as in Swiss watchmaking. In Switzerland, this practice was referred to by the specific term *chablonnage*, which is found in archival documents and literature. Since there is no equivalent English term, I use the expression 'knockdown production' to refer to this practice throughout this book. Knockdown production is generally a terminology used in the car manufacturing industry, but it designates a similar process of exporting components and assembling them overseas.

The main objective of such a practice was to avoid the high customs duties on finished watches. Cooperation with local case manufacturers also made it possible to launch products on the market that corresponded to consumer tastes, and thus to respond effectively to a wide variety of demands throughout the world. The share of movements in watch exports (number of pieces) highlighted the development of knockdown production. Until 1914, this practice was not perceived as dramatic by Swiss watchmaking circles. The export of movements was certainly on a continuous upward trend, rising from 297,000 pieces in 1890 to 1.2 million in 1914, but in relative figures, this growth was not so marked. The share of watch movements in Swiss watch exports (number of pieces) rose until 1906 (13.6% compared with 5.9% in 1890), but this was followed by a decline in the years leading up to World War I (11.9% in 1914).

Moreover, until 1920, knockdown production was mainly directed towards North America. The United States and Canada alone accounted for 50.3% of the volume of movements exported in 1900, 50.7% in 1910, and 79.4% in 1920.[8] Russia was the second outlet, with 15.3% in 1900 and 21.4% in 1910. Finally, Japan was in third place, with shares of 19.8%, 10.3%, and 10.9%, respectively. This practice, adopted in particular by Longines and Omega, explains the first place occupied by the American market for Swiss watchmakers after World War I.

The example of Russia, one of the main markets for Swiss watchmaking in the 1900s, is a good illustration of this phenomenon. The practice of knockdown production was a direct consequence of the industrial policy of the Russian authorities, who encouraged the establishment of foreign companies on their territory thanks to customs protectionism. The large American manufacturing companies thus opened production subsidiaries in Russia, following the example of the Singer sewing machine manufacturer (1897),[9] and Swiss watchmakers did the same. At the end of the nineteenth century, several of them made Russia their main outlet, in particular the Neuchâtel firms Paul Buhré, Moser, Zenith, and above all Ch. Tissot & Fils. They had branches there, to which part of the production activities (assembly, casing) were gradually transferred. In 1878, an engineer from Neuchâtel settled in Saint Petersburg and opened a watch factory in which about 20 Swiss watchmakers worked.[10] However, by putting an end to commercial relations with Swiss watchmakers, the new Bolshevik regime stopped the practice of knockdown production and cut itself off from an important source of know-how. It was only after World War II that a genuine domestic watch industry was created in Russia (see chapter 4, pp. 82–83).

The situation is different in the case of the United States and Japan, due to the continuity of industrial policy between the end of the nineteenth century and the interwar period. The gradual strengthening of customs protectionism led some Swiss watchmakers to extend knockdown production during the 1920s and 1930s. However, what watch manufacturers in Switzerland feared was that the techniques and know-how passed on with knockdown production in watch assembly workshops set up abroad would lead to the emergence of new industrial competitors, thus calling into question Switzerland's dominant position.

Challenging the Waltham–Elgin duopoly

Between 1890 and 1914, the American watch industry as a whole continued to develop along the lines of the model established in previous decades. However, knockdown production was an opportunity to challenge the duopoly of Waltham and Elgin at the beginning of the twentieth century.

The growth is significant: the total value of American watch production rose from 6 million dollars in 1889 to 11.9 million in 1904 and 14.3 million in 1914.[11] Moreover, although the proportion of exports was increasing (3.4% of production in 1889 and 10.2% in 1914), its level remained extremely low. The domestic market was the essential basis for the development of American companies. Moreover, national production was not sufficient to meet all demand. In 1914, imports of watches amounted to 3.4 million dollars, of which 2.7 million came from Switzerland.[12] Thus, at that time, American companies controlled approximately 80% of the domestic market.

American Watch (renamed Waltham Watch Co. in 1907) and Elgin National Watch continued to dominate the domestic industry. In 1900, they both had an annual production of more than 400,000 watches, which represented about half of the production of conventional watches (i.e. without the 'dollar watches'), the other half being manufactured by about 15 small companies.[13] This domination was also based on cooperation between the two firms, although this had been illegal since the adoption of the Sherman Antitrust Act of 1890. During the 1900s, these two manufacturers exchanged technical and commercial information on the launch of new products in order to join forces against possible competitors. The cartel also covered the selling price of watch movements, as well as the prices for the purchase of cases. Moreover, these companies put pressure on distributors and retailers to limit sales of watches from other US companies.[14]

However, the dominant position of the two American giants was challenged by three types of company, which managed to set up business models to overcome the difficulties linked to the Waltham–Elgin duopoly. First, there was the manufacture of entry-level mechanical watches, mass-produced and sold at extremely low prices, known as 'dollar watches'. This new product was the result of a collaboration between a Connecticut clock manufacturer, Waterbury Clock Co., and New York-based mail-order traders, the Ingersoll brothers. In 1892, Waterbury, which had started developing watches a few years earlier, first supplied its timepieces to the Ingersolls.[15] The unit price of one dollar was adopted four years later with the highly successful 'Yankee' model. In 1910, Waterbury reached a production of 3.5 million watches for R. H. Ingersoll & Bro. Six years later, R. H. Ingersoll & Bro. opened a factory in Britain, Ingersoll Ltd, to produce dollar watches for the British market. With the launch of this new product, positioned in the lowest market segment, Waterbury and Ingersoll established themselves as key players in the American watch market. The dollar watches represented an annual production volume that exceeded that of conventional watches from the early 1900s and reached double that of conventional watches in 1910.[16]

Second, there was the emergence and development of a third major generalist manufacturer: Hamilton Watch.[17] Many watch factories went bankrupt in the 1870s and 1880s because they were unable to produce and sell enough watches to amortise the investments made in the means of production. In 1892, the founders of Hamilton Watch entered the watch market with the development of

Figure 3.3 Advertisement for Hamilton Watch, 1920.

a special product: a watch for the railways (figure 3.3). Growth was rapid during the first decade of operations, with production volume rising from just over 5,000 pieces in 1894 to over 50,000 in 1902. The company then entered a phase of stagnation, as the specific market for railway watches had reached saturation point, but Hamilton managed to establish itself as a major manufacturer, despite opposition from the Waltham and Elgin factories (see box 3.1).

Third, and finally, some entrepreneurs used the knockdown production of Swiss watches to set up competitive firms on the American market. The best-known example is that of Bulova.[18] The company was founded by a Czech emigrant, Joseph Bulova, who founded a jewellery business in New York in 1875 and had been importing Swiss watches since 1887. In 1911, he opened a branch in Biel, Switzerland, to obtain direct supplies of Swiss products, and quickly transformed it into a watchmaking workshop. Thus, in the mid-1910s, the Bulova company had a two-headed organisation – one that produced in Switzerland and marketed in the United States. Other jewellers had a similar profile. Tiffany had a watchmaking workshop in Geneva from the early 1870s, and purchased watches through Patek, Philippe & Cie. However, Bulova was the only company to have organised itself sustainably on a transnational scale during this period. It was on this basis that it established itself as one of the world's largest watch manufacturers in the following decades (see chapter 4, pp. 80, 88).

Box 3.1 Waltham and Elgin manufacturers attempt to limit Hamilton Watch expansion: letter from American Watch to Ball & Co. (1904)

Dear Mr. Ball,

Last week in New York I had an important conference with Mr. Hulburd, President of the Elgin National Watch Company, who informed me, among other things, that he was about closing an arrangement with you to manufacture your 18 size watches, which you were proposing to transfer from the Hamilton factory to his. This is all right, and in the right direction, and I hope that it will result satisfactorily and profitably to both of you. If you had consulted me about it I should have strongly advised it. As you know, we are not able to handle it, in any event, and for reasons which you also know, would much prefer to see it go to the Elgin Company; besides the fact that for you to be associated with both the leading companies which are far the largest, is decidedly in your interests, and in my opinion for the best interests of the railroad watch business as a whole.

Mr. Hulburd asked me about prices, wishing some information in this direction so as not to conflict with us, and generally to avoid friction. He is entitled to this information, but as our arrangement is confidential I will first have to have your consent.

Source: Harvard Business School, Boston, Barker Library, MSS 598, American Waltham Watch Co, P. 3 V. 975, Letter from the management of American Watch (Waltham) to Ball & Co. (Cleveland), 26 May 1904.
Note: Ball & Co. was a small company specialising in watches for railways.

The growing dependence of the French watch industry on Switzerland

Between 1890 and 1914, the French watch industry experienced a phase of slow growth, in the general context of rising domestic demand. National production rose from around 1.3 million to 2 million pieces during this period. The city of Besançon thus continued its development.

However, the technological dependence of French watch companies on Switzerland increased. Blanks and regulating parts of the movement were still imported in large quantities from Switzerland. For example, the number of watch movements imported grew from 655,000 in 1900 to 998,000 in 1910. In 1911, the number of imported movements exceeded 1 million.[19] France thus played an increasing role as a final assembler for Swiss watchmakers. French foreign trade statistics highlight the importance of this function. In 1910, France exported 2.8 million complete watches, but only 99,000 were manufactured entirely in the country.[20] Moreover, French watch companies were not very competitive on the American market, which was by then the largest in the world. Between 1890 and 1914, France accounted for only 6% of American watch imports. It was even overtaken in this market by Germany (8%).[21] Furthermore, American imports from France fluctuated sharply, while those from Germany showed a general upward trend after 1898, reflecting the growing competitiveness of this industry (see figure 3.4).

Figure 3.4 US imports of French and German watches and watch movements, value in thousands of dollars, 1890–1914.

Source: Bureau of Foreign and Domestic Commerce, *Foreign Commerce and Navigation of the United States* (Washington, DC: US Department of Commerce, 1890–1914).

Figure 3.5 Japy Frères works, Beaucourt, circa 1910.

It should also be noted that French exports to the United States included a few re-exports of Swiss watches – which constituted the bulk of French watchmaking foreign trade. Swiss watchmakers tended to export directly to the United States. Their use of France as an intermediary was intended to given them access to particular markets. In 1900, French exports of complete watches (essentially re-exports of Swiss products) went to Britain (37.5%), Japan (12.1%), Spain (11.7%), and the British Indies (9.6%).[22] These four outlets accounted for more than 70% of all such exports.

This trade was also being encouraged by a change in French customs policy. The agreement signed with Switzerland in 1906 led to the lowering of import duties on many products, including watches, entering French territory. The number of finished watches imported into France went from 1.8 million in 1900 to 2.9 million in 1910.[23] After World War I, Besançon watch manufacturers denounced 'a sort of hold of Swiss watchmaking on the French market'.[24] Invoking patriotic arguments – 'while our workers were defending the soil, the Swiss made extensive use of our market, where they no longer had any competition, and poured enormous quantities of small-volume watches into it' – they demanded protectionist state intervention.

The Japy company is a good example of the difficulties French watch companies experienced in imposing themselves on a competitive market. Initially, the managers of this firm organised its production on a transnational scale, shortly after the adoption of the mass-production system. Wishing to internalise know-how related to the production of complete watches, in 1894 they opened two watch workshops to add to their long-established site in Beaucourt, one in Besançon and the other in La Chaux-de-Fonds, the latter being transferred to Biel in 1898.[25] As a result, the production of finished watches increased in value from 633,000 French francs in 1884 to 1.2 million in 1909.[26] However, this organisation was not enough to enable the company to compete against Swiss, American, and German manufacturers. It suffered from low profitability and organisational difficulties due to the strong diversification into small mechanics and ironmongery, which took place in the last third of the nineteenth century. Japy's Besançon workshop was closed in 1901 and the Biel factory in 1906.

The industrial development of the German watch industry

In February 1911, the newspaper *L'Impartial*, published in La Chaux-de-Fonds, Switzerland, featured an article entitled 'A fearsome competition for our watch industry: what is being prepared in Germany'.[27] Its author stated that:

> there will be very important improvements in the manufacture of German watches. Indeed, one of the most powerful and richest watch manufacturers in Germany is currently completing the installation of a complete set of equipment, from which will undoubtedly come a watch of serious quality, because it will be built on the most modern data and with the help of the best machines and the best workers.

The figures for German national production prove the Neuchâtel newspaper right. With the national volume of watches manufactured rising from around 1.3 million to 4.3 million between 1890 and 1914, Germany was the country with the second highest growth rate in the world, after the United States.

This success was based on a small number of large companies adopting US-inspired methods of mass production of standardised goods. Gebrüder Junghans was involved in the development and production of watches. In 1900, the company, already one of the world's largest manufacturers of alarm clocks, absorbed Thomas Haller AG, which had succeeded in organising the mechanised production of watches. Two years later, the engineer Oskar Junghans, son of one of the company's directors, studied at the Locle Watchmaking School, Switzerland, and set up a division for the production of pocket watches within the family business. In addition, the company extended its activities to other countries through the takeover of local companies. In 1902, it bought the company Gebrüder Resch in Austria and this first acquisition was followed by others in Austria, Italy, France, Poland, and Spain. The activities of these various subsidiaries are not known in detail, but several of them obviously set up watch assembly in parallel with the manufacture of alarm clocks. Junghans can thus be considered one of the first multinational companies in the watch industry. In 1906, its production of pocket watches amounted to approximately 1.5 million pieces.[28]

Alongside this industrial giant, several dozen smaller companies emerged, while some major alarm clock producers, such as Kienzle, followed Junghans' example and also launched themselves into the manufacture of watches. Finally, one should also mention the case of the manufacturer of high-precision watches,

Figure 3.6 Pocket-watch workshop, Gebrüder Junghans, 1925.

A. Lange & Söhne, which became truly industrialised at the turn of the century. In 1914, it reached a production of 70,000 pocket watches, compared with only 1,500 in 1891.[29]

The tremendous industrial boom in German watch manufacturing was finally coupled with a high level of competitiveness on the world market, expressed by the increase in sales in the United States after the end of the 1890s (see figure 3.4, p. 56). This threat on the world market caused the Swiss watchmaking elite to react. In 1914, the journal *La Fédération horlogère suisse* warned Swiss workers that Charles Junghans was passing through Biel 'with a view to hiring workers for his factory and introducing the manufacture of new types of watches in his country. Workers, don't believe in the fine promises made to you.'[30]

The emergence of a new watchmaking nation: Japan

During the years 1890–1914, Japan was the only non-Western country to attempt the industrial production of watches. These attempts took place in the context of the country's opening up to world trade and strong industrialisation based on the transfer of technology from Europe and the United States.[31] In the particular case of watchmaking, the Japanese market opened up in the early 1860s. It was controlled by a few Swiss traders based in Yokohama. They worked in

Figure 3.7 Workers leaving Hattori main factory, 1937.

collaboration with Japanese merchants who distributed their watches to a vast network of retailers established in the major cities. Until the 1890s, this was a niche market dominated by gold and silver watches.

However, these Japanese merchants aspired to have their own factories so that they would no longer be dependent on imports of Swiss and American watches. It was in this context that Japan's first watch companies appeared.[32] Technology transfer and knockdown production played a particular role in this process. The first two companies to attempt the industrial production of watches were set up by watch traders wishing to make their own watches. The companies Osaka Watch (1895–1905) and Japan Pocket Watch Manufacturing (1898–1901) produced several thousand watches using equipment and know-how from the United States and Switzerland, respectively. However, production volumes were too low to amortise the equipment, so they closed down after a few years of operation.

The only long-lasting enterprise that managed to establish itself during these years was the company founded by Kintaro Hattori in 1881, which became known as Seiko. It started as a shop in the Ginza district of Tokyo, selling mainly imported clocks and watches. In 1892, Hattori started manufacturing clocks, then diversified the company's production to watch cases (1893), pocket watches (1895), and alarm clocks (1899), with the aim of becoming a generalist manufacturer of timepieces. Clock production was booming – it rose from 24,000 pieces in 1894 to 41,000 in 1896 and 63,000 in 1897.[33] Soon thereafter the volumes exceeded those of its main competitors on the domestic market. This was a profitable activity which, together with the sales in imported watches, provided the bulk of the company's income until around 1910. The production of watches was more difficult to organise. The technical challenges and the financial obstacles were higher, but the other divisions of the company made it possible to finance the production of pocket watches at a loss for several years, until the rise in customs tariffs made it a profitable division. This particular management system allowed Hattori to succeed where others had failed.

In 1894, Hattori decided the company should start making watches. He entrusted the supervision of this operation to Tsuruhiko Yoshikawa, a mechanic in charge of the technical direction of the company who surrounded himself with new technical skills through the involvement of 'a young Japanese man who had spent a few years at the Locle Watchmaking School'.[34] Hattori also made a trip to the United States and Europe in 1899–1900, which took him to visit the Waltham and Elgin factories, as well as several watch and machine companies in Switzerland and Germany. He also brought back some German machine tools from this trip, then from the United States during a second trip in 1906. Finally, he adopted a strategy of acquiring watchmaking technology in Japan itself, by buying the machines and hiring the workers of the Japan Pocket Watch Co. and, probably, the Osaka Watch Co. The first watch models were copies of Swiss and American watches. The volume of production remained modest in its early days (24,000 watches in 1903).[35] Moreover, Hattori watches were not yet competitive against imported products: their average price was significantly higher. It was not until 1911 that the watch division recorded its first profit, thanks to successive

Figure 3.8 Registration of the brand Citizen by Rodolphe Schmid in Switzerland, 1918.

increases in import taxes (1899 and 1906), which made foreign products more expensive for the Japanese consumer.[36] At the same time, Hattori improved the company's technical capabilities. He started his own manufacture of parts, such as dials (1913). Between 1909 and 1917, he also launched six new watch models on the market, including the Empire watch (1909), the first model for mass production made with the company's new equipment. It was produced in improved forms until 1934, and was Hattori's great commercial success in the first part of the twentieth century.[37] In 1913, he also marketed the country's first wristwatch (Laurel), designed on the model of a Swiss watch.[38] By 1915, his company was employing more than 1,100 workers, who produced more than 500,000 clocks and 125,000 watches.[39]

Finally, a second enduring watch company was set up in Japan during this period. It grew out of knockdown production and was founded by a Neuchâtel watch manufacturer, Rodolphe Schmid. Born in Switzerland in 1871, Schmid moved to Yokohama in 1894, where he ran an import–export business while owning a watch factory in Neuchâtel, Cassardes Watch Co.[40] Directly affected by the rise in customs tariffs in 1906, he transferred part of his production to Japan. In 1908, he began importing parts, which he assembled in a small workshop in Yokohama and put into cases imported from Switzerland. The company moved to Tokyo in 1912 and employed around 30 people in 1913. In that year, a new stage in the transfer was reached with the manufacture of cases in Japan, which led to violent reactions in Switzerland. The Neuchâtel Cantonal Chamber of Commerce, Industry and Labour wrote to the Swiss federal authorities, arguing:

> the Watchmaking Federation has already pointed out, without naming the manufacturer, what such a process denotes of selfishness, as well as the serious harm that the creation of a silver case factory by Swiss people who have had all their experience with us can cause to our watch industry.[41]

However, despite the transfer of the case production, the manufacture of other parts was not carried out in Japan until the early 1930s. Schmid also launched new brands on the market, such as Japan Watch (1909), Gunjin Tokei for a model intended for the army (1910), and, above all, Citizen (1918), which would become the brand of the second Japanese watchmaking group in whose foundation the Neuchâtel merchant participated (see chapter 4, pp. 81–82).[42]

Conclusion

The organisational structure of the world watch industry underwent a profound upheaval during the years 1890–1914, against a backdrop of exploding demand and the widespread adoption of the mass-production model. Switzerland retained an undisputed dominant position on the world market thanks to the modernisation of production methods and dynamic trade. The emergence and development of knockdown production made it possible to overcome certain customs barriers and to adapt watches better to specific local demands. The phenomenon occasionally led to the transfer of certain productive activities abroad, as in the case of Bulova in the United States and Schmid in Japan. However, it was not yet perceived as a problem for Swiss watchmakers.

With the exception of Switzerland, the countries in which mass production was widely adopted experienced the strongest growth. In the United States, the Waltham and Elgin factories kept their dominance of the domestic market, which they strengthened through cartel-like cooperation. The new companies that managed to establish themselves were positioned in particular segments for which they mass-produced standardised goods (railway watches or dollar watches). Similarly, German watch companies had a very strong growth thanks to the use of mass-production methods and the strong increase in their domestic market. Finally, in Japan, this same organisational model enabled Hattori to develop successfully the first watch factory outside Western countries. The German and Japanese watch companies engaging in watch production also benefited from know-how acquired in the production of similar goods, mainly clocks and alarm clocks. The watch is certainly smaller and therefore more complex to produce, but the technologies involved are very similar.

On the other hand, Britain witnessed the decline and virtual disappearance of the watch industry on its territory, due to the lack of modernisation of productive structures in the context of an economy converted to free trade. This country was an important market, but it was controlled by non-British, mainly Swiss, merchants. As for France, it remained in a position of technological dependence on its Swiss neighbour, which only increased with the transition to a liberal customs policy in 1906.

In 1914, the world watch industry remained largely organised on a national basis. The virtual non-existence of foreign direct investment, due both to the specificities of the watch (a high value-added and light product, therefore easily exportable) and to the small size of watch companies compared with other sectors of the manufacturing industry, and the concentration of most watch manufacturers on their domestic market, make it possible to consider nations as the basis for competition in this industry. The British subsidiaries of a few American manufacturers, as well as the foreign workshops of Junghans, were exceptions in the global industry. However, knockdown production challenged the national bases of the world watch industry. The phenomenon led, during the interwar period, to the first phase of globalisation.

Notes

1 Donzé, *Du comptoir familial à la marque globale*, 105–108.
2 Landes, *Revolution in Time*.
3 Luchien Karsten, *Globalization and Time* (New York: Routledge, 2013).
4 Geoffrey Jones, *Multinationals and Global Capitalism: From the Nineteenth to the Twenty-First Century* (New York: Oxford University Press, 2005).
5 On the industrialisation of watchmaking during this period, see Koller, 'De la lime à la machine'; Donzé, *Histoire de l'industrie horlogère suisse*.

6 Koller, *'De la lime à la machine'*, 183.
7 Ibid., 374–380.
8 *Statistique annuelle du commerce extérieur de la Suisse*, 1900–1920.
9 Fred V. Carstensen, *American Enterprise in Foreign Markets: Studies of Singer and International Harvester in Imperial Russia* (Chapel Hill: University of North Carolina Press, 1984).
10 Société Générale de l'Horlogerie Suisse SA (ASUAG), *Historique publié à l'occasion de son vingt-cinquième anniversaire, 1931–1956* (Biel: Arts Graphiques SA, 1956), 16.
11 Bureau of the Census, *Biennial Census of Manufactures*, 1905, 1914.
12 Bureau of Foreign and Domestic Commerce, *Foreign Commerce and Navigation of the United States*, 1914.
13 Harrold, *American Watchmaking*, 49–51.
14 Baker Library, MSS 598, Correspondence between Waltham Watch and Elgin Watch, 1900–1906.
15 Glasmeier, *Manufacturing Time*, 123–124.
16 Harrold, *American Watchmaking*, 50.
17 Don Sauers, *Time for America: Hamilton Watch, 1892–1992* (Lititz: Sutter House, 1992).
18 Journal de Genève, 29 June 1873 and 2 June 1877.
19 *Statistique mensuelle du commerce extérieur de la France* (Paris: Ministry of Finances, 1900–1911).
20 *Documents statistiques réunis par l'administration des douanes sur le commerce de la France: années 1909, 1910 et 1911* (Paris: Ministry of Finance, 1911).
21 Bureau of Foreign and Domestic Commerce, *Foreign Commerce and Navigation of the United States*, 1890–1914.
22 *Statistique mensuelle du commerce extérieur de la France*, 1900.
23 Ibid.
24 *Mémoire sur les conditions actuelles d'importation de la petite horlogerie et la nécessité d'une tarification 'ad valorem'* (Besançon: Le Fabricant Français, 1922), 5.
25 Lamard, *Histoire d'un capital familial*, 269.
26 Ibid., 280.
27 *L'Impartial*, 11 February 1911.
28 Schmid, *Lexikon der Deutschen Uhrenindustrie*, 312–314.
29 Ibid., 387.
30 *La Fédération horlogère Suisse*, 19 December 1914.
31 Pierre-Yves Donzé, *'Rattraper et dépasser la Suisse': histoire de l'industrie horlogère japonaise, 1850 à nos jours* (Neuchâtel: Alphil, 2014).
32 Ibid.
33 Mitsuo Hirano, *Seikosha Shiwa* (Tokyo: Seiko, 1968), appendices.
34 Swiss Federal Archives (SFA), Bern, E6.172, Letter from Consul Ritter to the Trade Division, 6 December 1895.
35 Hoshimi Uchida, *Tokei kogyo no hattatsu* (Tokyo: Seiko Institute of Horology, 1985), 351.
36 Hoshimi Uchida, *Evolution of Seiko, 1892–1923* (Tokyo: Hattori Seiko, 2000), 108.
37 Hirano, *Seikosha Shiwa*, 97.
38 Ibid., 118.
39 Ibid., appendices.
40 *Archives de l'horlogerie* (Berne: Office Polytechnique d'Édition et de Publicité, 2 July 1903).
41 SFA, E6.178, Letter from the Neuchâtel Cantonal Chamber of Commerce, Industry and Labour to the Commerce Division, 16 April 1913.
42 *Archives de l'horlogerie*, various volumes.

4

The transformation of the watch industry, 1914–1945

One for all – All for one. The draft American customs tariff proposal provides for an average increase of around 300% for watchmaking products, with no justification. Such a project constitutes an unfriendly act towards Switzerland; it compromises part of its national economy. To react against the danger that threatens us and in a spirit of solidarity, we ask all industrialists, craftsmen, traders and consumers to ban all goods from the United States from their offices, factories, workshops, garages, shops and homes.[1]

This call for a boycott of American products was made by the Swiss watch organisations in April 1930, during a demonstration in the streets of Biel attended by nearly 15,000 workers, led by the Socialist mayor and national councillor Guido Müller.[2] They denounced the sharp increase in import taxes introduced in the United States by the Smoot–Hawley Tariff Act of 1930. The trade war raged during the interwar period (1919–1939). The various economic crises of this period led most governments to adopt protectionist policies to limit imports and support local businesses. For Swiss watchmakers, higher tariffs meant greater difficulty in accessing the various foreign markets on which they depended.

Generally speaking, the interwar period was one of slowing growth in the world production and consumption of watches, due to the economic, social, and political crises affecting all countries. Between 1914 and 1937, world production increased from 26.1 million to 48.5 million watches (see table 4.1). Switzerland strengthened its leading position, with a world market share of around 50% in 1937. This relative increase was mainly to the detriment of the United States, whose position as the second watchmaking nation was not, however, called into question. Indeed, watch production in Germany and France grew only slightly. The main change during these two decades was the strong development of watch manufacturing in Japan, a success that was almost entirely due to Hattori & Co. becoming the world's largest producer in the 1930s.

However, despite this apparent stability, the world watch industry underwent a profound upheaval in its organisation during the interwar period, characterised by the transfer and expansion of watch production outside Switzerland. Knockdown production was indeed the object of a formidable expansion throughout the world, which led the major watch companies and the Swiss authorities to take measures to put an end to technology transfer and industrial transplantation. The cartel gradually put in place during the 1920s and 1930s,

Table 4.1 World watch production, 1914 and 1937

Country	1914		1937		1914–1937
	Volume	%	Volume	%	Growth (%)
Switzerland	10,500,000	40.2	24,700,000	50.9	135
United States	8,500,000	32.6	12,100,000	24.9	42.4
France	2,000,000	7.7	2,900,000	6.0	45
Germany	4,300,000	16.5	5,700,000	11.8	32.6
Japan	100,000	0.4	1,000,000	2.1	900
Others	700,000	2.7	1,400,000	2.9	144
Total	26,100,000	100	48,500,000	100	85.8

Sources: See appendix.

known as Watchmaking Statute (Statut horloger in French), played a decisive role in maintaining and strengthening the competitiveness of the watch industry (see p. 73). The institutional measures adopted in Switzerland are a rare successful example of state intervention to prevent technology transfer.[3]

This success is the result of Switzerland's comparative advantage in technology during this period, particularly with regard to the quality (precision and durability) of certain components of the watch-regulating organ (assortments, barrels, springs, etc.). Thus, the concentration of this specific knowledge in Swiss companies enabled the Swiss authorities to exercise effective control over industrial transplantation until the end of World War II. In other industries, where knowledge was shared between various nations and companies, the control of technological flows was generally not feasible in the medium term.[4]

Moreover, in other sectors of the manufacturing industry, the absence of legal constraints such as the Watchmaking Statute led some companies to transfer their production to their main markets to overcome the constraints of customs protectionism that developed strongly during the interwar period. Although this period is rightly considered as a phase of 'de-globalisation', due to the sharp decline in international trade and the limitations on migratory movements, it corresponds to a phase of strengthening the global organisation of manufacturing companies.[5] In the automobile industry, for example, Ford opened more than 20 foreign factories around the world between 1918 and 1940.[6] Swiss companies in many industrial sectors (food, chemicals, machinery) were themselves actively engaged in this process of globalisation, with watchmaking an exception, the cause of which is discussed below. It is therefore appropriate in this chapter to examine the factors contributing to the worldwide expansion of watch production during the interwar period.

The evolution of demand on the world market

The transformation of the world watch industry between 1914 and 1945 was not solely the result of economic policies. There were also major changes in the structure of demand, which had a considerable impact on the conditions of competition. New companies, sensitive to the changing tastes and needs of consumers, managed to establish themselves as dominant players, while others, which were slow to adapt, lost their competitiveness and disappeared.

Demand on the global market underwent two major evolutionary changes. First, sales outside the traditional American and European markets boomed until the beginning of the twentieth century. Admittedly, after the forced opening of Japan to international trade in the 1860s, all the countries of the world represented a potential outlet for watch manufacturers. However, sales in Asia, Africa, and Latin America constituted only a small part of business until the 1900s. Then, during the interwar period, they became a growing market. The statistics of Swiss watch exports express this phenomenon well. In 1920, India, Japan, China, and Argentina were among the top 10 markets for Swiss watches (see table 3.2, p. 50). Eighteen years later, despite the economic and political crises of the 1930s, India, Australia, and Argentina were among the 10 largest outlets (table 4.2). Moreover, the combined market share of the 10 largest countries fell sharply between 1920 (70%) and 1938 (53.3%), which also reflects the growing geographical expansion of outlets for Swiss watchmaking.

Table 4.2 The 10 main markets of the Swiss watch industry, 1938

Country	Exports (millions of francs)	Market share (%)
United States	32.0	13.3
United Kingdom	28.6	11.9
Italy	17.4	7.2
Argentina	9.7	4.0
Germany	8.1	3.4
Sweden	7.5	3.1
Australia	6.8	2.8
British India	6.4	2.7
Czechoslovakia	6.1	2.5
France	6	2.5
Others	112.7	46.7
Total	241.3	100

Source: La Fédération horlogère suisse, 25 January 1939.

Second, a major product change took place during the interwar period, with the shift from the pocket watch to the wristwatch. The composition of Swiss watch exports between 1920 and 1940 illustrates this development perfectly (see figure 4.1). During these two decades, the proportion of wristwatches rose from 24.6% to 84.7% of the total volume of exports. The change was gradual but irreversible. The wristwatch was an innovation which dated back to the end of the nineteenth century and which became established during the interwar period.[7] It contributed to the development of a new market: ladies' watches. By becoming visible on the wrist, the watch is no longer just a useful object that tells the time. It becomes a fashion accessory. The wristwatch was also the

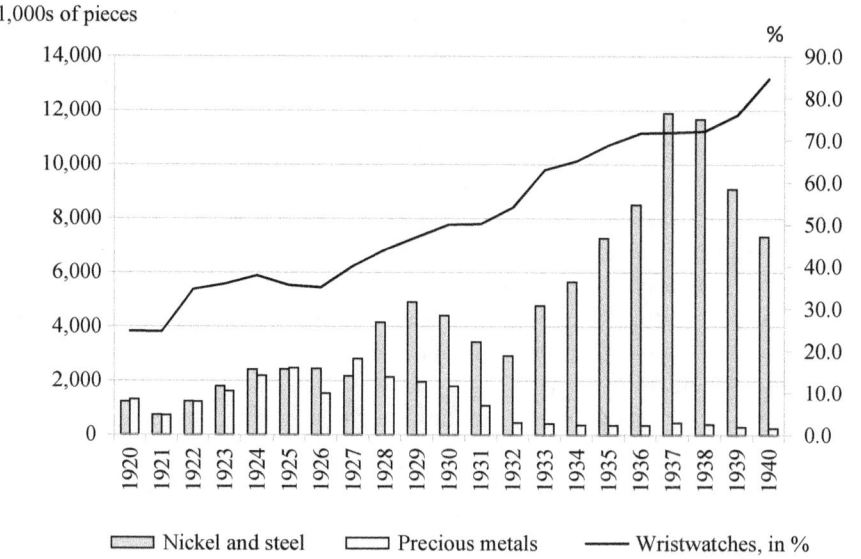

Figure 4.1 Swiss wristwatch exports, 1920–1940.

Source: H.-J. Siegenthaler and H. Ritzmann-Blickenstorfer, *Historische Statistik der Schweiz* (Zurich: Chronos, 1996), p. 627.

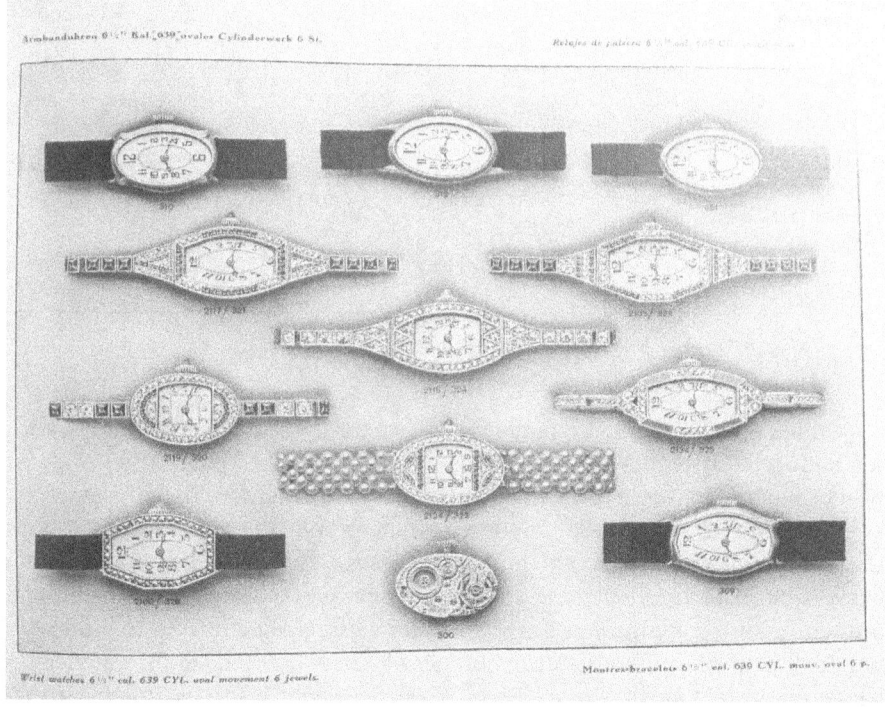

Figure 4.2 Catalogue of the Swiss watch company Numa Jeanin, 1931.

subject of technical innovations aimed at improving its durability, the main ones being the development of water resistance and the automatic movement, two innovations made by Rolex in 1926 and 1931, respectively.[8]

The switch to wristwatches also corresponded with the rise of simple and inexpensive watches for the general public. Until 1927, when wristwatches accounted for only one-third of Swiss exports, the share of precious metal watches (platinum, gold, and silver) was equivalent to that of steel and nickel products (see figure 4.1). However, after 1927, there was a collapse in the volume of precious metal wristwatches (to under 5% from 1935) and a tremendous growth in steel and nickel wristwatches. A large part of this volume was made up of Roskopf watches (i.e. simple and cheap mechanical watches, called 'pin-lever watches' in some countries).[9] In 1938, they accounted for 41.6% of total Swiss watch exports.[10] The growth experienced by the Swiss watch industry from the end of the 1920s was thus based on a democratisation of consumption. The situation was similar in other watchmaking nations.

The cartellisation of the Swiss watch industry

After World War I, the Swiss watch industry was confronted with a considerable growth of knockdown production, encouraged by the increase in customs protectionism around the world. The share of movements in total watch exports, which stood at 11.9% in 1914, rose to 21.1% in 1930, and 40.2% in 1940.[11] Moreover, this practice, which had been mainly limited to the United States and Japan at the beginning of the twentieth century, spread to many countries, particularly Germany, during the 1920s and 1930s. The risk of technology transfer and the emergence of new competitors therefore increased during this period. The second problem faced by the Swiss watch industry was a general downward trend in the prices of components (cases, dials, movement parts). The economic crises of 1921–1922 and 1930–1935, as well as the strong competition between Swiss manufacturers, led to a decrease in prices, which in turn put into question the profitability – and the existence – of many companies. The creation of a cartel that would govern both the conditions of export and the price of watch components was considered the best solution by a large proportion of entrepreneurs.

This view was reinforced by social and political factors. The Swiss watch industry was concentrated in the Jura mountains, outside the major cities, in a region that often had no other industrial activity. Industrial relocation to other countries would therefore have had disastrous effects in terms of jobs. Thus, several Socialist deputies intervened in the National Council in the 1920s and 1930s to call for a ban on knockdown production in the name of worker protection. They were supported by the population of the watchmaking regions, who in July 1931 submitted a petition, signed by 56,000 people, to the federal authorities. Affirming that 'knockdown production favours the manufacture of watches abroad and constitutes a serious threat for the future',[12] the petition called for state intervention to put an end to this practice. For the political authorities, it was not just a question of keeping jobs in Switzerland but more broadly of a decentralised production system, which helped to maintain social order. After the general strike of 1918, the political elites of the 1920s and 1950s were obsessed by the fear that industrial concentration in the urban centres would encourage trade unionism and communism. They sought to keep the workers in the local community and, from this perspective, supported the maintenance of industrial activity in the peripheral regions.

The cartellisation of the Swiss watch industry was a complex process that has been analysed in depth by Johann Boillat.[13] It had three main stages: the adoption of a series of conventions (1928), the creation of the Société Générale de l'Industrie Horlogère Suisse, more commonly known as Allgemeine Schweizerische Uhrenindustrie Aktiengesellschaft (General Swiss Watch Industry Co. Ltd), or ASUAG (1931), and legal intervention by the Swiss Confederation (1934). Initially, watchmaking circles sought an internal solution by bringing together the various companies of the sector in three groups according to their type of activity: watch manufacturers in the Swiss Federation of Watch Manufacturers' Associations (FH, 1924), manufacturers of blanks in the joint stock company Ébauches SA (1926), and parts manufacturers in the Union of Watch-Related Branches (Union des Branches Annexes de l'Horlogerie, UBAH, 1927).

The manufacturers of blanks played an essential role in this cartel. The three leading companies in this sector (Fontainemelon SA, A. Schild SA, and Ad. Michel SA), supported by the banks, merged to form the company Ébauches SA. With the support of the banks, more than 30 factories were bought up through to 1931. At that time, Ébauches SA controlled around 90% of production. Unlike the FH and UBAH, Ébauches SA was not an association but a company. It was the only real concentration in Swiss watchmaking in the 1920s. Its position as an

Figure 4.3 Advertisement for the manufacturer of watch movements O. Kessler SA, Grenchen, Switzerland, 1928.

oligopoly made it an essential player, since it was the company that supplied watch manufacturers with movement blanks.

In 1928, these three groups adopted a series of conventions known as the Watchmaking Conventions, focusing on three main points. First, the various member companies of these groups undertook to maintain commercial relations only with other signatory companies and to respect official minimum tariffs. Second, from 1931, these companies prohibited the export of dismantled watches throughout the world, with the exception of France and Germany. Third, the signatory associations decided to refuse the admission of companies created after 1929. Thus, these agreements aimed to control watch manufacturing by seeking to stabilise prices, prevent the establishment of new entrants, and avoid industrial relocation abroad. These agreements were first renewed in 1931 and then every five years. They remained in force until 1961.

However, the conventions had one weakness: dissent. They were private agreements, and it was not possible to make companies adhere to them. Several small watch manufacturers, who worked as assembly makers and exported unassembled watches – such as Rodolphe Schmid, the Neuchâtel watchmaker based in Yokohama – refused to be bound. To remedy this weakness, financial and political elites intervened with the creation in 1931 of a holding company, ASUAG.[14] The shareholders of ASUAG, whose share capital amounted to 10,006,000 francs, were made up of watch manufacturers (5 million francs), banks (5 million francs), and the federal government (6,000 francs in shares in return for 6 million francs in aid). In addition, the state granted an interest-free loan of 7.5 million francs and the banks loans of 15.5 million francs, making a total of 23 million francs, which was fully repaid in the early 1940s. The government justified the Confederation's financial commitment to a private company by the fact that ASUAG 'cannot of course be an ordinary public limited company for purely profit-making purposes. Its task is to safeguard the interests of the watch industry as a whole'.[15] Its board of directors had 30 members, five of whom were appointed by the Swiss government. Finally, the federal councillor (government minister) in charge of the Department of Public Economy automatically sat on the ASUAG board, which showed the importance the state attached to this company.

The aim of ASUAG was to strengthen the Watchmaking Conventions through a broad movement of industrial concentration. It acquired the company Ébauches SA and took over dozens of dissident blank factories, as well as companies active in the production of movement components. It thus functioned as a super-holding, controlling four holding companies: Ébauches SA (movement blanks), Société des fabriques de spiraux réunies SA (balance-springs), Fabriques d'assortiments réunies SA (assortments), and Fabriques de balanciers réunies SA (balance wheels), the last three being members of the UBAH. The strategy implemented by ASUAG in its concentration policy was to take a majority stake in these four holding companies in order to control them, but to leave a minority share to the managers of the companies acquired. The chosen path of industrial concentration, which did not clash head on with the interests of family capitalism, explains to a large extent the success of ASUAG.

The creation of ASUAG was an essential step in the reorganisation of the Swiss watch industry. It did not call into question the flexibility of the production system. The existence of dozens of independent watch manufacturers was an asset for the Swiss watch industry, enabling it to dominate the world market as it made it possible to supply a broad range of products. What the industrial and banking circles put in place, with the creation of ASUAG, was an industrial concentration at the level of watch movements. This strategy had two objectives. The first was the control of technology transfer and the maintenance of employment in Switzerland. The goal was to put an end to knockdown production. The second objective was to reduce the cost of movements. The rationalisation of production led to a certain standardisation of the various calibres. At Longines, for example, new calibres introduced in 1928 were produced according to various logics (size, thickness, type, etc.) and allowed cost control while guaranteeing a wide range of products.[16]

Thus, ASUAG's position was quite special within the Swiss watchmaking cartel: indeed, it was a real trust – that is, a company with a monopoly position. With the exception of manufacturers who produced their own movements – but obtained their components from ASUAG subsidiaries – all Swiss watch manufacturers were legally obliged to obtain blanks and certain parts (springs, balance springs, sets) from ASUAG. This control of the 'watch engine' market certainly helped to avoid knockdown production and industrial relocation abroad. But above all, it gave ASUAG omnipotence within the Swiss watch industry; its objective was to secure and make profitable the massive investments made by the banks. Until the quartz revolution, which made it possible for Swiss and foreign manufacturers to obtain cheap movements from elsewhere, ASUAG was the central player around which the Swiss watch industry was organised.

However, the industrial concentration achieved by ASUAG was not exhaustive and several new dissident companies emerged, leading to a maintenance of knockdown production. Ultimately, only legal intervention by the state was capable of putting an end to dissent. Watchmaking circles, opposed in principle to state legal intervention, tempered their reluctance during the crisis of the 1930s, which saw watch exports fall from 20.8 million pieces in 1929 to 8.2 million in 1932, and accepted state intervention, thus 'closing the circle'.[17] in the words of federal councillor Schulthess, head of the Department of Public Economy. The Confederation adopted three federal decrees between 1934 and 1936, which had the effect of legalising the Watchmaking Conventions of 1928. The first of these was on 12 March 1934, which made the opening of new watch companies, any increase in the number of workers, and the expansion, transformation (change of activity), and relocation of existing companies subject to a permit. In addition, the export of disassembled watches, blanks, and components was also subject to an official permit. The aim of this first decree was thus twofold: to exercise strict control over the structure of the watch industry as well as to control the

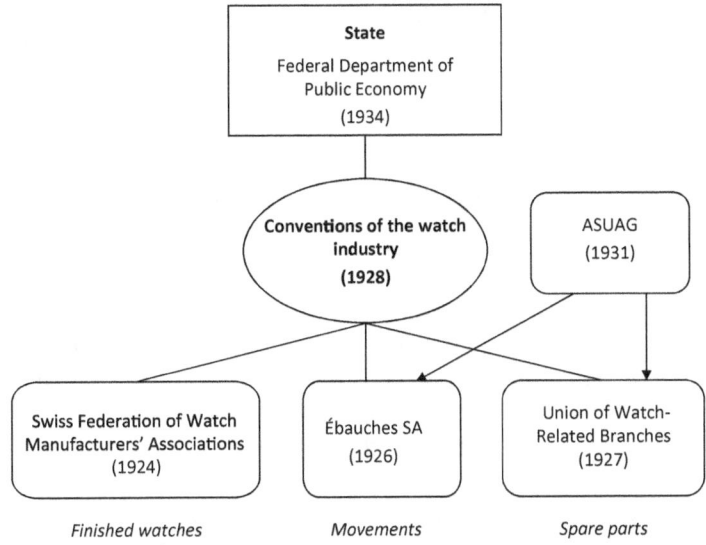

Figure 4.4 Organisation of the Swiss watchmaking cartel, 1934.
Source: Drafted by the author.

practice of knockdown production. The system was strengthened in 1936 with the adoption of two new decrees concerning the officialisation of minimum tariffs adopted within the framework of the 1928 convention, to which dissidents were now also subject (decree of 13 March 1936), and the regulation of home-based work, now limited to certain branches (decree of 9 October 1936). These three decrees were brought together and renewed once in 1937, then on numerous occasions until 1961. They formed the framework within which the Swiss watch industry operated for a quarter of a century, known as the Watchmaking Statute.

The massive state intervention in favour of the watch industry, both financial (ASUAG) and legal (the Watchmaking Statute), may seem surprising. The Swiss Confederation traditionally intervened little in industry, even in sectors in difficulty such as textiles. The crisis was certainly an influential factor, but it was not enough to explain this intervention, which was not observed as strongly in other sectors. Similarly, the desire to keep jobs in Switzerland was not a sufficient element, as other industries relocated massively in the interwar period without the public authorities being particularly concerned. The importance of the banks seems to be a decisive factor in state interventionism. They lent a lot, through a very broad credit policy, and invested, notably in ASUAG, during the interwar period. They also suffered heavy losses abroad, mainly in Germany. Some of them, like the Banque Populaire Suisse, which was saved by the Swiss Confederation in 1933, were facing serious financial difficulties. Bankers were able to play an essential role in encouraging state intervention in the watch industry. By legalising the 1928 agreements and the trust, the federal decrees of 1934 and 1936 stabilised the structure of the Swiss watch industry and secured the banks' financial commitments.

The domestic focus of the French watch industry

The French watch industry experienced a growth during the 1920s that enabled it to quickly return to and surpass pre-war levels. While national production can be estimated at 2 million watches in 1914, it amounted to about 2.5 million pieces in 1925, including about 200,000 gold watches.[18] However, French watchmaking lacked competitiveness on the world market and was strongly oriented towards the domestic market. Watch exports peaked at 164,000 watches in 1924 (less than 10% of total national production), and then entered a phase of long decline until World War II (see figure 4.5). For the 1920s as a whole, France accounted for only 1.8% of American watch imports (in value).[19] Furthermore, although the balance of trade was negative (to the benefit of Swiss watchmakers, who accounted for almost all French imports of complete watches), foreign watches represented only a small share of the domestic market. In 1925, they had a market share of only 10%. So, the assertion by Louis Trincano, director of the Besançon Watchmaking School, that World War I 'enabled Switzerland to invade our market'[20] was no longer relevant by the mid-1920s. French watch manufacturers thus dominated their domestic market but were largely absent from foreign markets.

Figure 4.5 French exports and imports of complete watches, volume, 1920–1937.

Source: *Statistique mensuelle du commerce extérieur de la France* (Paris: Ministry of Finance, 1920–1937).
Note: These figures do not include transit trade or trade with colonies.

Figure 4.6 Advertisement for Montres Lip, 1918.

However, despite a strong position on the domestic market, French watch manufacturers remained highly technologically dependent on Switzerland, particularly for the blanks and components. In 1926, there were only three small blank factories in Besançon, and the Japy company was no longer able to supply French watchmakers.[21] As a result, the French watch industry concentrated on assembly, case production, and decoration.

Some industrialists from Besançon, led by Louis Trincano, were nevertheless seeking to reduce this dependence and encourage the production of all watch components on national territory. In 1919, Trincano founded the Société Anonyme des Spiraux Français to promote the manufacture of balance springs.[22] Two years later, a trading association of watchmakers was set up, in order to 'no longer suffer the monopoly of certain foreign supplies'.[23] However, these various actions had little influence and did not reduce dependence on Switzerland.

The crisis of the 1930s hit the French watch industry hard. The companies that resisted best were those engaged in the production of wristwatches and that had adopted the mass-production system. They thus managed to offer the consumer products corresponding to the new fashion at affordable prices. The Lipmann factory in Besançon and a company in Villers-le-Lac introduced work lines and reduced the number of models in production.[24] However, these companies were small (see table 4.3). In 1930, the Lipmann factory, then the largest watch manufacturer in Besançon, employed only 245 workers.[25] Fred Lipmann, technical director of this company, was the main promoter of industrial rationalisation. A watchmaking standardisation office was created on his initiative in 1931.[26] In 1938, the French watch industry once again reached the production level of the mid-1920s, with an estimated volume of 2.7 million pieces.[27] World War II marked a new period of crisis for the industry, with national production falling to 850,000 watches in 1945.

Table 4.3 Watch companies in Besançon employing more than 20 people, 1930

Company	Activity	Number of employees
Lipmann	Watches	245
Japy	Watches	68
Zenith	Watches	62
Hatot	Watches	53
Société générale des Monteurs de boites	Watch cases	84
Lévy Frères	Watch cases	103
Rosa & Billot	Watches	30
Huguenin Fils & Cie	Hands	46
Société des compteurs	Meters	461
Etablissements de précision mécanique	Components	57
Beauchesne & Bredillot	Dials	125

Source: Daclin, *La crise des années 30 à Besançon*, 16.

The tremendous growth of the German watch industry

Germany is the European country whose watch industry had the strongest growth during the interwar period. Exports of complete watches rose from 1.1 million pieces in 1922 to a peak of 1.9 million in 1930.[28] The main markets were Britain and the Netherlands.[29] In 1928, German watch companies manufactured a total of 4 million watches.[30] Almost half of this volume was exported, which illustrates the high competitiveness of these products. The crisis of the 1930s abruptly interrupted this growth. Exports fell to an average of 1.2 million watches per year in 1932–1934, then to 1.3 million in 1935–1936.[31]

This boom was largely based on the development of several large companies, unlike the situation in France at the same time. In 1927, the German watch industry had around 25,000 workers, 20,000 of whom were in the Black Forest and 15,000 were employed by the six largest factories seeking to concentrate.[32] Most of these firms were founded in the second half of the nineteenth century and originally specialised in the manufacture of clocks (mainly wall clocks and alarm clocks). They adopted American mass-production methods and established themselves as the world's largest clock manufacturers. At the beginning of the twentieth century, they diversified into the production of watches.[33]

Table 4.4 The six largest German watch companies, 1927

Company	Locality	Number of employees
Gebrüder Junghans AG	Schramberg	5,500
Hamburg-Amerikanische Uhrenfabrik AG	Schramberg	2,000
Kienzle Uhrenfabrik AG	Schwenningen	2,600
Thomas Ernst Haller AG	Schwenningen	1,500
Friedreich Mauthe GmbH	Schwenningen	1,500
Vereinigte Freiburger Uhrenfabrik AG	Freiburg	1,750

Source: *Journal de Genève*, 3 October 1927.

These six companies discussed a merger in the mid-1920s, but the project was not carried out due to opposition from the Schwenningen companies. However, a mega-merger between Junghans, Hamburg-Amerikanishce, and Vereinigte Freiburger Uhrenfabrik took place in 1927–1928. Junghans' capital was increased from 15 to 21 million marks, allowing the acquisition of the other two companies.[34] The new firm became the largest clock factory in the world and an important producer of watches.[35]

The capital and mass-production technology of these large companies undoubtedly contributed greatly to the development of a watch industry in Germany during the interwar period. The role played by Switzerland in this process should also be emphasised. Knockdown production was indeed an important vector of technology transfer, particularly with regard to the manufacture of blanks and components. Several dissident Swiss watch companies – that is, not signatories to the 1928 conventions – opened subsidiaries in Germany, mainly in Pforzheim.[36] This eventually led to the emergence of a local watch component industry that made Germany independent of Switzerland in the mid-1930s, a process that was profoundly different from what happened in France at the same time.

Finally, in 1930 German manufacturers set up a cartel for the production and sale of cheap watches – an extension of the cartel of large watch manufacturers organised in 1917. It comprised all the houses in the industry, led by Junghans. This cartel not only decided on prices and delivery conditions, but also introduced quotas per firm for the domestic and export markets. A centralised sales office controlled the operation of the cartel.[37] German watchmaking was thus organised on a similar basis to that in Switzerland at the time, but without the intervention of the major banks and the federal state. This industry comprised only eight companies active in the manufacture of watches, of which only six produced cheap watches. Under these conditions, it was relatively easy to set up a cartel. It remained in force until World War II.

The transformation of the American watch industry

In February 1949, President Truman received the mayor of the city of Waltham and the governor of Massachusetts. They came to defend the interests of the large watch manufacturer in the suburbs of Boston, which had suspended its activities due to financial difficulties.[38] Waltham Watch had been conducting particularly effective lobbying in Washington for several decades. It was one of the main supporters of the development of customs protectionism. However, in 1949, the US federal government remained impassive, and Waltham Watch was declared bankrupt shortly afterwards. The transformation of the American watch industry during the interwar period was characterised by the development of new watch companies that were more competitive than the historical manufacturers.

The watch industry showed a similar dynamic to that of the entire industry and economy of the United States during the interwar period: after strong

Figure 4.7 Woman working on a drilling machine at Hamilton Watch, circa 1936–1937.

growth in the 1920s, it entered a phase of deep recession in the 1930s. The value of domestic production of watches (including movements and components) rose from 14.3 million dollars in 1914 to a peak of 39.4 million in 1929, before falling to 13.9 million in 1933. In 1939, production of complete watches alone rose to 47.7 million. In volume terms, available figures show that annual national production declined from about 11 million watches in the 1920s to 6 million in 1931 and 6.4 million in 1933.[39] It reached its pre-crisis level again in 1939, with 12.5 million watches.[40]

The crisis was violent and reinforced the lack of competitiveness of American companies. In 1914–1921, the value of watch exports amounted to an average of 2.7 million dollars, or less than 10% of domestic production. It then showed a general downward trend that accelerated during the crisis of the 1930s but that had begun prior to that. In addition, there was an extremely high level of watch imports, mainly from Switzerland, despite strong fluctuations. For Swiss watchmakers, dependence on the American market was also increasing during this period (21% of the value of watch exports on average over the period 1914–1945). The United States imported watches to a total value of 181 million dollars in 1914–1940, whereas it exported watches to a value of only 24 million dollars.[41]

Under these conditions, American manufacturers saw protectionism as a means of safeguarding their interests. They obtained successive customs

Figure 4.8 Exports and imports of watches and watch movements by the United States, value in thousands of dollars, 1914–1940.

Source: Bureau of Foreign and Domestic Commerce, *Foreign Commerce and Navigation of the United States* (Washington, DC: US Department of Commerce, 1914–1940).

increases, culminating in the adoption of the Smoot–Hawley Tariff Act of 1930. However, US customs protectionism led to an increase in smuggling and worsened relations between Switzerland and the United States until the signing of an agreement between the two countries in 1936, which led to a reduction in import duties.[42]

However, these protectionist measures were of little help to Waltham Watch, which lost its status as the leading American manufacturer. After reaching a peak in 1920, with a turnover of more than 8 million dollars and a production of 616,000 movements, it entered a phase of stagnation and decline, despite the favourable economic situation (5.9 million dollars of gross sales in 1928), mainly due to industrial unrest within the firm and a belated involvement in the production of wristwatches. In 1929, pocket watches still accounted for 40% of the volume of movements produced.[43] Waltham Watch barely survived the crisis but anyway went bankrupt in 1949. As for Elgin Watch, it had an annual production of more than 1 million movements in the 1920s and diversified into the development and manufacture of measuring instruments. Badly hit by the crisis, it entered a period of growth at the end of the 1930s thanks to the production of military equipment.[44] For its part, Hamilton managed to experience a new phase of development during the 1920s by diversifying its activities outside its original market of railway watches. This expansion was made possible in particular by the acquisition in 1928 of Illinois Watch, a company that had started developing wristwatches at an early stage.[45]

Customs protectionism and knockdown production, however, presented an opportunity for a new type of business to emerge and grow. Organised on a transnational scale, with factories in Switzerland and the United States, quality wristwatches were launched on the American market that met the tastes of local customers. Bulova is undoubtedly the best expression of this. Although it had had a factory in Switzerland since 1911, rising US tariffs encouraged it to transfer part of its production to American soil and make itself independent of Swiss manufacturing. In the 1920s, it thus developed a strategy of acquiring specific watchmaking know-how by buying up assortment and machine workshops in Switzerland. This technical mastery enabled it to open a blank factory in the United States at the beginning of the 1930s. However, it continued to produce certain movements on Swiss soil, which were assembled in the United States. In the 1930s, Bulova also became involved in the distribution of Swiss brands on the American market. In particular, it obtained the Vacheron Constantin agency and took control of the Longines-Wittnauer company. The role of these two Swiss manufacturers in the knockdown production trade to the United States is unclear, but it seems likely that the cooperation with Bulova led to the assembly in the United States of the watches of these two prestigious brands and enabled them to overcome serious financial difficulties during the crisis of the 1930s.[46] For Bulova, the transfer of technology during the interwar period was an economic success that enabled it to establish itself as one of the most important American watch companies, alongside traditional manufacturers such as Waltham Watch and Elgin Watch. Its turnover rose from 858,000 dollars in 1926 to 15.7 million dollars in 1938.[47] Bulova's transnational organisation was also adopted by smaller American companies, such as Benrus Watch and Gruen Watch, which also had branches in Switzerland.

In Switzerland these companies were considered Swiss, mainly due to the location of the management of their subsidiaries. From the 1920s, Bulova's Swiss subsidiary was managed by a Swiss citizen and received financial support from the Cantonal Bank of Berne, a local bank heavily involved in lending to regional watch companies.[48] The Swiss subsidiary of Gruen Watch was also managed by a Swiss national in the 1940s,[49] and both companies were signatories to the 1928 conventions and members of the Swiss watchmaking cartel. During the 1930s, they negotiated with the Swiss watchmaking organisations (FH, Ébauches, and UBAH) over the possibility of exporting components to their American factories, on the basis that they considered this to be an internal matter. In January 1943, Gruen obtained an export permit and in exchange undertook to buy at least 300,000 movements a year in Switzerland, not to manufacture components in the United States, and to limit its American production to two types of movements.[50] Bulova, accused in the 1930s of having signed a secret agreement with ASUAG[51] – which has not been found in the archives – signed a contract similar to Gruen's in 1948.[52]

The rise of watchmaking giants in Japan: Seiko and Citizen

Japan was the country with the strongest growth in watch production during the interwar period. It rose from around 100,000 pieces in 1914 to a peak of more than 1.7 million in 1940,[53] an increase that was almost exclusively due to Hattori & Co. (90% of national production in the 1920s and more than 70% in the late 1930s). The founding of the company Citizen Watch in 1930 did not challenge Hattori's dominant position in Japan. In 1935, with a production of more than 700,000 watches, it could be considered the largest watch factory in the world.

This success was based on a particular strategic positioning: the mass production of high-quality watches.[54] Hattori surrounded itself with engineers from the best universities in the country. They selected a small number of high-precision Swiss watches, including models manufactured by Longines and Nardin, on the basis of which they developed their own watches. Hattori made the country's first wristwatch in 1913 and launched the Seiko brand in 1924. In all, the company produced only 14 models between 1924 and 1934. These watches were massproduced in the ultra-modern factory opened in Tokyo after the earthquake of 1923 and equipped with machine tools imported from Switzerland. Hattori also depended on Switzerland for the supply of specific components, particularly springs, but invested in research and development (R&D) during the 1930s to master these technologies.

As for Citizen Watch Co., it was born in 1930 from the meeting between a watch manufacturer based in Yokohama, Rodolphe Schmid, who had already registered the brand Citizen in Switzerland in 1918, and Japanese watch

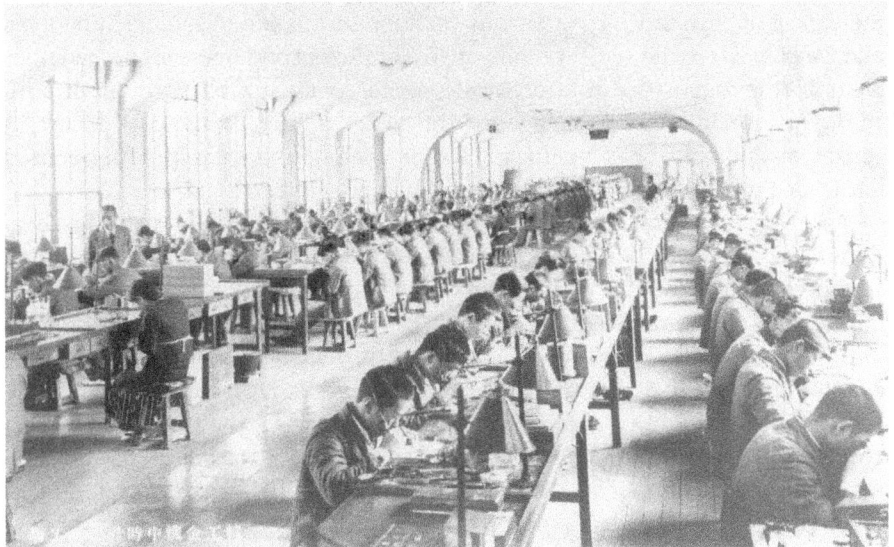

Figure 4.9 Seikosha, watch assembly workshop, circa 1930.

merchants who wanted to have their own factory rather than import products. While the Japanese watch merchants provided capital and access to their distribution networks, Schmid brought technology and know-how. He imported Swiss machine tools (1933) and ordered plans for new calibres from a Geneva engineer (1934). Watches manufactured by Mido, which Schmid imported into Japan, served as models for the three new types of wristwatches that Citizen marketed until the end of World War II (1931, 1935, and 1941). This technological boom enabled Citizen to enter a development phase, marked by the opening of a new factory in 1934. In 1939, Citizen reached a volume of around 250,000 watches.

The development of a watch industry in Japan caused great concern in Switzerland in the early 1930s, mainly because the country had by then become an important outlet for Swiss watchmaking (6.9% of watch exports between 1920 and 1929). However, Hattori and Citizen did not represent threats outside the Japanese market. In 1937, Japanese watch exports amounted to only 14,000 pieces – that is, less than 1% of national production. Moreover, the Pacific War put a – temporary – end to Hattori's expansion.

A new watchmaking nation: the Soviet Union

The Soviet watch industry did not originate from knockdown production and assembly of Swiss watches on its territory. Such activities are evidenced at the beginning of the twentieth century, but the revolution of 1917 put an end to them. It was not until the mid-1930s that a Swiss watch company, Tavannes Watch, attempted to revive watch production in collaboration with the Soviet authorities.[55] In 1935, it applied to the Federal Department of Public Economy, which had been monitoring the application of the watchmaking conventions regulating the export of parts since the previous year, for permission to sell machine tools and watch parts to the Soviet Union and to train Soviet engineers in the Tavannes factory. This request led to a political scandal, against a background of anti-communism and the struggle against the Socialist Party on the part of certain conservative media, with federal councillor Obrecht declaring himself opposed to the idea of 'handing over our manufacturing secrets to Russia'.[56]

However, it was indeed from a transfer of technology and industrial relocation that a Soviet watch industry emerged during the 1930s. By putting an end to commercial relations with Swiss watchmakers, the new Bolshevik regime also put an end to the practice of knockdown production and cut itself off from an important source of know-how. Thus, when they wished to develop their own watch industry, the Soviet authorities adopted an active policy of technology transfer. They bought two American companies in 1930, the Dueber-Hampden Watch Co. (Ohio) and Ansonia Watch Co. (New York).[57] In addition, about 20 American technicians moved to Russia to organise the factories and launch production.

The acquisition of know-how thus enabled the official start of watch manufacturing in Moscow's Factory No. 1 in 1930. Other industrial sites were set up in the following years: Moscow Factory No. 2 (1931), Pensensky Factory (1933), and Uglitch Factory (1940).[58] Production sites were also opened in Minsk and Leningrad. Together, these factories produced an estimated 500,000 watches up to World War II, with technical assistance from Swiss watchmakers and mechanics.[59] French watch engineers also went on technical assistance missions to the Soviet Union in the 1930s.[60] Finally, a new watch factory was opened in 1941 in Tchistopol (Tatarstan).[61] It was the result of the relocation of Factory No. 1 due to the war and specialised in the production of watches for soldiers.[62] However, the war with Germany had disastrous effects, pushing back the real development of the Soviet watch industry after 1945.

Conclusion

The world watch industry continued to grow between 1914 and 1945. The evolution of production technologies (mass production) and modes of consumption (wristwatches) supported this development. Mass production also facilitated the expansion of the watch industry into new nations, such as Japan, Germany, and Russia. In all these countries, large companies made the industrialisation of watch production possible. They also had the means to invest in R&D and to free themselves gradually from their technological dependence on Switzerland for the supply of blanks and regulating components. From this perspective, the trajectory of the French watch industry, composed solely of SMEs, illustrates the difficulties of building an independent watch industry.

On the eve of World War II, Switzerland was faced therefore with a growing number of competitors. However, it retained its comparative advantage thanks to an organisational model that incorporated both modern production technologies (mass production of blanks and components under the supervision of ASUAG) and the flexibility and adaptability of watch manufacturers to the varied tastes of customers around the world (final assembly of the watch by hundreds of independent factories). The production of Swiss watches more than doubled between 1914 and 1938, and from 1934 the Watchmaking Statute guaranteed control of technology transfer and industrial transplantation.

Furthermore, the competitors of Swiss watchmakers remained largely concentrated on their own domestic market during this period. American, French, and Japanese manufacturers were virtually absent from the world market. Only the German manufacturers managed to export, but volumes amounted to around only 1 million watches in the mid-1930s, while the Swiss exported more than 20 million. The threat remained relative.

State action made a decisive contribution to the development of the world watch industry during the interwar period. Customs protectionism allowed the development of watch companies in their own domestic markets in the United States and Japan. In addition, it reinforced knockdown production in these countries. Finally, in Switzerland, the watchmaking cartel found real stability thanks to the intervention of the federal authorities. Thus, unlike other sectors of manufacturing industry, multinational companies did not transform the watch industry during the 1920s and 1930s. Companies organised internationally proved to be extremely rare and were not representative of the general dynamics of the watch industry. Only new American factories such as Bulova or the German watch giant Junghans had workshops in more than one country. In other industries, on the contrary, customs protectionism reinforced direct investments by manufacturing companies. For example, between 1920 and 1940, Nestlé opened condensed milk and chocolate factories in 18 new countries.[63]

The specificities of the watch (a high value-added product that is easy to transport, and therefore to export) and the technical difficulties in implementing mass production of standardised movements made it difficult and costly to transplant factories abroad. Assembly workshops were a solution to these difficulties, but only Swiss entrepreneurs or those sourcing Swiss-made watch components were able to open such workshops around the world. The concentration of component production in a small number of companies (Germany, United States, Japan) or technological dependence on Switzerland (France) meant that knockdown production was strongly linked to Switzerland. This was also what gave meaning – and effectiveness – to the Watchmaking Statute.

These various factors explain to a large extent why the world watch industry remained organised on a national basis when World War II broke out. Competition in the watch market was not only between companies, but also, and even more importantly, between nations. Major changes occurred in the following decades.

Notes

1. *La Fédération horlogère suisse*, 30 April 1930.
2. Ibid., 3 May 1930.
3. Pierre-Yves Donzé, '*Swiss Made* but global: from technology to fashion in the watch industry, 1950–2010', in *Industries and Global Competition: Business Beyond Borders*, eds Bram Bowens and Pierre-Yves Donzé, and Takafumi Kurosawa (New York: Routledge, 2017), 195–214.
4. Pierre-Yves Donzé and Shigehiro Nishimura, eds, *Organizing Global Technology Flows: Institutions, Actors, and Processes* (New York: Routledge, 2014).
5. Jones, *Multinationals and Global Capitalism*.
6. Mira Wilkins and Ernest Frank Hill, *American Business Abroad: Ford on Six Continents* (Detroit: Wayne State University Press, 1964), 434–435.
7. Sylvie Béguelin, 'Naissance et développement de la montre-bracelet: histoire d'une conquête (1880–1950)', *Chronometrophilia*, vol. 37 (1994): 33–43.
8. Harry Borer, '1878–1978. Centenaire de la manufacture des montres Rolex SA, Bienne', *Neues Bieler Jahrbuch* (1979): 101–109; Donzé, *Histoire de l'industrie horlogère suisse*, 174–176.
9. Jean-Michel Piguet, ed., *Le drôle de montre de Monsieur Roskopf* (Neuchâtel: Alphil, 2013).
10. Swiss Social Archive (SSA), Zurich, SMUV, 04–0063, statistics on Roskopf watches.
11. *Statistique annuelle du commerce extérieur de la Suisse*, 1914–1940.
12. *Feuille fédérale* (1931), 206.
13. Boillat, *Les véritables maîtres du temps*.

14 Also known as the Société Générale de l'Horlogerie Suisse.
15 *Feuille fédérale* (1931), 213.
16 Linder, *Au cœur d'une vocation industrielle*.
17 *Feuille fédérale* (1950), 76.
18 Louis Trincano, *L'industrie horlogère française* (Besançon: Chambre Intersyndicale des Fabricants d'Horlogerie de l'Est, 1927).
19 Bureau of Foreign and Domestic Commerce, *Foreign Commerce and Navigation of the United States*, 1920–1929.
20 Trincano, *L'industrie horlogère française*, 5.
21 Aimée Moutet, *Les logiques de l'entreprise: la rationalisation dans l'industrie française dans l'entre-deux-guerre* (Paris: Éditions EHESS, 1997), 122.
22 Claude Briselance, 'Les écoles d'horlogerie de Besançon: une contribution décisif au développement industriel local et régional (1793–1974)' (PhD diss., University of Lyon II, 2015), 368.
23 Trincano, *L'industrie horlogère française*, 6.
24 Moutet, *Les logiques de l'entreprise*, 122.
25 Pierre Daclin, *La crise des années 30 à Besançon* (Besançon: Belles Lettres, 1968), 16.
26 Moutet, *Les logiques de l'entreprise*, 279.
27 Briselance, 'Les écoles d'horlogerie de Besançon', 564.
28 *Deutsche Uhrmacher Zeitung*, 1923–1931.
29 *L'Impartial*, 4 March 1924.
30 *Die Uhrmacher Woche* (1930), 802.
31 *Deutsche Uhrmacher Zeitung*, 1932–1936.
32 *Journal de Genève*, 3 October 1927.
33 Schmid, *Lexikon der Deutschen Uhrenindustrie*.
34 *Journal de Genève*, 3 October 1927.
35 Schmid, *Lexikon der Deutschen Uhrenindustrie*, 312–315.
36 Koller, *'De la lime à la machine'*, 388–391 and 452–459.
37 *La Fédération horlogère suisse*, 13 December 1930.
38 *Journal de Genève*, 4 February 1949.
39 Bureau of the Census, *Biennial Census of Manufactures*, 1914–1939.
40 Jean-Jacques Bolli, *L'aspect horloger des relations commerciales américano-suisses de 1929 à 1950* (La Chaux-de-Fonds: La Suisse horlogère, 1956), appendix XII.
41 Bureau of Foreign and Domestic Commerce, *Foreign Commerce and Navigation of the United States*, 1914–1940.
42 Bolli, *L'aspect horloger des relations commerciales*.
43 Moore, *Timing a Century*, 218.
44 Alft and Briska, *Elgin Time*.
45 Sauers, *Time for America*, 76.
46 Koller, *'De la lime à la machine'*, 419–431.
47 *Moody's Industrial Manual*, 1929 and 1939.
48 Koller, *'De la lime à la machine'*, 421–423.
49 SFA, E7004, 1967/12, 80, Note from the Federal Department of Economic Affairs, 6 May 1958.
50 SFA, E7004, 1967/12, 80, History of Gruen Watch Mfg. (undated); Archives Cantonales Jurassiennes (ACJ), Porrentruy, Fonds Péquignot, 100, contract between the watchmaking organisations and Gruen Watch, 11 January 1943.
51 Koller, *'De la lime à la machine'*, 423.
52 ACJ, Fonds Péquignot, 100, contract between the watchmaking organisations and Bulova Watch, 7 April 1948.

53 Hirano, *Seikosha Shiwa*.
54 Pierre-Yves Donzé, 'The hybrid production system and the birth of the Japanese specialized industry: watch production at Hattori & Co. (1900–1960)', *Enterprise and Society*, vol. 12, no. 2 (2011): 356–397.
55 Koller, *'De la lime à la machine'*, 434–439.
56 Ibid., 439.
57 Harrold, *American Watchmaking*, 35–36.
58 Lucien F. Trueb, *The World of Watches: History, Technology, Industry* (New York: Ebner Publishing International, 2005), 155.
59 Marc Perrenoud, 'Mouvements migratoires et mouvement ouvrier neuchâtelois dans les années 1930', *Revue d'Histoire Neuchâteloise*, no. 1–2 (2001): 37–54.
60 André Donat, 'L'industrie horlogère russe', *Production Horlogère Française*, vol. 12 (1958): 2.
61 *L'Impartial*, 17 August 1972.
62 *International Watch*, November 2006, 187.
63 *Nestlé 150 Years: Nutrition. Health and Wellness, 1866–2016* (Vevey: Nestlé, 2016), appendix, 302–303.

5

The first wave of foreign direct investment, 1945–1970

In 1966, the leaders of UBHA, the trade association of watch component manufacturers and one of the three main organisations of the Watchmaking Statute, denounced the new FH policy in these terms:

> The leaders of the FH intend to allow the Chinese to sell watches assembled in Hong Kong with Asian cases and dials under the Swiss name. In addition, the FH is prepared to tolerate that Swiss-made movements be assembled with Chinese supplies. [...] The UBAH vigorously protests against this policy of abandoning the Swiss watch and calls for its immediate review.[1]

A few days earlier, Gérard F. Bauer, president of the FH, had announced the signing of an agreement with the Hong Kong watch manufacturers on technical assistance to enable them to improve the quality of the cases, dials, and bracelets they had recently been supplying to Swiss watchmakers. Such a measure seemed to profoundly contradict the entire watchmaking policy pursued since the 1920s. What happened after World War II? What prompted the FH to support the internationalisation of watch production?

The impact of World War II on the watch industry was seemingly very limited. The volume of world production was at a similar level in 1937 and 1950, amounting to just under 50 million watches per year (see table 5.1). Moreover, the balance between nations remained more or less the same. Switzerland had slightly strengthened its domination of the world market (more than 50%), while most of the warring nations had experienced a slight decline in the volume of their production, due to a repositioning towards arms production during the world conflict, which continued after 1945, particularly in the United States. But the most striking phenomenon of the immediate post-war period was the emergence of the Soviet Union in 1950 as the world's fifth-largest watchmaking nation.

However, beyond these apparently stable figures, World War II had a considerable influence on the dynamics of the watch industry until 1970. The production of armaments enabled companies in the precision-instruments industry, such as watches, cameras, and sewing machines, to acquire new knowledge related to mass production (product standardisation, use of high-quality machine tools, introduction of gauges and tolerance standards, etc.).[2] Applied to watch manufacturing in the 1950s and 1960s, these production technologies enabled the global watch industry to experience tremendous growth. Between 1950 and 1970, the volume of world watch production rose from around 48 million pieces to over 179 million. An important part of this production was made up of Roskopf watches. Quartz and electronics were mainly technologies that were then limited to the R&D departments of large companies. It was therefore not *product innovation* but innovation in production methods (*process innovation*) that made the growth of the years 1945–1970 possible.

Moreover, this strong growth favoured the emergence of new nations in the watch industry, although Switzerland retained its leading position with 73.6 million watches and more than 40% of world production in 1970. However, the

Table 5.1 World watch production, 1937–1970

Country	1937		1950		1970	
	Volume	%	Volume	%	Volume	%
Switzerland	24,700,000	50.9	25,000,000	52.4	73,600,000	41.0
United States	12,100,000	24.9	9,780,000	20.5	19,400,000	10.8
France	2,900,000	6.0	3,200,000	6.7	10,900,000	6.1
Germany	5,700,000	11.8	5,200,000	10.9	11,500,000	6.4
Japan	1,000,000	2.1	700,000	1.5	23,800,000	13.3
Soviet Union	700,000	1.4	2,150,000	4.5	21,700,000	12.1
Hong Kong	–	–	–	–	5,700,000	3.2
China	–	–	–	–	5,000,000	2.8
Others	1,400,000	2.9	1,670,000	0.6	7,700,000	4.3
Total	48,500,000	100	47,700,000	100	179,300,000	100

Sources: See appendix.

Table 5.2 Main world watch companies in 1970

Name	Production (millions of watches)	Turnover (millions of francs)	Watchmaking as % of turnover
US Time-Timex (United States)	20.0	860	75
Hattori (Japan)	12.0	779	89
SSIH (Switzerland)	10.0	470	100
Citizen (Japan)	7.0	226	88
Slava (Soviet Union)	6.0	175	100
SGT (Switzerland)	3.8	175	90
Bulova (United States)	2.0	682	71
ASUAG (Switzerland)	0.5	700	100
Hamilton (United States)	0.4	382	35
Junghans (Germany)	0.4	145	100

Source: Jean-François Blanc, *Suisse–Hong Kong: le défi horloger: innovation technologique et division internationale du travail* (Lausanne: Éditions d'En bas, 1988), 23.
Note: The original source also mentions Elgin (United States), with a production volume of 1 million watches, but as this company ceased to exist in 1968, it has been excluded from this table.

extraordinary development of the Japanese and Soviet watch industries, which both overtook the United States in 1970, should be highlighted. Hong Kong and China also saw the emergence and development of a watch industry on their territory. As for France and Germany, they faced a slight decrease in their market share, despite an increase in absolute figures.

The years 1945–1970 finally saw the development and strengthening of a few large companies that dominated the world market. In 1970, the 10 largest of these companies had a cumulative production of around 62 million watches – almost 35% of world production (see table 5.2). At that time, these companies were headquartered in the major watchmaking nations, but most of them were multinationals: they had production units in other countries and were gradually organising themselves on a global scale. This represented a profound transformation of the structures of the global watch industry.

The liberalisation of the Swiss watch industry

The rise of American and Japanese watch companies, as well as the emergence of new watchmaking nations, resulted in increased competition on the world market. The challenge was no longer so much to design precision watches as to produce them at an ever-lower cost. From the early 1950s, some Swiss watch company managers called for the abolition of the cartel, which had not prevented other countries from acquiring and developing watchmaking technologies. In particular, these managers wished to be free to organise themselves as they wanted, in order to adopt the technology (product standardisation, mass production, assembly-line work) essential to strengthening their competitiveness. The concentration of companies and the relocation overseas of low value-added activities required the liberalisation of the watch industry. In 1959, the secretary general of the Federal Department of Public Economy (DFEP), Karl Huber, declared that 'what is decisive is to maintain the competitive capacity of the entire Swiss watch industry, which is an indispensable condition for achieving all the other objectives that can be proposed'.[3]

The abandonment of the cartel was at the heart of watchmaking policy at the end of the 1950s. However, this question was by no means unanimously accepted in the watch industry, which was unable to present a common position to the federal authorities.[4] The most reticent were the producers of parts and movements, grouped together within the UBAH and the company Ébauches SA. ASUAG in particular was openly critical of proposals to abandon manufacturing permits and export controls on movements. For ASUAG, the main challenge was to maintain its monopoly position as a supplier of movements to the Swiss watch industry. The case and dial manufacturers defended the principle of compulsory tariffs and the ban on mass-produced supplies from outside the country. In contrast to watch manufacturers, the parts producers were positioned on a national market and feared that liberalisation would mainly benefit foreign competition.

Figure 5.1 Advertisement for Movado, 1951.

The main promoters of decartelisation were indeed the manufacturers of complete watches. Present on the world market and faced with foreign competition, they demanded the liberalisation of their branch in order to implement the modernisation of their production apparatus. The liberalisation ultimately met with a growing number of supporters in the general context of a trend towards decartelisation of the Swiss economy in the 1960s.[5] A first revision of the Watchmaking Statute was adopted by the Federal Assembly in 1961. However, liberalisation proceeded smoothly, with a transitional regime in the years 1962–1970, during which export controls on parts of movements and blanks were maintained. Similarly, until 1965, the state continued formally to control production (opening of enterprises, hiring of personnel, etc.), although it applied these measures very leniently. Finally, by 1971, the watch industry had been totally liberalised. The Swiss Confederation withdrew from the capital of ASUAG in 1984.[6]

However, the end of the watch cartel did not mean the total liberalisation of watchmaking in Switzerland. Two types of measures were adopted in parallel with the decartelisation: technical control of watches (1962) and the protection of the label 'Swiss Made' (1971). The aim of these two measures was to ensure that a certain quality of Swiss production was maintained in order to preserve the comparative advantage of the reputation of Swiss watches in a liberalised and competitive market. Introduced in 1962, technical control of watches was a response to a widespread fear of a proliferation of watch manufacturers who would lower the quality of their products in order to benefit from low selling prices. Such a policy could ultimately harm the entire industry. Technical inspection of watches and watch movements manufactured in Switzerland should therefore be introduced 'in order to prevent the export of watchmaking products which could seriously damage the reputation of the Swiss watch industry'.[7] However, in practice, only a small minority of products were actually inspected. From 1972 to 1979, the Institute for Official Quality Control in the Swiss Watch Industry, an independent non-state body, inspected a total of 1.8 million watches, but this was only 0.3% of watches exported.[8] In addition to this technical control, the definition of 'Swiss Made' for watches was adopted by the legislator at the time of liberalisation (1971). The use of this label had to meet a certain number of criteria, the main one being the assembly and production of at least half the value of the movement's components on Swiss territory.

The end of the cartel had two effects on the Swiss watch industry: first, the concentration of companies and the birth of groups; second, the relocation of certain production activities to Asia, mainly to Hong Kong (see pp. 104–109). In the whole Swiss watch industry, between 1950 and 1970, the number of companies declined from 1,863 to 1,618, while the number of employees rose from 60,239 to 89,448. More than 200 companies disappeared, while the industry was growing rapidly.[9]

Industrial concentration was particularly marked in the years 1966–1971, a period during which three main watch groups emerged in Switzerland. They were among the 10 largest watch companies in the world (see table 5.2, p. 88) and in 1971 accounted for more than a quarter of the country's watch production (see table 5.3). This first phase of concentration, which aimed at rationalisation of the

Table 5.3 Main concentrations in the Swiss watch industry, 1971

Name	Foundation	Main brands	Production (millions of pieces)	Share of national production (%)
SSIH	1930	Omega, Tissot, Lanco, Aetos, Agon, Buhler, Ferex, Continental	10.2	14.6
Société des Garde-Temps (SGT)	1968	Waltham, Avia, Helvetia, Silvana, Solvil, Titus, Invicta, Sandoz	3.3	4.7
General Watch Co.	1971	Certina, Edox, Eterna, Mido, Oris, Rado, Technos, Longines, Rotary	5.3	7.6

Source: 'Les concentrations dans l'industrie horlogère suisse', *Annales biennoises* (1971): 50.

means of production, strengthened the country's two largest watch companies: SSIH and ASUAG.

The company Société Suisse pour l'Industrie Horlogère SA (SSIH), which resulted from the merger of Omega and Tissot in 1930, was the country's leading watch company in terms of production. In the early 1970s, it was the third-largest watch company in the world, behind the American Timex and the Japanese Seiko. In the early 1960s, it embarked on a strategy of all-out corporate acquisitions, with the successive takeovers of Rayville SA Montres Blancpain, which specialised in ladies' jewellery watches (1961), and Langendorf Watch Co. (Lanco), a producer of complete watches (1965). In 1969, SSIH acquired a stake in the Aetos Group, which brought together companies producing Roskopf watches. In 1971, it became a majority shareholder in the Economic Swiss Time Holding group, a company of manufacturers of low-end watches (pin-lever) whose aim was to compete with the American Timex. These multiple acquisitions were as much a response to a desire to increase production capacity as to a new marketing strategy based on a desire to be present in all segments of the market. In the 1960s, SSIH adopted a policy of segmenting the group's brands. Thus, the group's two main companies, Tissot and Omega, had a distinct profile in 1970: the volume of their production was similar (1.2 million pieces for Tissot and 1.6 million for Omega) but the value of their turnover was very different (22 million francs for Tissot and 62 million francs for Omega).[10]

The second group in 1971 was General Watch Co. (GWC), founded that year by ASUAG, which held 60% of its capital. The decartelisation of Swiss watchmaking and the emergence of electronic watches called into question the monopoly position occupied by the super-holding since the 1930s. The latter diversified its activities by acquiring watch manufacturers. At the beginning of the 1960s, the GWC had 11 companies, the main ones being Longines, Rotary, and Rado.

The third group was Société des Garde-Temps (SGT), created in 1968 and bringing together various manufacturers of low-end mechanical watches and electronic watches. SGT also distinguished itself by its international dimension, acquiring the American company Waltham Watch and entering into a licence agreement with Elgin Watch in 1973. At the time, it was the largest foreign investment by a Swiss watch company. Although these two American companies had a prestigious history, both were focused on the lower end of their national market and did not offer an important opportunity for growth. Above all, they offered SGT access to the American market.[11] A rationalisation of production was achieved in 1971 with the centralisation of the manufacture of movements. However, the exclusive orientation of the group towards the lower end of the range posed serious problems of competitiveness on the world market and led to the bankruptcy of the company at the beginning of the 1980s.

Finally, it is worth mentioning, during this first wave of concentration, the creation in 1966 of a financial company, Chronos Holding SA, founded in Biel with a share capital of 21.15 million francs.[12] It had its own watch group, Synchron SA, founded in 1968 with a capital of 2.4 million francs, that brought together

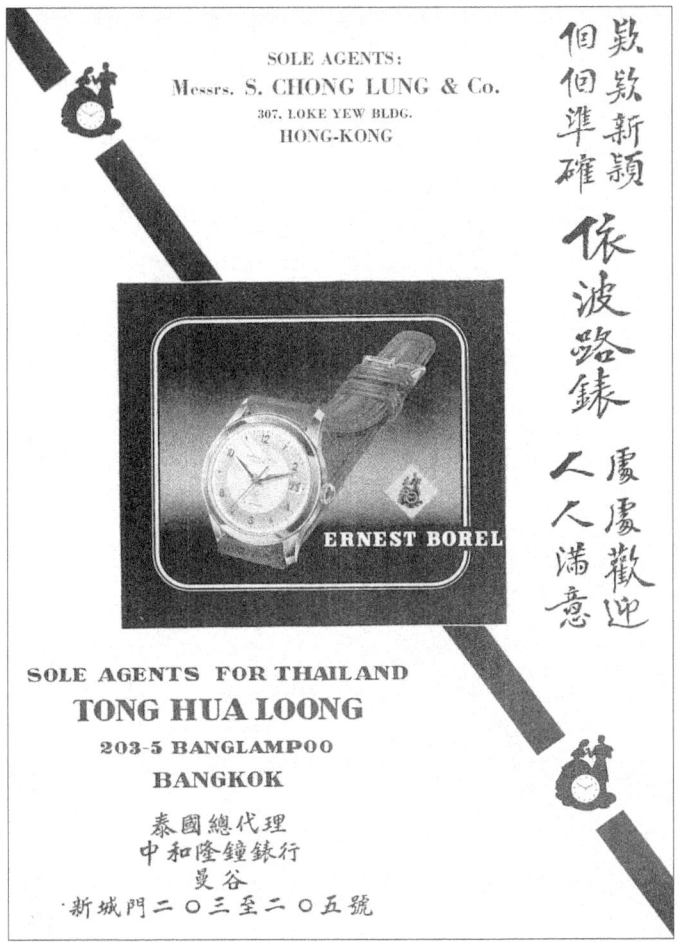

Figure 5.2 Advertisement for Ernest Borel, 1953.

the Cyma, Ernest Borel (see figure 5.2), and Doxa brands, whose production volume in 1971 amounted to 250,000 pieces. At the same time, it held financial stakes in SGT (14% of the capital in 1971) and in the Saphir group, which gathered Favre-Leuba and Jaeger-Lecoultre (23% of the capital). In liquidation, Synchron SA closed its companies and sold the brands in 1978 to the family company Aubry Frères SA, which at the same time adopted a strategy of expansion by buying out other companies.[13]

These regroupings strengthened the competitiveness of Swiss watch companies. However, in 1970, almost three-quarters of Swiss production was carried out by the hundreds of independent companies that were encountering increasing difficulties in the face of American and Japanese competitors, especially in the United States. The American watch market was the largest in the world in the decades following World War II. It absorbed, on average, a quarter of Swiss exports (in value) between 1950 and 1970. The Swiss watchmakers were up against the new American watchmaking giants, Bulova and Timex. It was also on this market, as well as in Hong Kong, the second outlet for Swiss watchmakers in 1970, that Seiko concentrated its efforts from the mid-1960s to penetrate the world market.

Table 5.4 The 10 main markets of the Swiss watch industry, 1970

Country	Exports (millions of francs)	Market share (%)
United States	515.9	19.6
Hong Kong	247.8	9.4
Germany	190.7	7.3
Italy	169.4	6.4
United Kingdom	150.6	5.7
Japan	113.3	4.3
Spain	93.4	3.6
United Arab Emirates	92.3	3.5
France	85.6	3.3
Argentina	54.3	2.1
Others	916	34.8
Total	2,629.0	100

Source: Federation of the Swiss Watch Industry (personal communication with author).

The transformation of the American watch industry

During the 1950s and the 1960s, the American watch industry underwent a profound transformation, which is only partially illustrated by the growth in the volume of its production. Although the volume doubled during these two decades, the United States saw its share of the world market halved.

American watchmaking had four major characteristics. First, the large American companies of Waltham and Elgin, which had been at the vanguard of the industrialisation of watch production in the United States, disappeared in 1949 and 1968, respectively. These two companies, which had enjoyed an oligopolistic position in the US market, had already lost their ability to innovate during the interwar period and survived mainly thanks to customs protectionism.[14] The survival of Elgin Watch until the end of the 1960s was based on a diversification of activities outside the watch industry (electronic components, military equipment, various instruments), a sharp reduction in the number of workers, and the import and sales of watches from Switzerland, even going so far as to establish a branch in Neuchâtel in 1959 to ensure its supply.[15] However, these measures were not enough to ensure Elgin's survival.

Second, American watchmakers were actively engaged in the development of new technologies relating to time measurement. Several companies were carrying out R&D into the use of electrical and electronic technologies. Hamilton launched an electric watch in 1957, followed three years later by Bulova, with its Accutron tuning-fork watch.[16] These activities were undoubtedly related to the boom in the production of electronic components for the defence industry by these same companies. Table 5.2 (p. 88) illustrates the fact that non-watchmaking activities were important for Bulova and Hamilton. Hamilton set up a Defence Orders Division in 1949, which led it to diversify into electronics to develop components for missiles, and was active in the production of military equipment during the Korean War.[17] As for Bulova, it had even been led since 1958 by a former US army general, Omar Bradley.[18] It experienced strong growth – its turnover went from 46.5 million dollars in 1945 to 66.6 million in 1960 and 158 million in 1970.[19] While it had established itself as one of the most important watch companies in the world, it remained heavily dependent on the American market.

Third, the Virgin Islands played a key role in the development of the American watch industry in the 1960s. In their desire to develop the economy of their island possessions, the American authorities passed a legislative act in 1954 according to which products manufactured in these territories could be imported duty free into the United States, provided that the value of the foreign parts was less than half the value of the object. Watch movements, which were heavily taxed on importation into the United States, were a typical industry of this delocalisation.[20] The first watch company to open a production unit in the Virgin Islands was the American Standard Watch Co. (1959). In 1965, there was 12 watch companies, employing a total of 474 people, all of which were linked to American importers or manufacturers, such as the assembly companies Antilles Industries Inc. (General Time Co.), Master Time Co. (Elgin National Watch Co.), and Virgo Co. (U.S. Time Co.). The process was similar for all companies – they imported parts and assembled movements on site. These were generally low-end watches, sold in the US market under the brands of the importers, not the manufacturers. In the second half of the 1960s, many foreign manufacturers opened assembly units in the Virgin Islands. In 1967, 2.9 million watches were assembled there, mainly by Japanese companies (72%), followed by German (14%), French (12%), and Swiss (2%) companies.[21] The import of cheap mechanical watches into the United States via this territory decreased at the end of the 1970s, following the evolution of American policy, which lowered its customs tariffs and since 1970 has limited the possibilities of duty-free imports from island possessions.[22] Shortly afterwards, these products also faced competition from quartz watches.

Fourth, and finally, the main characteristic of American watch companies was their worldwide expansion. Like Elgin Watch, mentioned above, most of them invested in setting up foreign production subsidiaries or in joint ventures with watch manufacturers in other countries. Thus, the US foreign trade figures, which suggest a low competitiveness of US watch manufacturers (the share of watch production exported between 1958 and 1970 averaged only 1.6%),[23] provide an inaccurate picture of the reality of the companies. They produced in the

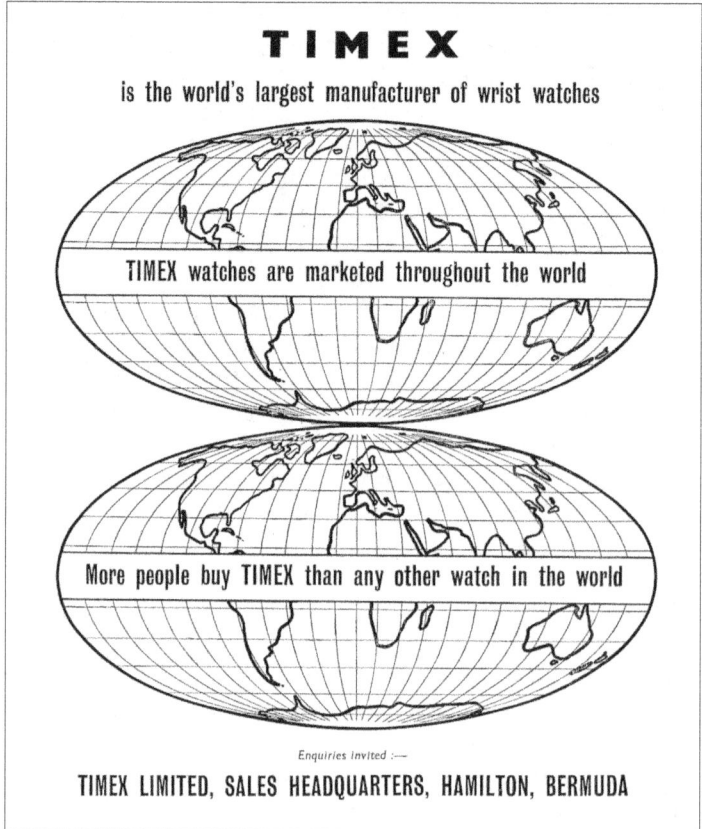

Figure 5.3 Advertisement for Timex, 1956.

United States for the American market and in their foreign subsidiaries for sales to other markets.

United States Time Co. (Timex) was the company most intensely committed to building a global organisation.[24] It must be considered the first modern multinational company in the global watch industry. Founded in 1941 to produce military equipment, after the war it focused on the mass production of Roskopf watches and adopted an active policy of foreign direct investment by opening assembly and component production plants around the world. In 1971, Timex employed a total of 7,000 workers in its American factories and production centres in Hong Kong and Taiwan for Asia, as well as in Besançon (France), Chaneca de Caparica (Portugal), Dundee (Scotland), Feltham (England), and Pforzheim (Germany) for Europe.[25] This worldwide deployment enabled the American company to increase its production from 8 million watches in 1960 to 22 million in 1969.[26]

The other major American companies based their internationalisation on cooperation with manufacturers in other countries. Bulova, which continued to develop its Swiss subsidiary, signed an agreement with the Japanese company

Citizen in 1958 whereby Citizen would supply movements to Bulova for the American market, where the watches were marketed under the Caravelle brand, while Bulova would supply its own movements, notably for tuning-fork watches, to Citizen for the Japanese market. In 1970, the two companies strengthened their cooperation and set up a joint venture in Japan to manufacture tuning-fork watches in this country.[27]

Hamilton had a similar strategy. In 1957, it signed a technical cooperation agreement with a small Japanese watch manufacturer, Takano, with the aim of penetrating Asian markets. The agreement provided for the production of Hamilton watches under licence by Takano and the distribution of Takano watches by Hamilton on the American market. The bankruptcy of Takano in 1961 led Hamilton to approach Ricoh, an instrument manufacturer that was trying to enter the watchmaking business by taking over Takano's assets. In 1962, the two partners founded the joint venture Hamilton-Ricoh Watch Co. Ltd, with 60% American capital. Its objective was the production of electric watches in Japan, with Hamilton supplying the electrical parts and the Japanese factory producing the mechanical parts. But the commercial failure of this product – in Japan as in the rest of the world – led to the closure of this company in 1965.[28] In the meantime, Hamilton also invested in Switzerland. It took over the watch manufacturers A. Huguenin Fils (1959) and Büren Watch AG (1966). This enabled it to source Swiss movements for its American watches.

Thus, American watch companies adopted a strategy of worldwide redeployment during the 1950s and 1960s. They became true multinationals, as can be seen in other sectors of the manufacturing industry. American watchmaking thus gradually lost its national character, so that by the end of the 1960s it became difficult to consider the existence of an 'American watch industry'. This redeployment also had consequences in the countries in which the subsidiaries of American companies were located. France is an excellent example of the challenges facing these countries.

The French watch industry under the control of foreign firms

The French watch industry has a paradoxical character which illustrates its insertion into a production system that had become increasingly global. While the volume of its watch production increased threefold between 1950 and 1970 and its share of world production remained stable (around 6%), no French company was present in the ranking of the 10 largest watch manufacturers in the world in 1970. However, this situation did not reflect an industry dominated by SMEs, but rather resulted from the presence on French territory of foreign companies that had grown significantly.

In 1974, Banque de France stated in an official report that:

> the French watch industry is nevertheless controlled to a certain extent by foreign interests (Swiss, German, American): at present some fifteen watch, watch parts and clock factories have foreign holdings in their capital ranging from 20 to 100%.[29]

ASUAG, a holding company controlling the production of blanks and parts in Switzerland, had had a 30% stake in the capital of the French watch manufacturer Lip since 1967, which was increased to 43% in 1970. It also held stakes in several French watch component factories. These are the roots of French subsidiaries of Swatch Group today.

However, France's largest company, Kelton, was owned by US giant Timex.[30] This multinational company, which specialised in Roskopf watches (18.9% of French production in 1963 and more than 50% in 1971 and 1972), invested in France during the 1950s, and in 1962 opened a factory in Besançon, which enjoyed tremendous growth for more than 10 years. While the number of its employees rose from 143 in 1960 to a peak of nearly 2,800 in 1975, its watch production reached 4.8 million movements in 1975 – that is, approximately one-third of French national production (see figure 5.4).

With the exception of Kelton and Lip, most of the watch factories owned by French capital were small, family-owned companies that were unable to remain competitive on the world market. There were two main consequences of the foreign domination of the French watch industry. First, the industry was not very export-oriented and focused sharply on the domestic market – foreign companies set up in France to sell watches there. In 1970, the domestic market absorbed 67% of French watch production. Exports, mainly to European countries, accounted for only a third of production. French watches were virtually absent from the world's largest watch market, the United States.

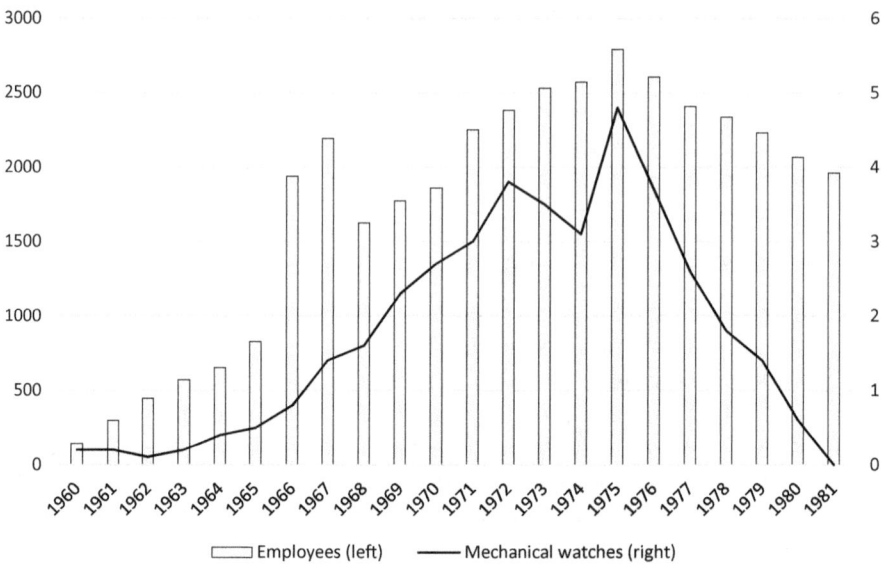

Figure 5.4 Kelton–Timex employee numbers and production volume (millions of pieces), 1960–1981.

Source: Archives Nationales, Paris, 19910207/2, Various documents on Timex.

Second, foreign-owned companies did not invest in R&D in their French factories, while local SMEs did not have the capital to do so. As a result, the French watch industry experienced technological backwardness in the early 1970s.

These two commercial and technological factors led to a serious crisis in the 1970s, which ended with the disappearance of the watch industry in France (see chapter 6, pp. 132–134).

Division and renaissance of the German watch industry

The German watch industry underwent major reorganisation after 1945, marked not only by the reconstruction of companies after the end of the war but also by the deep division between West Germany (German Federal Republic) and East Germany (German Democratic Republic). The watch industry had indeed experienced a boom in several regions of the country, but until the early 1990s it was divided for political reasons.

As in France, investments by foreign companies were also important in Germany, but they did not have the same consequences. In 1959, US Time Corporation (Timex) bought the Durowe AG watch blanks factory and the watch factory Lacher & Co. AG, both owned by the same entrepreneur. The former occupied a key position in the German watch industry. Durowe was founded in 1924 in Pforzheim, from a workshop that had been relocated from Switzerland in the context of knockdown production. In the mid-1950s, it employed 1,400 people and produced almost 1 million blanks a year, while the total volume of German watches at that time was just over 5 million pieces. However, Timex was mainly interested in acquiring the Durowe's know-how in the field of electric watchmaking. The Durowe-Laco complex was disposed of in 1965 and sold to the Swiss company Ébauches SA, which made it its entry point into the European Economic Community (EEC) market.[31] However, with the exception of this company, most German watch manufacturers were controlled by domestic capital, particularly producers of finished watches.

Germany's largest watch company was still the general timepiece manufacturer Junghans, from Pforzheim.[32] At the beginning of the 1960s, it alone had an annual production of more than 1.5 million watches, which were exported worldwide. It was also engaged in R&D activities that enabled it to launch automatic watches on the market during the 1950s. Other German watch companies employing more than 500 people in 1970 (see table 5.5) were mainly high-volume manufacturers of alarm clocks and watches. Some of them, such as Kienzle and Mauthe, also produced wristwatches, but they were still a minority. In fact, the watch industry in West Germany was mainly based on the Junghans factory.

As for the East German watch industry, concentrated in the Glashütte region, Saxony, it underwent a profound industrial transformation following the establishment of a communist regime in the country. All the watch companies in

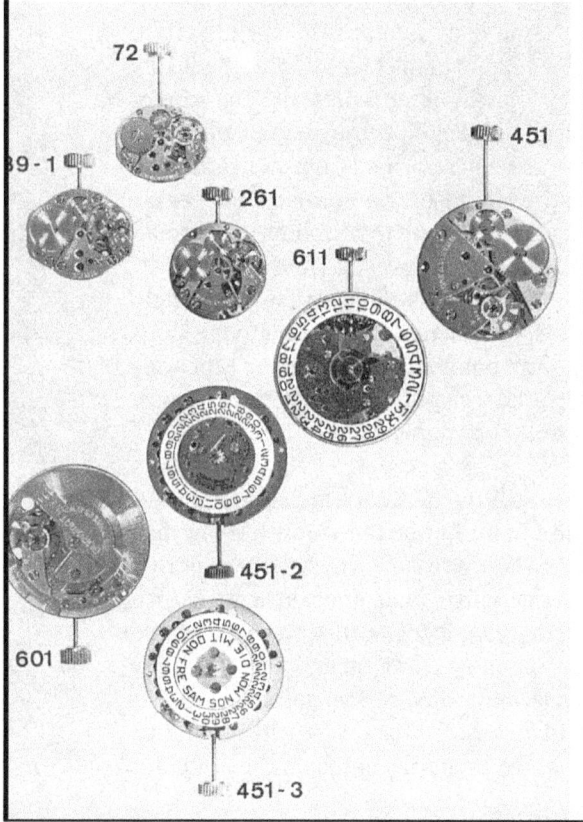

International Concentration for the Distribution of Watch Components by EBAUCHES S.A.

The extension of watch production at the world level and the growth of international competition give rise to many problems, ranging from the manufacture of watches to their consumption: dispersal of forces, non-specialised channels of distribution, hesitation on the consumer's part as regards quaity, customer service, etc. An event marking a new stage in the collaboration between the German and Swiss watch industries is therefore to be welcomed as an attempt to achieve better coordination of the manufacturers' efforts and to support the traditional watch trade. The event in question is the acquisition, by Ebauches S.A., Neuchâtel, of the Durowe ebauche plant, in Pforzheim, whereby a German undertaking has been incorporated into the world's largest ebauche-producing complex. (Last year, the sixteen companies affiliated to Ebauches S.A. manufactured over thirty-eight million ebauches, i.e. thirty per cent of the world production).

Figure 5.5 Acquisition of Durowe by Ebauches SA, 1968.

Table 5.5 The largest watch companies in West Germany, 1970

Company	Location	Number of employees	Turnover (millions of Deutschmarks)	Share of exports (%)
Junghans	Schramberg	4,300	128	40
Europa-Uhren	Senden	2,100	87	65
Kienzle	Schwenningen	3,000	82	33
Blessing	Waldkirch	1,600	40	60
J. Kaiser	Villingen	1,300	30	50
Mauthe	Schwenningen	1,200	30	50
Bifora-Uhren	Schwäb. Gmünd	700	25	30
Kundo	St Georgen	550	25	30

Source: Villingen-Schwenningen City Archive – VDU 4.9 / 864 industry report, Commerzbank/watch industry (April 1972), 20 (quoted at http://www.sozialgeschichte-uhrenindustrie.de/2014/06/22/vom-niedergang-der-uhrenindustrie-strukturwandel-in-der-region-schwarzwald-baar-heuberg/, accessed 8 April 2019).

this city, including A. Lange & Söhne, were merged in 1951 into a state-owned conglomerate: VEB Glashütter Uhrenbetriebe (GUB). In 1967, it merged with another state-owned watch manufacturer, Ruhla.[33] Both companies possessed automated production technologies and set up a system for the mass production of standardised products. Their production volume amounted to approximately 2.2 million watches, which were mainly sold on the domestic market, in other Eastern European countries, and in the Soviet Union.[34]

Thus, during the 1950s and 1960s, Germany as a whole saw its watch production double but its share of world production decline. Its performance certainly appeared weaker than that of France. However, production was highly concentrated in a few large and well equipped companies owned by local players. Furthermore, the German watch industry was competitive on the world market. In 1957, half of its watch production was exported.[35]

The formidable growth of Japanese watchmakers

Japan is the country that experienced the greatest expansion of its watch industry during the period of strong growth following World War II. The production volume rose from 700,000 watches in 1950 to 24 million in 1970. At that time, Japan established itself as the world's second-largest watch producer, behind Switzerland, with a share of 13.3%, compared with only 1.5% in 1950.

This tremendous growth was mainly through two large companies: Hattori (the watch brand produced by Seiko) and Citizen. They were among the world's largest watch manufacturers in 1970, ranking second and fourth, respectively (see table 5.2, p.88) and totally dominating their domestic industry. For the 1960s as a whole, Seiko had an average share of 54.4% of Japanese watch production and Citizen 30.7%. It was therefore an extremely concentrated industry. Moreover, these two companies, and Seiko in particular, pursued a strategy put in place during the interwar period, namely the mass production of quality watches – not unlike the business model adopted by Rolex. For example, it did not engage in the manufacture of Roskopf watches, unlike the American and Swiss companies, which aimed at mass production of entry-level products. Japanese watch manufacturers benefited from the know-how of former Imperial Navy production engineers, who brought to private industry the experience they had gained in the development and manufacture of weapons during the war. Seiko is an excellent example of this process.[36]

In 1946, Daini Seikosha, Seiko group's watch manufacturing subsidiary, hired its first production engineer in the person of Dai Matsumoto.[37] Born in 1918, Matsumoto graduated from the Department of Arms Production of the University of Tokyo in 1941. He joined the Navy as an officer engineer and ran a torpedo production workshop in Yokosuka Arsenal. After his arrival at Daini Seikosha, he spent a year in an assembly workshop, where he was responsible for drawing up plans for watch parts and movements. In particular, he introduced tolerance standards into the drawings, a principle that had not existed until then and which was essential to ensure quality control of the manufacturing process and the establishment of a mass-production system based on the perfect interchangeability of parts.[38] During the 1950s, Matsumoto supervised the introduction of work lines and new machines, and then the automation of assembly at the end of the following decade. In 1970, he became a member of the board of directors of Daini Seikosha, and in 1982 he became managing director of its subsidiary Seiko Seiki, which produced machine tools. In addition, Matsumoto was assisted by the many university engineers who joined Seiko group in the 1950s – 49 in all, from the country's top universities. They took over the workshops at the expense of qualified watchmakers. Control over the organisation of assembly was at the heart of this change, with the perfect interchangeability of parts leading to the adoption of line work – and the replacement of skilled workers by unqualified women.[39]

In parallel with the transformation of production technologies, Seiko engineers worked on the standardisation of watch models. New products were launched on the market in the years following the end of the war: an extra-flat pocket watch (1946), a men's wristwatch (1946), a women's wristwatch (1948), and a pocket chronograph (1949).[40] In the years 1951–1955, Seiko launched four more new models. All these products were copies of Swiss watches. Meanwhile, Daini Seikosha's engineers were working on the launch of their first watch designed in-house for mass production, the Marvel (1956), which was a great success on the domestic market, and then the Grand Seiko (1960), a quality watch designed to compete with Swiss watches on the world market. Automatic watches were developed in the second half of the 1950s.

This rationalisation of production allowed Seiko to mass-produce quality watches at extremely low prices. This was the source of the company's competitive advantage on the world market. It should also be pointed out that Citizen followed a similar organisational model and that the strong competition between the two firms improved their competitiveness on the world market. The development of automatic watches is a perfect illustration of this phenomenon. This type of watch was developed successively by Seiko (1956) and Citizen (1958).[41] However, this was not just a feat designed to show the world Japanese watchmakers' technical capacity, but a voluntary commitment to the mass production of quality watches. Thus, in the factory of the Suwa Seikosha subsidiary, the production of automatic watches began in 1959 and reached 450,000 pieces in 1960. In 1964, it surpassed the volume of hand-wind watches and reached 1.7 million pieces in 1965.[42] In addition, the strong competition between Seiko and Citizen on the domestic market stimulated innovation, characterised by a reduction in the number of movement parts, in order to reduce production costs. Around 1960, the Seiko Matic movement comprised a total of 145 parts,

Figure 5.6 Dial fitting work through a conveyor belt system at Seiko, circa 1960.

including 37 for the automatic module alone, while the Swiss watch Universal, taken as a reference by Japanese manufacturers, had 196 parts, including 48 for the automatic module.[43]

Moreover, the rivalry between Seiko and Citizen took place in the context of a domestic market largely protected from foreign competition. After the war, the Japanese state adopted a policy of control and restriction (quotas) on watch imports. This system was abandoned in 1961, but liberalisation was accompanied by high import taxes until the early 1970s. However, unlike in France, for example, Japanese protectionism was not intended to reserve the fruits of the domestic market for local companies, but to prepare them for global competition. Seiko and Citizen benefited from a system of organised competition that strengthened their competitiveness. When the country liberalised the import of watches, they were ready to set out to conquer the world and challenge the historical domination of Swiss watchmakers. The share of domestic watch production that was exported averaged only 3.8% in the 1950s. It passed the 40% mark in 1966 and the 50% mark in 1971. Japanese watchmakers thus established themselves as major players on the world watch market long before the development of the quartz watch. Electronic technology strengthened their competitiveness after the end of the 1970s, but it was in no way its origin.

The strong growth of the Japanese watch industry during the 1950s and 1960s was therefore the result both of strategies implemented at company level and of industrial policy aimed at strengthening the competitiveness of the latter. Seiko and Citizen largely maintained their production facilities in the Japanese archipelago until 1970. The rare investments made abroad (Citizen in India in 1961 and Seiko in South Korea in 1963) were aimed at accessing protected markets. They did not lead to a real internationalisation of the production system, and technology transfers were limited, with the exception of Hong Kong, where Japanese watchmakers opened parts production and assembly units, as did their Swiss and American competitors.

The birth of a subcontracting industry in Hong Kong

During the 1950s, after the independence of India (1947) and the establishment of a communist regime in China (1949), Hong Kong became one of the major watch-trading centres in Asia. It was particularly from the British colony that Swiss watchmakers exported their products, often smuggled, into the countries of the region.[44] For the period 1950–1965, Hong Kong was one of the main destinations for Swiss watch exports (6.2% of the volume), behind the United States (25.6%). Japanese watchmakers were also present in this city. They signed distribution contracts with Hong Kong trading houses with sales networks throughout South-East Asia, Gilman & Co. for Citizen (1962) and Thong Sia for Hattori (1963).[45] These two companies then opened their own sales subsidiaries (Hattori, 1968; Citizen, 1970). However, Hong Kong's function in the global watch industry was not only commercial. It established itself in the 1960s as the main place in the world for

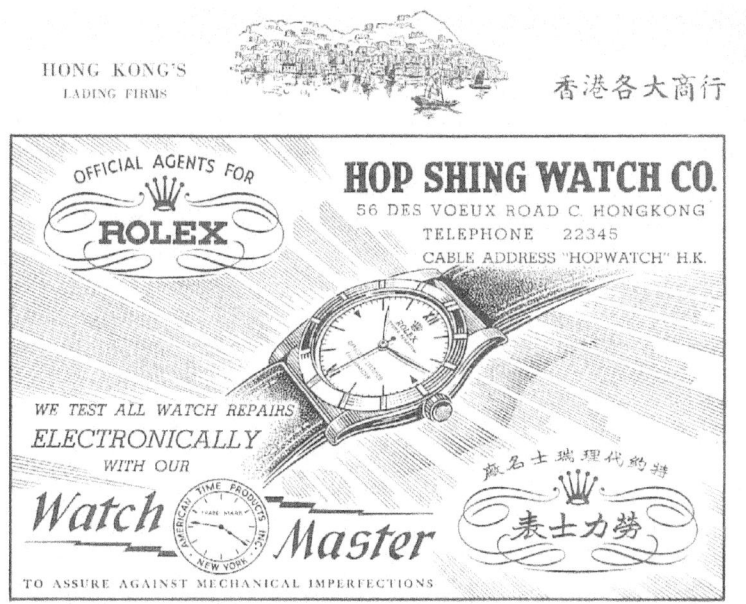

Figure 5.7 Advertisement for Rolex in Hong Kong, 1951.

American, Swiss, and Japanese watch manufacturers to relocate their low value-added manufacturing activities.

The first major company to embark on such relocation was the American trading company Shriro, which specialised in trading with Asia. In 1948, it founded the subsidiary Shriro (China) Ltd and began selling Swiss watches. It imported Swiss movements from the United States and assembled them in cases made in Hong Kong. Three years later, it opened an office in Biel to source components.[46] For the watch industry, this marked the beginning of an international division of labour centred on Hong Kong. At first, Swiss watch dealers accused Shriro of undercutting prices and ruining their business. In a 1950 letter to the Federal Political Department, the Swiss Consulate in Hong Kong admitted that 'Shriro's methods are not always very orthodox and he has cut the grass from under the feet of Swiss importers. But Shriro is very strong, cunning, and he knows that nothing can be proven against him.'[47] This company had established itself as one of the leading distributors of Swiss watches in the Far East and is said to have bought 22 million francs' worth of watches in Switzerland in 1951 and 16 million in 1952.[48]

After 1960, Hong Kong remained a major hub for the watch trade in Asia, absorbing 9.9% of Swiss watch exports in 1970 and 15.9% in 1980,[49] and 26.2% and 24.5%, respectively, of Japanese watches.[50] However, its main feature was its emergence as a centre for the production of watch parts and assembly, in a subcontracting relationship for American, Japanese, and Swiss companies. This transfer of production was made possible not only by the low cost and abundance of local labour, but also by transformations in the production system. The widespread mass production of mechanical watches led to a standardisation of parts and models, which facilitated the transfer of certain manufacturing operations abroad. Finally, in the case of Switzerland, an institutional factor must be stressed – the abandonment of the cartel system during the years 1961–1965 (see above) made the international division of labour possible.[51]

The 1960s saw a significant increase in the number of watch companies in Hong Kong, with 61 firms in 1960 and 229 in 1970. This increase was not primarily due to the multiplication of small independent workshops, since at the same time the average number of employees was maintained at around 40 per firm (see table 5.6).

Table 5.6 Hong Kong watch industry, 1960–1990

	1960	1965	1970	1975	1980	1985	1990
Number of companies	61	102	229	471	1,509	1,805	1,690
Total number of employees	2,433	4,556	9,773	15,783	49,454	36,692	27,154
Average number of employees per company	39.9	44.7	42.7	33.5	32.8	20.3	16.1
Employees as % of total manufacturing industry	1.1	1.3	1.8	2.3	5.5	4.3	3.7

Source: *Hong Kong's Manufacturing Industries* (Hong Kong: Hong Kong Government Industry Department, 1996).

Although these are very small units in comparison with the Japanese watchmaking giants – Citizen Watch Co. employed 4,500 people in 1970[52] – they are comparable to the situation in Switzerland, where the average number of employees per company was 43.6 in 1965.[53] However, the watch industry remained of secondary importance to the British colony's economy, accounting for less than 2% of manufacturing employment in the 1960s.

These watch companies created since the end of the 1950s were part of a relationship of economic and technological dependence on the world's major watchmaking groups. The Hong Kong companies active in the watch industry can therefore be divided into two categories: manufacturers of watch parts and assemblers of complete watches.

Manufacturers of parts were almost exclusively active in external components (cases, dials, bracelets), and their entry dates back to the second half of the 1950s. In December 1958, the Hong Kong & Kowloon Clock & Watch Trade Merchants' Association included 13 case manufacturers, 6 glass manufacturers and 3 dial manufacturers among its members. Shriro was also one of the few companies to develop its production activities in the early 1960s. Shriro founded a new subsidiary, Shriro Precision Engineering, to manufacture watch parts for the American market, in order to compete with Bulova Watch, which at the time had a dominant position.[54] The United States was the main market for parts for watches made in Hong Kong. For the period 1962–1964, it accounted for 77.4% of the value of Hong Kong exports, which totalled 7.6 million Hong Kong dollars, far ahead of Switzerland (4%), where the use of foreign parts was still strictly regulated, and Japan (1.2%).[55]

With the exception of Shriro, all these subcontractors were Chinese companies. The origin of the technology transfer is not known, but it should be noted that the parts for watch cases were of rudimentary technology and were the first watch part whose production was delocalised. Hong Kong developed as a centre for watch-case production in the mid-1960s. The liberalisation of the Swiss watch industry and, above all, the adoption of the ordinance regulating the use of the Swiss name for watches (1971), which provided that Swiss movements fitted abroad could bear the 'Swiss Made' label, encouraged this development.[56] As a first step, the Federation of the Swiss Watch Industry took action to improve the quality of watches produced in Hong Kong. In 1966, it signed a technical assistance agreement with the Federation of Hong Kong Industries.[57] In a second phase, the major Swiss watch groups invested directly. They opened subsidiaries, such as Swiss Watch Case Centre (1968) and Swiss Time Hong Kong (1969), as well as joint ventures with manufacturers and traders established in Hong Kong, such as Swiss Plating Co. (1968) and Swikong Manufacturing (1971).[58] For the Swiss watch industry, Hong Kong became essential for its supplies – while Swiss imports of cases rose from 1.6 million pieces in 1961 to 8 million in 1970, Hong Kong's share also increased sharply, from 21.9% in 1961 to 60.8% in 1970.[59] Although Japanese watch companies did not invest directly in the British colony, they made it a major source of parts. Japanese imports of such parts from Hong Kong rose from 141,000 yen in 1960 to 34.8 million yen in 1970 and 1.3 billion yen in 1980.[60]

The second type of company to develop in Hong Kong were assemblers of finished watches. This international division of labour was the result of a desire to minimise production costs on the part of the major watchmaking groups. Mass-production methods, followed by the automation of watch-movement manufacturing, had been generalised since the 1960s. However, manufacturers had not succeeded in integrating casing or assembly of movements, which remained the least automated operations. These activities were relocated to Hong Kong, or to the Virgin Islands for the American market. The first major watch company to open a subsidiary for the assembly of its mechanical movements was the American company Timex Corporation, which founded Timex Hong Kong Ltd in 1967.[61] In 1968, the Japanese Hattori group opened a production unit, Precision Engineering, followed a few years later by Asian Precision (1974) and Epson Engineering (1976).[62] The Swiss companies were also present. In the low-range segment (pin-lever watches) was the Baumgartner Frères Granges subsidiary BFG Far East (opened in 1970),[63] a joint venture between four of Switzerland's largest manufacturers – Swiss Watch Manufacturing (1971),[64] Asian Swiss Industrial Company (1969), Ronda Ltd (1971), and Swiss Ebauches Production (Sepro) Ltd (1973) – that started assembly in Hong Kong.[65]

These various industrial relocations had a considerable impact on the development of the international watch trade. First, there was a high growth in Swiss watch exports to Hong Kong. The decade 1965–1974 saw a sharp rise in their value, from 87.2 million francs to 418.4 million francs. Furthermore, Hong Kong's share of the Swiss watch trade doubled during this period, with its market share rising from 4.8% to 11.3%. This extremely favourable dynamic is explained by the growing industrial interdependence between Switzerland and Hong Kong. Complete watches, which accounted for more than 90% of the value of exports until 1965, fell to 51.1% in 1974. In 1974, the Swiss also exported a large proportion of watch movements (38.7%) and watch parts (10.2%).[66]

Second, the Japanese watch industry made a completely different use of Hong Kong, marked by a relative withdrawal from production. While Japanese watch exports rose from 49.6 million yen in 1960 to 10.3 billion yen in 1970, the share of complete watches rose sharply from 69.4% to 82.5%.[67] Switzerland and Japan thus made very distinct use of Hong Kong in their international division of labour. During the 1960s, the major Japanese watchmaking groups implemented a system of mass production in their Japanese factories, which did not require the transfer of activities abroad.[68] Seiko and Citizen mainly exported finished watches and this commercial activity was partly located in Hong Kong.

Third, and finally, Hong Kong established itself as one of the world's leading watchmaking regions during the 1960s. The value of its exports rose from 7 million US dollars in 1960 and 10 million in 1965 to 44 million in 1970 (see table 5.7). In 1970, Hong Kong was still far behind Japan (116.3 million US dollars) and Switzerland (610 million US dollars), but it entered into a growing trade dynamic that would be reinforced in the following period. Moreover, this increase was based on a significant change in the nature of products. In 1970, complete watches accounted for 68.5% of the value of Hong Kong's total watch exports, whereas the category 'complete watches' had been non-existent in the official export statistics five years earlier.[69]

Table 5.7 Watch exports from Hong Kong, Japan, and Switzerland, in millions of US dollars, 1960–2010

	1960	1970	1980	1990	2000	2010
Hong Kong	7	44	1,604	3,839	5,614	7,417
Japan	3	116	1,613	2,208	1,386	1,084
Switzerland	293	610	2,121	4,883	6,098	16,200

Sources: *Hong Kong Trade Statistics Export and Re-export* (Hong Kong: Census Department, 1960–2010); *Nihon gaikoku boeki tokei* (Tokyo: Ministry of Finance, 1960–2010); *Statistique annuelle du commerce extérieur de la Suisse* (Berne: Direction Générale des Douanes, 1960–2010).
Note: Data converted into US dollars according to indices of the Japanese Bureau of Statistics (http://www.stat.go.jp).

However, these figures do not mean that Hong Kong was moving from a commercial hub to the final stage (that of assembly) in the international watch production division. Despite the emergence of this productive function, Hong Kong remained the major centre of watch distribution in Asia. The volume of watches re-exported doubled during the 1960s (721,000 pieces in 1960 and 1.5 million in 1970).[70] We must therefore stress the twofold function of the British colony in the global watch industry. Moreover, Chinese entrepreneurs in Hong Kong remained technologically dependent on American, Japanese, and Swiss companies, whose movements they merely assembled and fitted together. The design, development, and production of the movement, which represented the core of watchmaking technology, largely escaped the control of Hong Kong companies. The advent of electronic watches in the early 1970s was a major breakthrough in their emancipation.

The emergence of new watchmaking nations: the Soviet Union, China, and India

Direct investments by Western and Japanese companies were not the only means by which hitherto non-watchmaking nations could see the development of a watch industry on their territory. After World War II, many so-called emerging countries, often former colonies that had become independent, adopted voluntary economic development policies based on protectionism and the active involvement of the state in the industrialisation process.[71]

A watch industry was formed in this context in several countries. These were mainly countries with a large domestic market, a necessary condition for the development of a new consumer goods industry protected from imports. The Soviet Union, China, and India saw the development of watch production during this period. However, the conditions for technology transfer, state involvement, and relations with foreign companies differed for each of these nations.

Birth of a watchmaking giant: the Soviet Union

The war had almost put an end to the watch industry in the Soviet Union, which had been booming since the 1930s. In 1945, production barely amounted to 60,000 watches.[72] However, the Soviet watch industry made a new start and in the mid-1950s the Soviet Union became the world's second-largest producer of watches in terms of volume, behind Switzerland and ahead of the United States, before being overtaken by Japan at the end of the 1960s.[73] While its annual production was estimated at less than 150,000 pieces at the end of the 1930s, the Soviet watch industry reached a volume of 1.5 million watches in 1950, 21.7 million in 1970, and nearly 40 million in 1980. Figures for watches alone are not known for the 1980s (when the figures include clocks), but the Soviet watch industry continued to grow until the early 1990s (see figure 5.8).

The tremendous development of the Soviet watch industry between 1945 and 1990 was based on protected markets. The domestic market (180 million inhabitants in 1950 and 289 million in 1990)[74] was the most important outlet. As for

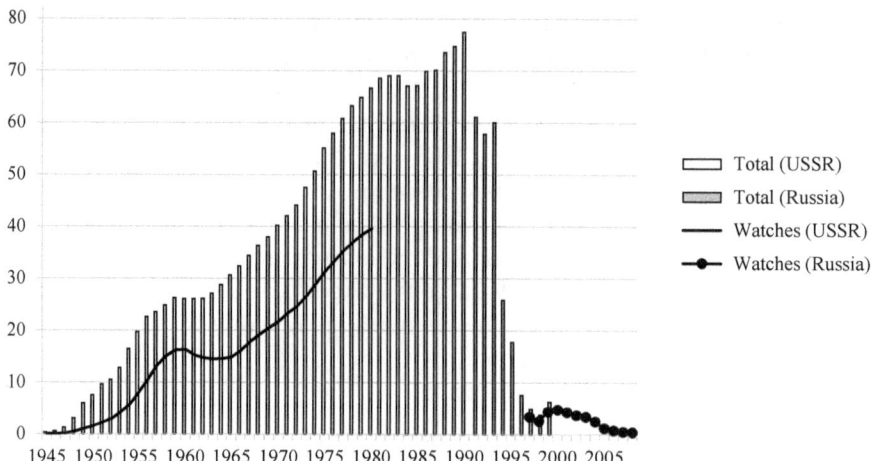

Figure 5.8 Watch and clock production (millions of pieces) in the Soviet Union and Russia, 1945–2008.

Sources: Roger A. Clarke and J. I. Dubravko, *Soviet Economic Facts, 1917–1981* (New York: St Martin's Press, 1983), 127; *Industrial Commodity Statistics Yearbook* (New York: United Nations, 1980–2008).

exports (27% of production in 1970 and 34% in 1980), they were destined for both Communist Bloc countries and Western states. In 1980, the largest markets were Panama (3.5 million pieces), Poland (3.3 million), the Netherlands (1.9 million), Britain (1.6 million), France (1.5 million), Romania (1.4 million), Hungary (1.1 million), and East Germany (1 million).[75] Although the Soviet Union had access to some Western European markets, where simple and cheap Soviet watches were competitive in the entry-level segment, there was an over-representation of communist countries, which had been its main customers since the 1950s, with a mostly limited presence in the West at the end of the 1970s.

State planning and the absence of marketing considerations allowed the adoption of a production system characterised by a only a small variety of models and their mass production. Western and Japanese industrialists and engineers who had the opportunity to visit watch factories in Moscow and the rest of the country all reported similar testimonials. They were impressed by the gigantism and modernity of the production equipment – including the presence of the most modern Swiss machine tools. They also praised the good quality of the watches – all anchor escapement watches with a minimum of 15 stones – but deplored the lack of attention paid to decoration and design.[76]

The beginnings of the Chinese watch industry

Although China became a growing market for Swiss and Japanese watchmakers during the interwar period, there was no transplantation of production units there before World War II. The Chinese watch industry was born at the beginning of the 1950s as a result of the intervention of the new communist state, which was eager to industrialise the country and reduce dependence on foreign trade.

Until the mid-1950s, watches produced in China were mainly limited to imported movements in Chinese-made cases. These assembly workshops, located mainly in the Shanghai region, were places where people could learn how to make watches. The first actual Chinese watch factories appeared around 1957–1960. One of the most important was the Shanghai Wristwatch Factory, which opened in 1957.[77] Equipped with Swiss and Soviet machine tools, it aimed to achieve an annual production of 100,000 pieces and produced its first watches in 1958. Other factories were opened elsewhere in the country during the years 1958–1960, such as in Beijing, Guangzhou, Liaoning, and Tientsin.

These business start-ups caused a stir in Switzerland. In February 1958, Gérard Bauer, who had shortly before taken up the post of president of the FH, expressed to the Swiss ambassador posted in Beijing, Bernoulli, his fear that China might follow Japan's example. The latter shared his concern, arguing that 'among these enormous peoples of 100, 200 and 600 million, we find the intelligences and talents necessary for the efficient creation of any industrial branch'.[78] So, in July 1958, the FH sent one of its employees, Gilbert Étienne, to China to study the watch market and industry. He was received at the Tientsin factory, which originated in a former clock factory where a group of workers began studying watchmaking in 1955, before setting up a company two years later. Production was on the rise, with 120 pieces in May 1958 and more than 200 in July of the same year, but remained very modest, despite a target of 200,000 pieces for 1960. The visit left Étienne doubtful about the development capacities of a Chinese watch industry, as the conclusion of his report shows:

> Seeing the semi-artisanal character of this factory where manual work plays an important role, one wonders whether this company will really manage to make the big leap forward next year.[79]

Despite Étienne's doubts, the Chinese watch industry showed strong growth during the 1960s (see figure 5.9). The volume of national production amounted to a few hundred thousand watches at the beginning of the decade. It reached 1.1 million pieces in 1965 and 3.6 million in 1970. It then experienced extraordinary growth in the second half of the 1970s thanks to the switch to the production of quartz watches. China thus became a watch-producing nation in the 1960s. In 1976, an official delegation even donated six watches to the International Museum of Horology in La Chaux-de-Fonds, a symbolic gesture that enabled the country to assert its entry into world watchmaking history. At the ceremony for the presentation of these timepieces, Wang Chung-Yuan, a representative of the Chinese embassy in Bern, declared that the watches were still manufactured 'with Swiss technical support'.[80]

The technical assistance provided by the Soviet Union and East Germany played an important role in the development of a watch industry in China, particularly through the supply of machine tools and watch design. For example,

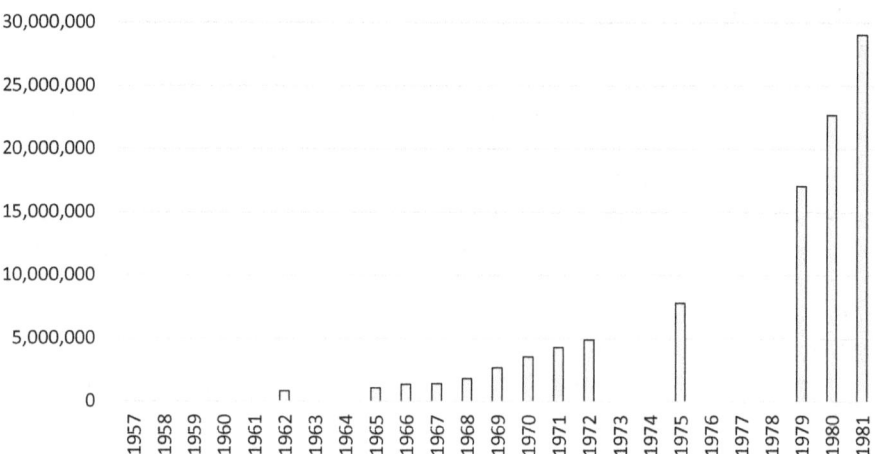

Figure 5.9 Chinese watch production volume, 1957–1981.
Source: Yuming Yang, 'L'industrie horlogère suisse et ses relations avec la Chine de 1949 à 1982' (PhD diss., Geneva: Institut Universitaire de Hautes Études Internationales, 1984), 110.

the first watches manufactured in the Liaoning factory were copies of Soviet products. However, the Chinese watch industry was not born out of a simple transfer of technology via its communist neighbour. Moreover, the deterioration of relations between the Soviet Union and China led to the departure of Soviet watch engineers after 1960.[81]

Switzerland also participated fully in this industrial boom, in particular through its deliveries of parts and machine tools.[82] Above all, it was springs, a difficult part to produce and necessary to ensure the precision of watches, that interested Chinese manufacturers at the beginning of the 1950s. Fabrique suisse de ressorts d'horlogerie SA was one of the main suppliers. Its customers in the 1950s included the New Light Watch Co. in Shanghai. Golay-Buchel & Cie, then producing watch stones and other supplies, also contacted the embassy in Beijing in 1957.[83]

Machine tool manufacturers participated in the modernisation of the equipment of these factories.[84] In 1958, the Swiss consul general in Shanghai, Kurt Hofmann, had the opportunity to visit the city's brand-new watch factory. There he observed the machines and tools of Swiss origin in the various workshops. The companies involved represented the cream of the Swiss machine tool industry: Hauser AG (Biel), Pétermann SA (Moutier), Bergeon & Cie (Le Locle), Lambert AG (Grenchen), Tesa SA (Renens), and Tripet SA (Biel). However, the number of machines and tools was extremely low. Their acquisition was not intended to implement a mass-production system, as was the case in the Japanese archipelago at the same time, but to be able to manufacture the various components of the watch. The Shanghai factory was still in its infancy, and rationalised industrial production was not implemented until the following decade.

Finally, the contribution of the Chinese state to the development of a watch industry on its territory should be underlined. In 1965, the Shanghai Department of Light Industry set up a watchmaking research centre in the city.[85] The state's efforts bore fruit and, at the beginning of the 1980s, China had around 70,000 watchmaking workers, spread over some 30 production sites.[86] National production increased from 3.6 million pieces in 1970 to 29.1 million in 1981, and 95% was sold on the domestic market.[87]

The emergence of watch production in India

After independence, India adopted a policy of industrialisation based on technology transfer. Until the end of the 1950s, imports of timepieces remained possible but were subject to quotas. The main exporters were Switzerland for watches, Germany for alarm clocks, and Japan for clocks. The Indian authorities then decided to launch the country's own watch production and approached foreign partners.

A Swiss watchmaking mission was sent to India in 1958 and several major companies, such as SSIH (Omega and Tissot), Favre-Leuba, and Enicar, considered opening production units there. However, due to the restraint of the federal authorities and the Swiss watchmaking associations, which controlled direct foreign investment until the mid-1960s, no industrial project materialised.[88] The conditions imposed on a watch investment in India (majority of Swiss capital, Swiss management, sale only of complete watches, export ban, guarantee against the risks of nationalisation, guarantee of repatriation of profits to Switzerland, etc.) were too strict and unrealistic in the context of Indian economic policy.[89]

As for French and German watch companies, they developed cooperation in this part of the world in the early 1960s. For example, watch manufacturers in Besançon set up Indo-French Time Industries Private Ltd in Bombay with Indian manufacturers, and the German company Kasper & Co. of Pforzheim founded Asika Time Industries Private Ltd in Konoor with local partners. The two companies assembled movements imported from France and Germany, respectively.[90] But it was, above all, Citizen Watch that made a name for itself, thanks to a major industrial investment: the creation of a joint venture in Bangalore with the state-owned company HMT (Hindustan Machine Tools), which was active in the production of precision machines.[91] The Japanese watch company supplied its Indian partner with machine tools, blanks, and components until the latter was capable of producing its own movements. It also trained around 50 HMT engineers in its factories in Japan.

Indian watch production began in 1962 and was booming. Between 1965 and 1980, it grew from 208,000 to 4.8 million pieces.[92] As a result, Swiss watchmakers saw a sharp drop in exports to India (430,000 watches in 1950 and 12,000 in 1980). As for the Japanese competitor, although it did not record an increase in its exports to India, it did benefit from Indian orders for parts and movements.

In 1980, Japan exported only 50 complete watches but 158,000 movements and parts to a value of more than 1.6 million yen.[93]

Conclusion

The 1950s and 1960s corresponded with a period of profound transformation of the world watch industry, marked by three main characteristics. First, the period saw the triumph of very large companies engaged in the mass production of watches. The world market experienced a tremendous expansion, with large Swiss, American, Japanese, and German companies emerging as the leading players in the industry. In addition, these firms organised themselves as multinational companies, such as Timex and ASUAG, which opened production centres abroad. Eventually, these companies found themselves in a situation of direct confrontation. They competed on the world market.

Second, low value-added activities such as components manufacturing and assembly were outsourced to countries with cheap labour, mainly Hong Kong. The strong competitiveness of the world market led the largest firms to relocate some of their workshops in order to reduce their production costs. This process gave rise to a watch industry in Hong Kong, but it remained dependent on American, Swiss, and Japanese clients.

Third, the birth of multinational watch companies and the internationalisation of production systems did not prevent the emergence of a watch industry in new countries. This is particularly the case in the Soviet Union, China, and India, countries largely closed to international trade and investment by foreign firms on their territory. The state was a key player in these three countries, where watch production was launched in a non-competitive context and taken over by state-owned companies which benefited from a monopoly situation.

The period 1945–1970 thus appears as a first phase of globalisation of the watch industry based on new organisational forms: the multinational company and international subcontracting networks. Institutional and technological factors contributed to making this globalisation possible. First of all, the adoption of a policy of liberalisation of foreign trade by Western countries and Japan led to the end of protected markets and the need to strengthen the competitiveness of firms. In Switzerland, the end of the watchmaking cartel favoured company mergers and allowed the internationalisation of production. The impact of mass-production technologies should also be emphasised. The standardisation of watch components and models facilitated the transfer to other countries of certain activities such as assembly.

Thus, at the beginning of the 1970s, the world watch industry was no longer fundamentally organised on national bases but instead on large companies that had become largely international. Competition between firms prevailed over competition between nations. In the middle of the decade, however, a technological paradigm shift, with the arrival of electronics, changed the conditions of global competition.

Notes

1. *L'Impartial*, 16 November 1966.
2. For the example of Japan, see Pierre-Yves Donzé, 'The Department for Arms Production of the University of Tokyo and the beginnings of the Japanese precision machine industry (1930–1960)', *Osaka Economic Papers*, vol. 61, no. 1 (2011): 37–59.
3. ACJ, Porrentruy, Fonds Péquignot, 122. Presentation by Karl Huber at a meeting of representatives of watchmaking organisations, 8 May 1959.
4. *Feuille fédérale* (1960), 1526.
5. Harm Schröter, 'Cartels', in *Dictionnaire historique de la Suisse*, https://www.dhs.ch (accessed 15 June 2009).
6. *Feuille fédérale* (1984), 848.
7. *Feuille fédérale* (1961), 1604.
8. *Feuille fédérale* (1980), 1329.
9. Convention patronale, *Recensement 2007* (La Chaux-de-Fonds: CPIH, 2008), 13.
10. Hélène Pasquier, *La 'recherche et développement' en horlogerie: acteurs, stratégies et choix technologiques dans l'arc jurassien suisse (1900–1970)* (Neuchâtel: Alphil, 2008).
11. *La Suisse horlogère et revue internationale d'horlogerie*, December 1974–January 1975: 39–40.
12. 'Les concentrations dans l'industrie horlogère suisse', *Annales biennoises* (1971): 50.
13. Pierre-Yves Donzé, 'Des montres et des pétrodollars: la politique commerciale d'une PME horlogère suisse. Aubry Frères SA, 1917–1993', *Revue Suisse d'Histoire* (2004): 384–409.
14. Glasmeier, *Manufacturing Time*; Alft and Biska, *Elgin Time*, 87–92.
15. *L'Impartial*, 17 April 1959.
16. Pasquier, *La 'recherche et développement' en horlogerie*. The stable frequency of the tuning-fork vibration is used as a resonator to measure the time flow.
17. Sauers, *Time for America*, 162; Glasmeier, *Manufacturing Time*, 184.
18. 'Bulova Corporation', in *International Directory of Company Histories* (Detroit: St James Press, 2001), 70–72.
19. *Moody's Industrial Manual*, 1948, 1962, and 1973.
20. F.-E. Oxtoby, 'The role of political factors in the Virgin Islands watch industry', *Geographical Review*, vol. 60, no. 4 (1970): 466.
21. Ibid., 469.
22. F. Knickerbocker, *Note on the Watch Industries in Switzerland, Japan, and the United States* (Boston: Harvard Business School, 1974), 14.
23. *U.S. Commodity Exports and Imports as Related to Output* (Washington, DC: US Census Bureau, 1960–1970).
24. 'Timex', in *International Directory of Company Histories* (Detroit: St James Press, 1999), 479–482.
25. Blanc, *Suisse–Hong Kong: le défi horloger: innovation technologique et division internationale du travail* (Lausanne: Éditions d'En bas, 1988), 45.
26. *Kokusai tokei tsushin* (1970), 477; Landes, *Revolution in Time*, 423.
27. Donzé, *'Rattraper et dépasser la Suisse.'*
28. Ibid.
29. *L'Industrie de l'horlogerie* (Paris: Banque de France, 1974), 7.
30. Archives Nationales, Paris, 19910207/2, Memorandum on Timex, 10 August 1979.
31. Schmid, *Lexikon der Deutschen Uhrenindustrie*, 382–383.
32. Ibid., 317–318.
33. Ibid., 190.

34 *L'Impartial*, 25 August 1967.
35 Hans Rieben, Madeleine Urech, and Charles Iffland, *L'Horlogerie et l'Europe* (Lausanne: Centre de Recherches Européennes, 1959), 32.
36 Pierre-Yves Donzé, 'Les origines militaires du 'miracle économique' japonais: l'essor technologique de Canon et de Seiko des années 1930 aux années 1960', *Entreprises et Histoire*, vol. 85 (2016): 12–25.
37 Seiko Museum, Tokyo, *Hiaringu tokei gijutsushi shirizu*, vol. 33.
38 Ibid., 9–10.
39 Ibid., vol. 11: 7.
40 *Seiko tokei no sengoshi* (Tokyo: Seiko, 1996), 32–37.
41 Ibid., 95.
42 Ibid., 96.
43 Ibid., 94.
44 Centre Jurassien d'Archives et de Recherches Économiques (CEJARE), Saint-Imier, Aubry Frères SA, Francis Foëx, 'Histoire de la West End Watch Co' (unpublished manuscript, 1973).
45 *Nihon keizai shimbun*, 19 June 1962.
46 SFA, E2200.136, Letter from the delegations meeting to Péquignot, 11 April 1951.
47 SFA, E2200.10, Hong Kong, Letter from the Swiss Consulate to the DPF, 1950.
48 SFA, E2200.10, Hong Kong, Letter from Th. Von Mandach, lawyer for Shriro in Switzerland, to Péquignot, 15 September 1953.
49 *Statistique annuelle du commerce extérieur de la Suisse*, 1970 and 1980.
50 *Nihon gaikoku boeki nenpyo* (Tokyo: Ministry of Finance, 1970–1980).
51 Donzé, *Histoire de l'industrie horlogère suisse*, 151–154.
52 *Kaisha yoran* (Tokyo: Daiamondo, 1971), 928.
53 Convention patronale, *Recensement 2007*, 13.
54 SFA, E2200.10 Hong Kong, Letter from Consul General Mossaz to Trade Division (10 March 1960).
55 *Hong Kong Trade Statistics Export and Re-export* (Hong Kong: Census Department, 1962–1964).
56 Pierre-Yves Donzé, 'National labels and the competitiveness of European industries: the Example of the 'Swiss Made' Law since 1950', *European Review of History*, vol. 26, no. 5 (2019): 855–870.
57 SFA, E2200.10, Hong Kong, Agreement between the Federation of Swiss Watch Manufacturers and the Federation of Hong Kong Industries, 2 November 1966.
58 Blanc, *Suisse–Hong Kong*, 149.
59 Pierre-Yves Donzé, 'Le district industriel horloger suisse de la cartellisation à la globalisation: L'exemple de l'industrie de la boîte de montres au cours du XXe siècle', in *Histoires de territoires. Les territoires industriels en question, XVIIIe–XXe siècles*, eds Laurent Tissot et al. (Neuchâtel: Alphil, 2010), 343.
60 *Nihon gaikoku boeki nenpyo* (Tokyo: Ministry of Finance, 1960–1980).
61 *Tokei no honkon shijo chosa hokokusho* (Tokyo: Nihon kikai zushutsu kumiai, 1980), 4.
62 'Seiko gurupu no kaigai senryaku', *Noryoku Kaihatsu Shirizu*, vol. 87 (1982): 14–15.
63 Blanc, *Suisse–Hong Kong*, 148.
64 Its four shareholders were BFG, Basis Watch (Tecknau), Claro Watch (Biel), and Ritz (Chiasso). *L'Impartial*, 3 June 1971.
65 Blanc, *Suisse–Hong Kong*, 148.
66 *Statistique annuelle du commerce extérieur de la Suisse*, 1960–1974.
67 *Nihon gaikoku boeki nenpyo*, 1960–1970.
68 Donzé, 'The hybrid production system.'

69 *Hong Kong Trade Statistics Export and Re-export*, 1960–1970.
70 Ibid.
71 Giuliano Garavini, *After empires: European integration, decolonization, and the challenge from the global south 1957–1986* (Oxford: Oxford University Press, 2012).
72 Roger A. Clarke and Dubravko J. I. Matko, *Soviet Economic Facts, 1917–1981* (New York: St Martin's Press, 1983), 127.
73 Landes, *Revolution in Time*. On Soviet watchmaking, see Pierre-Yves Donzé, 'Les relations horlogères entre la Suisse et la Russie au cours du 20e siècle', *Revue économique et sociale*, vol. 72 (2014): 15–25.
74 Angus Maddison, *The World Economy* (Paris: OECD, 2006), 183.
75 *Foreign Trade Statistics of the USSR* [Внешние экономические связи СССР] (Moscow: Ministerstvo vneshneĭ torgovli, Planovo-èkonomicheskoe, 1970 and 1980).
76 *L'Impartial*, 19 October 1960; Kinuyuki Motomochi, 'Soren no tokei kogyo ni tsuite', *Nihon tokei gakkaishi*, vol. 4 (1957): 49–54.
77 SFA, 220.174, 1971/46, Translation of an article published in the newspaper *Sin Wen Jih Pao*, 2 January 1957.
78 SFA, 220.174, 1971/46, Letter from Bernouilli to Bauer, 27 February 1958.
79 SFA, 220.174, 1971/46, Report by Gilbert Étienne, 24 September 1958.
80 *L'Impartial*, 25 February 1976.
81 Yuming Yang, 'L'industrie horlogère suisse et ses relations avec la Chine de 1949 à 1982' (PhD diss., Geneva: Graduate Institute of International Studies, 1984), 101–102.
82 SFA, E2200.174, 1968/3, Correspondence between the Swiss consulate in Shanghai and Swiss watch companies, 1953–1957.
83 SFA, 220.174, 1971/46, Letter from Shanghai consulate to Beijing embassy, 28 April 1958.
84 Ibid.
85 Yang, 'L'industrie horlogère Suisse', 102.
86 Ibid., 106.
87 Ibid., 107 and 111.
88 SFA E7004, 1973/8, Band 37, Submission by six companies interested in producing in India to the DFEP, 5 October 1964.
89 Ibid., Note of 4 November 1964.
90 Ibid., Memorandum from six companies interested in producing in India to the DFEP, 5 October 1964.
91 Utpal Chattopadhyay and Pragya Bhawsar, 'Effects of changing business environment on organization performance: the case of HMT Watches Ltd', *South Asian Journal of Business and Management Cases*, vol. 6, no. 1 (2017): 36–46.
92 Indian Engineering Association, *Handbook of Statistics, 1970–1990 and Industrial and Economic Statistics Compendium* (Mumbai: All-India Manufacturers' Organization, 1967).
93 *Nihon gaikoku boeki nenpyo*, 1980.

6

The impact of electronics, 1970–1985

In 1983, the Korean conglomerate Samsung launched its first watches on the market, equipped with Longines and Seiko movements. The tremendous boom in quartz watches over the previous decade could not leave this electronics giant indifferent: watchmaking offered new prospects for growth and it was necessary to master time-measurement technologies. This is why Samsung founded a joint venture with Swiss and Japanese companies that year. This cooperation enabled it to establish itself as a leader in the Korean domestic market in the 1990s. In 1994, Samsung continued to expand on its own and acquired a Swiss watch-case factory.[1] Although Samsung was unable to extend its competitiveness beyond national borders to become a watch player of global importance, the collaboration initiated in 1983 was highly representative of the opportunities offered by the advent of the quartz watch. The mastery of particular know-how related to the design and production of mechanical movements was no longer a fundamental resource for watch companies. It became easy to supply electronic movements and to launch watches on the market.

The years 1970–1985 represent a pivotal moment in the global history of the watch industry. It was during this period that old watchmaking nations such as Switzerland, France, Germany, and the United States declined, and Japan and Hong Kong emerged as major new players. The evolution of world watch production illustrates this new balance perfectly (see table 6.1). All former watchmaking nations experienced negative growth between 1970 and 1984. The most marked decline was that of the United States, with a real collapse in watch production, which fell during these 15 years, from almost 20 million pieces to 1 million. As for Switzerland, it lost its position as the world's largest watch manufacturer, which it had held since the beginning of the nineteenth century. The Soviet Union showed a growth, mainly because its domestic market was closed to foreign producers, and in particular the import of cheap watches from Asia. But it was above all the Asian nations that were showing tremendous growth. The growth rate in Hong Kong was close to 4,000%, making it the world's largest producer by the end of the period. Japan experienced weaker growth because its production level was already high in 1970. Finally, China and other Asian countries (mainly South Korea, Singapore, and Taiwan) were becoming important players in the watch industry. Moreover, this shift towards East Asia

Table 6.1 World watch production, 1970 and 1984

Country	1970		1984		1970–1984
	Volume	%	Volume	%	Growth in %
Switzerland	73,600,000	41.0	36,000,000	6.0	−51
United States	19,400,000	10.8	1,000,000	0.2	−95
France	10,900,000	6.1	7,800,000	1.3	−28
Germany	11,500,000	6.4	9,800,000	1.6	−15
Japan	23,800,000	13.3	120,000,000	20.0	+404
Soviet Union	21,700 000	12.1	37,000,000	6.2	+71
Hong Kong	5,700,000	3.2	226,000,000	37.6	+3,865
China	5,000,000	2.8	73,000,000	12.2	+1,360
Others	7,000,000	4.3	90,100,000	15.0	+1,802
Total	179,300,000	100	600,700,000	100	+235

Sources: See appendix.

was only partially in line with the previous period. The first wave of direct investment, which appeared in the 1960s, ended in brutal failure in the early 1980s. The years 1970–1985 witnessed a profound rupture in terms of industrial organisation and competitiveness.

These years are known as the 'quartz revolution', to use the term coined by American historian David S. Landes.[2] The phenomenon has attracted the attention of many historians, management scholars, and essayists.[3] The result of these writings is a technocentric, simplistic, and distorted view of reality, which nevertheless retains a great impact on the general public because of the evocative power of the story about the advent of quartz. Quartz watches would indeed be a new technology in which the old watchmaking nations did not believe but which enabled Asian watch companies, mainly Japan, to establish themselves on the world market.

The quartz watch is certainly a *product innovation* that changed the conditions of competition. However, it is inaccurate to claim that Swiss and American watchmakers were lagging behind Japan because of their lack of interest. After World War II, watch companies throughout the world pursued R&D activities aimed at integrating electronic technologies into watches. In fact, it was a Swiss company, the Centre Électronique Horloger (CEH), which presented the first prototype quartz watch, in 1967. In the United States, in the same year, a Swiss engineer founded the company Intersil, which specialised in the development of integrated circuits, in particular the CMOS semiconductors that would equip Seiko watches.[4] Two years later, on Christmas day, Seiko launched the first quartz watch on the market. In the years that followed, several American, Swiss, and Japanese companies presented their quartz models.

However, it was not the ability to develop such watches that upset the conditions of competition, but rather the ability to mass-produce them. A *process innovation* enabled Japanese manufacturers, mainly Seiko and Citizen, to win on the world market.[5] The Swiss watch industry, fragmented among hundreds of independent SMEs, was not capable of setting up a mass-production system for standardised movements. As for American watch companies, they made technical choices during the 1950s and 1960s that made it difficult to adopt quartz.

Figure 6.1 shows the impact of the quartz revolution. Until the mid-1970s, there was no real upheaval in competitive conditions, despite the launch of the first electronic watches. The United States had the largest watch industry, ahead of Switzerland and Japan – if clocks are included. However, when Japan managed to complete its mass-production system in the second half of the 1970s, it experienced rapid growth and established itself as the world's leading watchmaking nation between 1978 and 1986. The American watch industry collapsed – the value of production was halved between 1978 and 1985. In the same years, Switzerland experienced a phase of stagnation and crisis, before entering a phase of renewal after the mid-1980s – which will be discussed in the next chapter.

In addition, the importance of the monetary factor in the competition between Swiss and Japanese watchmakers should be stressed. After 1971, the

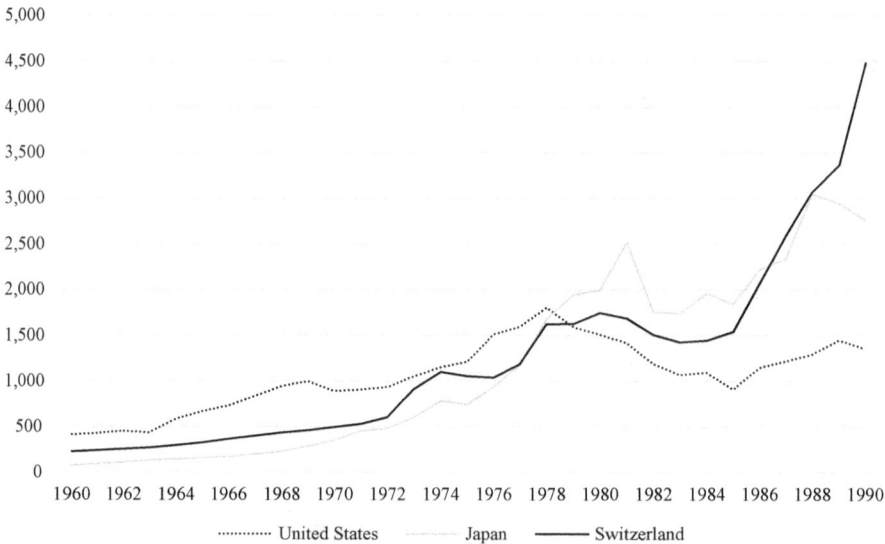

Figure 6.1 Clock and watch production in the United States, Switzerland, and Japan, in millions of US dollars, 1960–1990.

Sources: *Statistique annuelle du commerce extérieur de la Suisse* (Berne: Administration Fédérale des Douanes, 1960–1990); *Annual Survey of Manufactures* (Washington, DC: US Census Bureau, 1960–1990); *Kikai tokei nenpo* (Tokyo: MITI, 1960–1990).
Note: Swiss watch production is evaluated on the basis of the value of exports to which has been added 5% for the domestic market.

end of the Bretton Woods system and the transition to a floating exchange rate regime had disastrous consequences for Switzerland. Between 1970 and 1980, the dollar lost more than 60% of its value against the franc, but only 33% against the yen.[6] Japanese watchmakers thus benefited from a monetary context that strengthened their competitiveness on the American market, which was then the largest in the world. This advantage continued until the Plaza Accord (1985), which led to an increase in the value of the yen and the end of the monetary advantage for Japanese watchmakers.

Japan, the world's leading watchmaking nation

The Japanese watch industry experienced tremendous growth and became the leading producer of watches in terms of value, ahead of Switzerland, between 1978 and 1986 (see figure 6.1). Although Hong Kong was the largest manufacturer in terms of volume, Japanese watch companies produced relatively few digital watches and specialised in multi-function quartz watches, products with higher added value than their Hong Kong competitors, which explains their position as world leader.

The development of quartz watches was part of the strategy implemented at Seiko after 1945 – namely, to conquer the world market with high-quality watches produced in large quantities and offered at low prices. Electronic technologies enhanced the competitiveness of Japanese watches by improving their precision. In order to achieve this goal, Seiko began R&D activities in the 1960s and succeeded in marketing the first quartz watch in 1969. The transition to quartz was extremely rapid. For the Japanese watch industry as a whole, electronic watches still accounted for only 8.5% of national production in 1975. It reached 62.4% in 1980 and 82.7% in 1985. It was therefore towards the end of the 1970s that quartz became the dominant technology in this industry.

Moreover, the advent of quartz was an opportunity for an outsider – Casio – to enter the watch industry. Originally founded in 1946 in Tokyo, Casio specialised in the production of office equipment and calculators.[7] At the beginning of the 1970s, it began a diversification strategy due to the fierce competition in the calculator market in the second half of the 1960s (a 'calculator war' with Sharp).[8] It was in this context that Casio launched in 1974 the first digital quartz watch (Casiotron), which was the result of its research into LCD (liquid crystal display) and quartz technologies, the electronic pocket calculator using similar technologies. The principles of the watches made by Casio were based on all-electronics (no mechanical watches, no analogue display until 2004) and low prices (experience from the calculator war).[9] Casio enjoyed phenomenal success until the early 1980s. Its watch turnover rose from 4.8 billion yen in 1976 to 58.7 billion yen in 1981 and 68.9 billion yen in 1985. During this period, watches played an increasingly important role in Casio's business, with their share rising from less than 10% to more than a third during the first part of the 1980s.[10] The launch of the G-Shock model (1983) helped establish Casio as a manufacturer of quality digital watches. Above all, the considerable importance of Casio in the Japanese watch industry must be emphasised. Its share of the value of domestic watch production (including mechanical watches) rose very rapidly, from 2.2% in 1976 to 18.7% in 1985.

The international expansion of Japanese watch companies also strengthened during this period. It was essentially based on exports and not much on foreign direct investments. The highly automated factories of the Japanese watch companies enabled the production of cheap watches, which were then exported worldwide. The share of domestic production exported, which amounted to 47.6% in 1970, was 54.8% in 1975 and 68.5% in 1985. The domestic market thus remained important but became a minority during this period. It should also be pointed out that the strengthening of expansion on foreign markets was visible from the first part of the 1970s – that is, it predated the quartz revolution. Japanese mechanical watches were competitive and challenged the dominant position of Swiss watchmakers, particularly in the United States.

However, despite the importance of exports, Japanese watch companies invested abroad, mainly in low-wage countries where they opened production centres for assembly parts. The Seiko group, which had opened watch-assembly subsidiaries in Hong Kong (1968) and Singapore (1969), set up a watch-case factory and a company specialising in gold plating on cases[11] in Singapore in 1980. It also owned the majority of the capital of a component producer based in Hong Kong, Asian Precision (1976).[12] Finally, in 1980, Seiko signed an agreement with the Chinese authorities for the opening of a watch-case production centre, in collaboration with watch manufacturers in Beijing and Xian.[13]

The relocation also involved the manufacture of complete watches. In 1970, shortly after opening its first assembly centre in South Korea, Citizen created a joint venture in Hong Kong, Sunciti Manufacturers, in collaboration with Sun International, a company close to Gilman & Co, Citizen's distributor in South-East Asia. This joint venture was active in the assembly of movements, with parts were imported from Japan and then put into cases produced locally. As for Seiko, it owned a major factory in Singapore, the Singapore Time Pte company, formally founded in 1973 but which opened its doors in 1975, after having trained 100 Malaysian workers in the group's Japanese factories. It assembled low-end mechanical watches and electronic watches, all parts of which were manufactured locally. In 1979, its production volume reached a total of 1.7 million pieces, including 400,000 quartz watches, and grew rapidly.[14] Finally, Seiko undertook technical cooperation with the French watch group Matra (1982) and invested in a joint venture with Samsung in South Korea (1983), in order to strengthen its presence in protected markets.

The striking feature of these relocations was the import of finished movements – particularly quartz movements – a phenomenon that had not existed in the 1960s. The number of movements manufactured abroad in 1980 totalled 5.4 million pieces, representing 6.3% of Japanese watch production. During the 1970s, Japanese watch companies took the path of the international division of

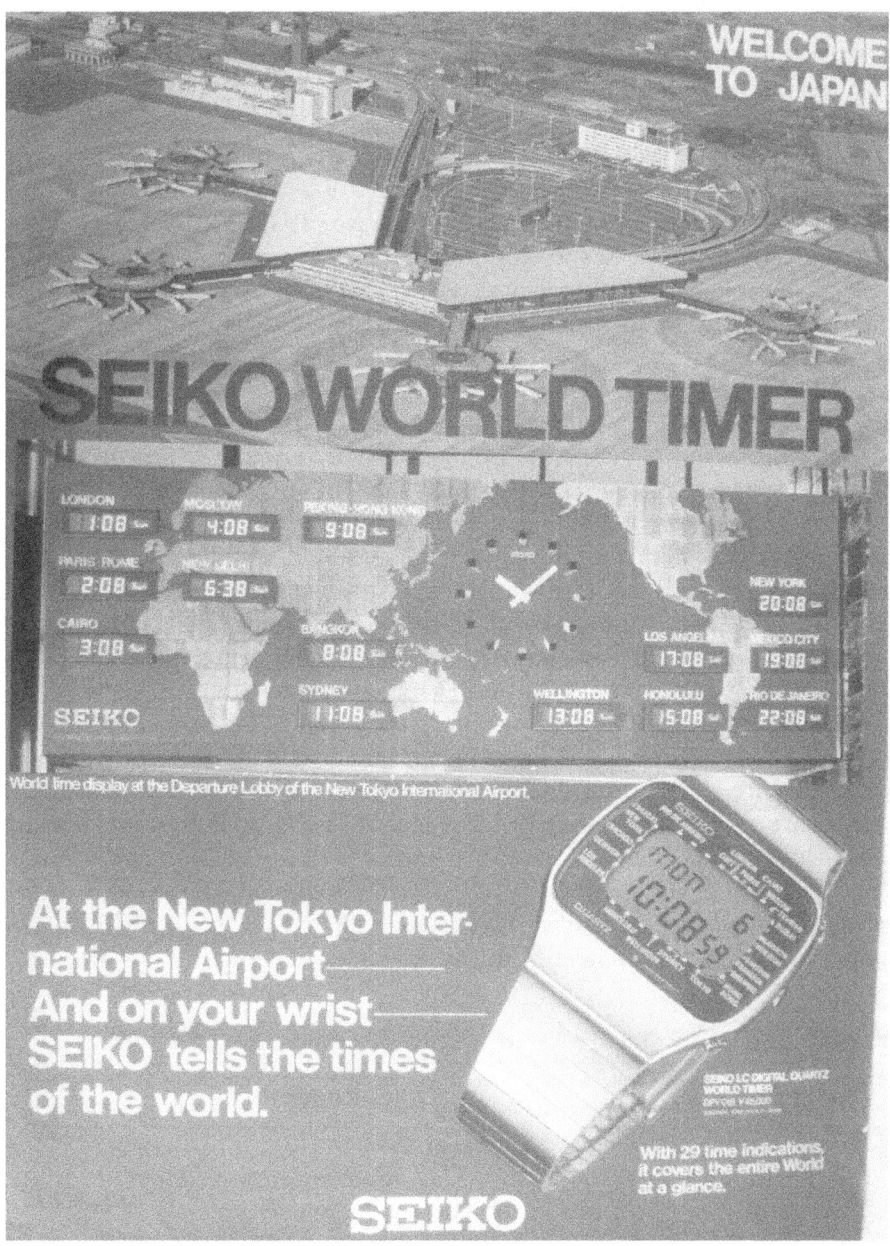

Figure 6.2 Advertisement for Seiko, 1977.

labour, a strategy that only became more pronounced thereafter. At the end of the 1990s, Japanese watches produced abroad accounted for a quarter of the total volume of production.[15]

The empowerment of Hong Kong watchmakers

The sudden emergence of Hong Kong as the world's leading watch producer between 1970 and 1984 was the result of the quartz revolution. Electronic technologies enabled the British colony's watchmakers to emancipate themselves from their historical dependence on Swiss, Japanese, and American watch companies. Whereas they had been subcontractors specialising in casing and assembly, the easy acquisition of quartz movements made them autonomous.

The assembly, then production, of analogue quartz watches in Hong Kong began in 1975, and digital watches the following year. The gains in market share, in terms of volume, were extremely high. In 1976, Hong Kong's domestic production amounted to 4 million quartz watches, making it the world's second-largest manufacturer, behind Japan (7.3 million).[16] The transition to quartz was rapid – the share of electronic watches already amounted to 68.3% of the total value of Hong Kong watch exports in 1980, then 88.2% in 1985 and 94.8 % in 1990.[17] Moreover, they represented a growing value in absolute terms: 285.8 million US dollars in 1975, 1.6 billion in 1980, and 3.8 billion in 1990.

The industrial structure of the Hong Kong watch industry underwent a profound change with the advent of many firms owned by local entrepreneurs. The latter occupied a growing share of Hong Kong's watchmaking workforce. Between 1974 and 1978, foreign capital invested in Hong Kong watchmaking declined, although the number of firms grew, and the number of employees remained stable. However, the position of these foreign-owned firms in the local watch industry weakened. They accounted for only 25% of watchmaking employment in 1978 compared with 49% in 1974 (see table 6.2).

Table 6.2 Hong Kong watch companies with foreign capital, 1974–1978

Year	Foreign capital (HK$ millions)	Number of companies	Number of employees	Employees as % of total watchmaking workforce
1974	184	12	4,643	49%
1975	188	20	5,391	71%
1976	133	22	4,676	36%
1977	135	25	4,894	32%
1978	137	27	5,024	25%

Source: *Tokei no honkon shijo chosa hokokusho* (Tokyo: Nihon kikai zushutsu kumiai, 1980), 10.

The official business census shows that these new companies were mainly SMEs. While the total number of watch companies grew from 229 in 1970 to 1,509 in 1980 and 1,805 in 1985, the average number of employees was declining. It fell from 42.7 to 20.3 between 1970 and 1985 (see table 5.6, p. 106). Finally, it is worth mentioning the progressive importance of the watchmaking sector in the colony's economy. It employed 1.8% of workers in manufacturing industry in 1970 and 5.3% in 1980.

Due to the lack of sources, it is difficult to know the exact nature of these companies and their function within the global watch industry. Some of these new watch manufacturers were former subcontractors, engaged in the production of watch covers during the 1960s, such as Stelux or Crystal Electronic, as well as a few foreign-owned firms, such as Asian Swiss Industrial Co.[18] However, these were exceptions. A study of the Hong Kong watch industry published in 1980 by JETRO (Japan External Trade Organization), an organisation supporting Japanese exporters, shows that all the major watch producers were companies without foreign capital, such as Collins Industrial (founded in 1974), Lambda Electronics (1975), IC Instruments (1975), National Electronics & Watch Co. (1975), Tinic Watch (1978), Larnol Enterprises (1978), and Betatronic Industries (1978).[19] By 1978, all of these companies had produced over 1 million watches and adopted a similar model: the assembly in Hong Kong of quartz movements with imported electronic components and the export of finished watches to the world market.

Although electronics represented a technological opportunity for them to establish themselves as watch manufacturers independent of large foreign companies, Hong Kong entrepreneurs were still dependent on external suppliers for the supply of components such as CMOS integrated circuits and digital LCD displays. However, the manufacturers of these components were not watch companies, but electronics firms that were absent from the watch market – and therefore did not compete with Hong Kong watch manufacturers. At the end of the 1970s, the main suppliers of integrated circuits were Japanese (Oki Electric and NEC) and American (Intersil and Litronix). As for digital display devices, they were mainly produced by Siemens & Beckman, Fairchild, Motorola, Hitachi, and Mos Technology. Several of these electronics manufacturers opened sales subsidiaries in Hong Kong (Hitachi, Intersil, Siemens & Beckman, etc.); some of them also relocated part of their production there. This is notably the case of the American company Fairchild, which in 1980 owned the subsidiary Fairchild Semiconductor Hong Kong. As for the Swiss multinational Brown Boveri Co. (BBC), it opened a subsidiary specialising in the assembly of electronic display systems, BBC Electronics Hong Kong (1978).[20] Finally, it is worth mentioning the special case of the Japanese watchmaker Citizen Watch, one of the few foreign watch producers that managed to take advantage of the change in Hong Kong. In 1979, it adopted a new strategy based on specialising in the mass production of quartz watch movements and exporting them to a Hong Kong watch-case producer who engaged in the manufacture and sale of finished products.[21]

The quartz revolution played a key role in the emergence of a watch industry in Hong Kong because it gave entrepreneurs from this British colony access to the world market. They quickly acquired skills in terms of marketing and distribution. In 1987, Hong Kong watch companies participated for the first time in the Basel Fair.[22]

The Swiss watch crisis and its consequences

Between the mid-1970s and the early 1980s, the Swiss watch industry faced a deep crisis that called into question its very existence. The volume of Swiss watch exports, which had reached an all-time high of 84.4 million pieces in 1974, fell to 30.2 million pieces in 1983.[23] It started to grow again in 1984 thanks to Swatch sales, but this collapse in exports had dramatic effects on watch companies. Between 1970 and 1985, their number decreased from 1,618 to 634, while the number of employees fell at the same time from 89,000 to 33,000.[24] The Swiss watch industry thus lost almost two-thirds of its workforce during the crisis. This led to industrial action, particularly at Bulova, which employed around 1,700 people in its factories in Biel and Neuchâtel. In 1976, the workers of the latter factory went on strike, but this did not prevent its closure in 1977. The Bulova group ceased production in Switzerland in 1982.[25]

This is commonly seen as a consequence of the quartz revolution and the inability of Swiss watch manufacturers to adopt this innovation. However, while it is true that Swiss companies encountered major difficulties in the transition to the industrialisation of electronic movements, as Hélène Pasquier has shown,[26] it also took several years for their Japanese competitors to impose this technology. Consequently, the Swiss watch crisis was only indirectly the result of a technological change linked to the nature of the product.

Figure 6.3 Demonstration in support of the strikers occupying the Bulova factory, 1976, Neuchâtel.

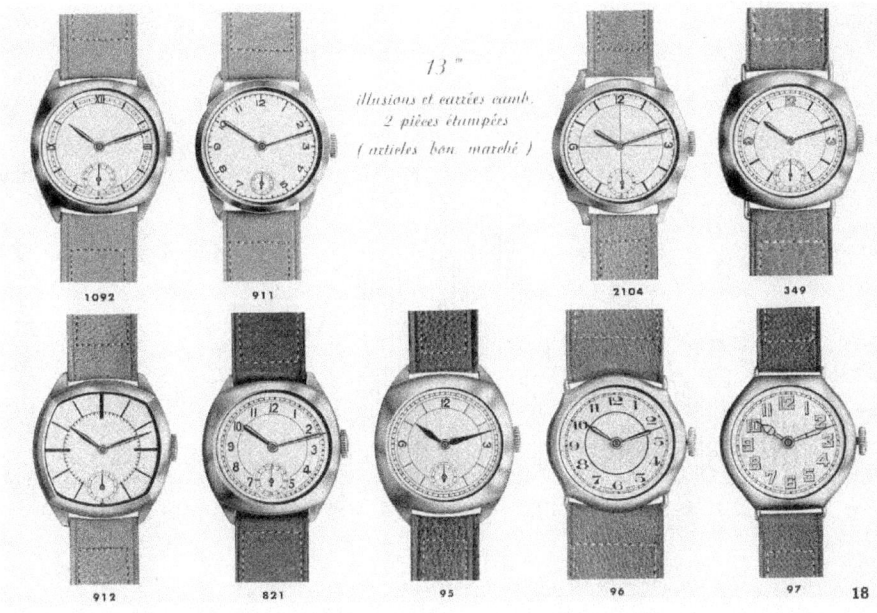

Figure 6.4 Roskopf watches in the catalogue of Bader-Hafner, Switzerland, circa 1940.

By keeping the structure of an industrial district made up of hundreds of SMEs, which were interdependent but autonomous, the Watchmaking Statute delayed a concentration that would allow the rationalisation of production and marketing necessary on a world market that had become extremely competitive. Furthermore, the rise in the value of the franc after the end of the Bretton Woods monetary system had exacerbated the difficulties of Swiss watchmakers, particularly in the United States. For example, the sports chronograph manufacturer Heuer-Léonidas, which made 50% of its sales on the American market in 1970, suffered heavy losses and was taken over by Manufacture d'Horlogerie Nouvelle Lémania SA (1982), then the investment company Technique d'Avant-Garde (1985).

Roskopf watch manufacturers were the only ones to have facilities for mass production.[27] However, they were hit hard by the advent of quartz watches, which were cheaper and more accurate products. In 1973–1974, Swiss watchmakers exported more than 35 million Roskopf watches and movements, which then accounted for half of all exports (see figure 6.5). The volume of Roskopf watches and movements fell to 29.5 million pieces in 1975, 12.9 million in 1980 and 1.2 million in 1985. Moreover, while they accounted for almost 50% of the volume of Swiss exports of mechanical watches in 1974, Roskopf watches saw their share fall to 34.6% in 1980 and to less than 5% from 1988 onwards.

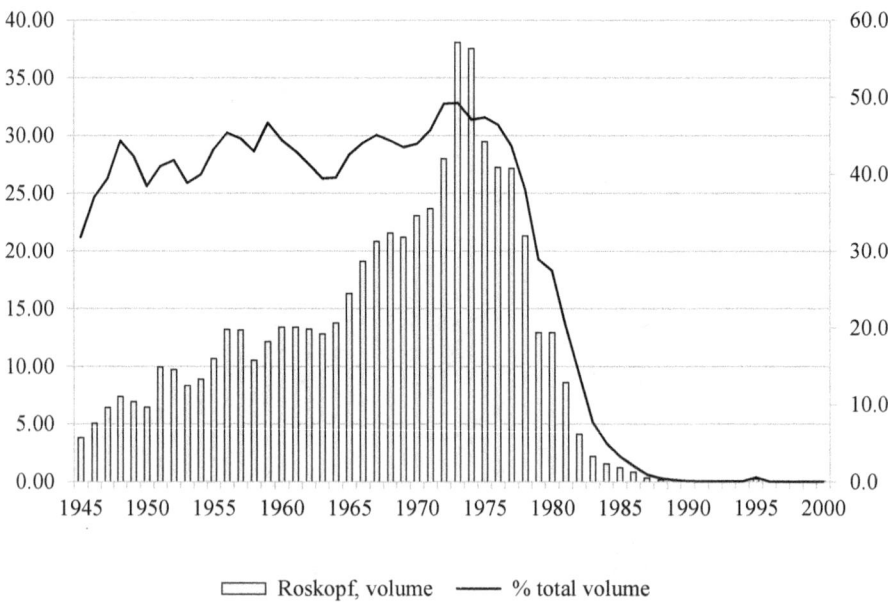

Figure 6.5 Swiss exports of Roskopf watches, volume (millions of pieces) and share of total exports (%), 1945–2000.
Source: Data from the Federation of the Swiss Watch Industry (personal communication with author).

This collapse of the Roskopf watch had disastrous consequences for many firms. BFG, in Grenchen, which had become one of the largest watch companies in the world in terms of volume, laid off staff and ceased recruitment from 1975 onwards. It closed its doors in 1982, with the stock and all production worldwide being taken over by one of its former customers, Sanzer, a subsidiary of the Hind Group in Hong Kong. Two years later, Ebosa SA, also in Grenchen, stopped operations. Finally, only Ronda, among the major manufacturers of Roskopf watches, was able to continue its business, thanks to a rapid conversion to the production of quartz movements and the globalisation of its production system. It opened a production centre in Thailand in 1972.[28]

The disappearance of Roskopf watches also had consequences for the major watchmaking groups, such as the SSIH (Omega group) and ASUAG, which had invested and diversified in this sector in the early 1970s. The situation was particularly problematic in the case of the SSIH, where the strategy of growth by volume ultimately proved to be a dead end. The importance acquired by Roskopf watches following the takeover of the Economic Swiss Time group (1971) explains the impact of the crisis on the entire Omega group. Sales of Roskopf watches fell from 9.5 million pieces in 1973 to 5.7 million in 1975 and only 470,000 in 1980.[29] The consequences were considerable in terms of finance, due to the heavy investments made in the takeover and modernisation of the various companies. After several restructurings, the SSIH management decided to liquidate the company Economic Swiss Time, which distributed the group's Roskopf watches in the United States (1979). Two years later, the production subsidiary in Switzerland was sold to one of its major customers, the Zurich-based company Nimex AG.[30]

Therefore, the Swiss watch industry faced a need for concentration and rationalisation in the field of quality mechanical watches. The disappearance of many small watch companies initially strengthened the position of the country's two largest, ASUAG and the SSIH, which in 1979 accounted for almost half of the Swiss watchmaking workforce.[31] However, this domination should be put into perspective, mainly due to the crisis suffered by the other companies. In reality, ASUAG and SSIH experienced serious industrial and financial difficulties. They ultimately owed their survival solely to the support of the banks.

ASUAG struggled to manage its growth and the diversification of its activities. While it had built its growth since the 1930s on its monopoly position as a producer and distributor of movements, the advent of the electronic watch fundamentally challenged this traditional function. In 1971, it attempted to diversify to complete watches with the creation of General Watch Co., a strategy that had a profound impact on its finances and management. Between 1970 and 1974, the company's balance sheet rose from 54.5 million to 234.1 million francs. Turnover rose steadily during these five years of economic boom: it was 760 million francs in 1970 and reached a peak of 1.4 billion in 1974. However, growth was fragile. ASUAG depended more and more on external capital, which made the creation of General Watch Co. possible: it represented 28.3% of the balance sheet in 1974, against 23.7% in 1970. Thus, when the Swiss watch industry entered recession, ASUAG's turnover fell to less than 1.2 billion francs per year during the 1975–1978 period, and dependence on bank capital continued to grow.[32]

The SSIH also faced a major crisis after 1974, resulting from diversification in all directions, particularly in the low-end mechanical watch sector (see chapter 5). Between 1974 and 1982, the SSIH collapsed. Turnover dropped from 733 million to 537 million francs. At the same time, the number of employees decreased from 7,300 to 3,400.[33] The banks, which ensured the company's survival by granting medium-term loans, supported the reorganisation of the SSIH. A restructuring committee was set up in 1980, led by the Union Bank of Switzerland (UBS), the Swiss Bank Corporation (SBS), and Credit Suisse. The following year, a former UBS director, Peter Gross, took over as chairman of the board of directors. Between 1981 and 1983, the banks injected more than 900 million Swiss francs into SSIH and ASUAG and sought a solution to return to profitability.[34]

The two main difficulties faced by the SSIH and ASUAG were the management of industrial groups with little rationalisation and the unsuitability of the products to the market. Only a policy of industrial restructuring and marketing rationalisation could ensure their survival. The banks turned to the advice of the consultant Nicolas G. Hayek to carry out this reorganisation. Born in Beirut in 1928 and trained at the University of Lyon, Hayek had founded his consulting company, Hayek Engineering, in Zurich in 1963. He worked in particular for several watch companies, whose restructuring was a necessity in the context of the changes taking place at that time (liberalisation, appearance of electronic watches, foreign competition).[35] In his report to the banks, Hayek proposed as the main measure the merger of ASUAG and the SSIH into a single entity, the Société Suisse de Microélectronique et d'Horlogerie (SMH). The operation was carried out in 1983 and gave birth to the world's largest watch company, which took the name Swatch Group in 1998. In 1985 Hayek acquired the majority of the capital of the SMH and the following year became chairman and president of the group management board. As the head of this company, he had the opportunity to implement an innovative industrial policy that made a major contribution to the renaissance of the Swiss watch industry (see next chapter).[36]

The collapse of the American watch industry

The American watch industry experienced a dramatic decline, with the volume of domestic production falling from nearly 20 million pieces in 1970 to 1 million in 1984 (see table 6.1, p. 119). Although the United States remained one of the world's largest watch markets, it was beyond the reach of local companies.

American watch imports are a good illustration of the growth of this market: they rose from a value of 71.7 million dollars in 1970 to 613.3 million in 1980. The billion-dollar mark was passed in 1985. This growth mainly benefited Japanese watchmakers. While Switzerland's share collapsed, falling from 83.1% of imports in 1970 to a low of 15.3% in 1983, followed by a slight jump due to Swatch (21.5% in 1985), Japan's share rose from 4% in 1970 to a peak of 37.7% in 1984 (36.8% in 1985).

The loss of competitiveness of American watch manufacturers was not the result of factors common to all companies. Three main models can be distinguished. First, the failure of Timex should be highlighted. This company, which had asserted itself as the leading multinational in the contemporary watch industry, was a direct victim of the quartz revolution. As was the case for its Swiss competitors, its Roskopf watches lost all competitiveness to electronic watches. Facing severe competition after the mid-1970s, particularly in the US market, where electronic companies such as Texas Instruments and Fairchild undercut prices with their digital watches, Timex was unable to enter the quartz watch industry. It recorded its first deficits in 1979, attempted clumsy diversification into electronics (including the launch of its own computer in 1982), optics, and medical technology, but was forced to close its many production sites around the world, leading to a strike in Britain and the intervention of prime minister Margaret Thatcher (1983). The company then refocused on the production of electronic watches for sport but lost its status as a global watchmaking giant.[37]

Second, the Bulova and Hamilton companies, which were at the top end of American watch production, faced difficulties resulting from technical choices that delayed or prevented the adoption of quartz technologies.[38] Bulova, for example, established itself as an innovative company with the launch of its tuning-fork watch in 1960, but this technical choice delayed the adoption of quartz and contributed to the company's downfall. In 1976, Bulova founded a subsidiary, Bulova Systems & Instruments, which specialised in government contracts, mainly in the defence sector, but this did not allow the company to return to growth. The company was bought by a Hong Kong investor that year.[39] Bulova's turnover fell from 228 million dollars in 1975 to 148 million in 1985.[40] Hamilton had a similar trajectory. In the mid-1950s, it began to develop electric watches, a technical choice in which it persisted over the following decade, notably creating a joint venture in Japan with the Ricoh company for the production of these watches in the archipelago (1962). However, faced with competition from Bulova's tuning-fork watches and internal difficulties linked to mass production and after-sales service, Hamilton ceased production of electric watches in 1969 and was unable to develop competitively the production of digital quartz watches, even though it had been in the market since 1970.[41]

Third, and finally, the American watch industry saw the arrival of many new entrants during the 1970s. The development of digital watches was an opportunity for several companies in the electronics industry to launch their own collections. This is the case, for example, with Microma Inc., General Electric, Intersil, Fairchild Camera & Instrument, and Texas Instruments. Some of them collaborated with Swiss watch companies in the development of digital watches, notably Texas Instruments, which in 1972 presented a prototype watch produced jointly with Ébauches SA and Longines.[42] However, these electronics

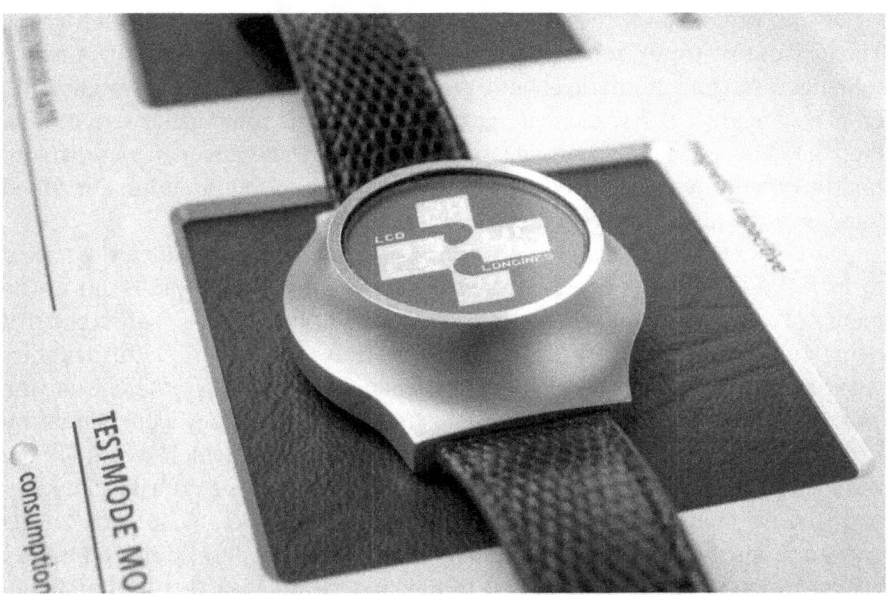

Figure 6.6 Digital watch developed by Texas Instruments, Ébauches and Longines, 1972.

manufacturers were unable to survive in the global watch market, mainly due to the lack of a clear marketing strategy and a sufficiently powerful sales organisation.[43]

Thus, none of the American companies involved in watchmaking during the 1970s managed to adapt to the new technological and commercial environment. At the beginning of the 1980s, the United States was still one of the world's leading watch markets, but it was now controlled by foreign companies. In this context, it is worth noting the foundation in Dallas in 1984 of a company specialised in the sale on the American market of watches produced in Hong Kong: Overseas Productions International. Two years later, it launched the Fossil brand and experienced tremendous growth, heralding the emergence of new forms of organisation of the international division of labour in the global watch industry.

Difficulties of German and French watchmakers and the protectionist reaction of the European Economic Community

German and French watch manufacturers went through a phase of decline during the years 1970–1985. However, the decline was less marked than in Switzerland or the United States. Moreover, Germany and France had different trajectories, which can be explained by different industrial organisation. In Germany, the production of watches was mainly based on a few large companies, the main ones being Junghans in the West and the public conglomerate Glashütter Uhrenbetriebe in the East. They certainly faced difficulties but maintained their competitiveness in the mid-1980s.

On the other hand, the French watch industry underwent a deep crisis. The collapse of Timex, whose Besançon subsidiary was France's largest watch manufacturer, had dramatic effects. While it produced 4.8 million watches and employed nearly 2,800 workers in 1975, it ceased its manufacturing activities on French territory in 1981. As for the Lip company, also in Besançon, it was dismantled in 1973 and was occupied by the workers – an episode that has remained famous in the history of French trade unionism.[44]

The French watch industry as a whole encountered serious difficulties linked to its lack of competitiveness. These difficulties were largely the result of the focus of French watchmakers on their domestic market. In 1970, it absorbed 67% of national production. French manufacturers thus exported only a third of their watches, mainly to European countries. They were virtually absent from the world's largest watch market, the United States. Moreover, they were benefiting from an uncompetitive situation on the domestic market, which meant French watches accounted for 87% of sales in France in 1970. However, the development of quartz watches, mass imported from Asia, had a considerable impact. On the one hand, the French market expanded rapidly, with watch sales rising from 6.7 million pieces in 1970 to more than 12 million in 1978 and 1979. On the other hand, it was mainly imported watches that benefited from the increase in demand, so that the share of French production was only 35% in 1979 (see figure 6.7).

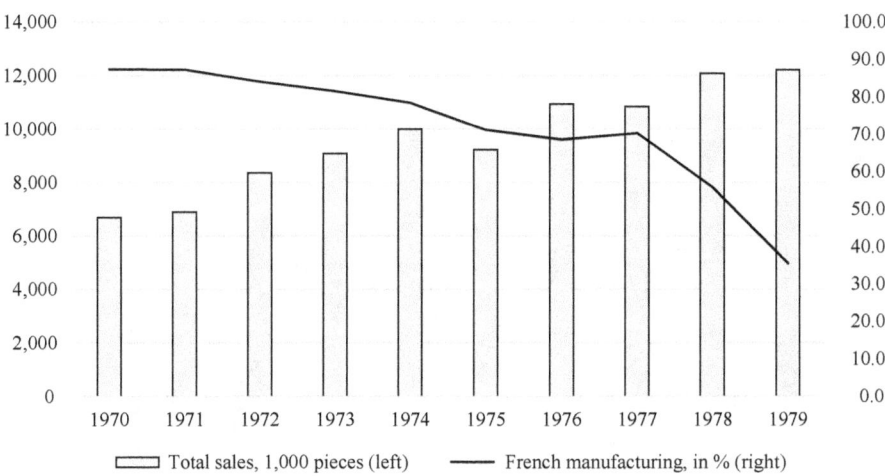

Figure 6.7 The French watch market, 1970–1979.
Source: Archives Nationales, Paris, 19910207/8, Statistics on the watch industry.

The technological backwardness of the French watch industry was the main cause of its lack of competitiveness. In the early 1970s, two companies established in France were engaged in the production of electronic watches: Lip and Timex. However, this technical base did not provide a path to the development of quartz watches. While Lip closed its doors in 1973, Timex transferred its production of electronic watches to Asia. As a result, France lost all capacity to innovate. In 1975, French and Swiss banks and industrialists, supported by the state, tried to reorganise Lip under the name Compagnie Européenne d'Horlogerie, with the aim of launching the production of quartz watches. The technical difficulties and lack of commitment on the part of ASUAG, which was a shareholder (40% of the capital in 1970) but had no interest in seeing the emergence of a new competitor, made it impossible to achieve this goal or to ensure the company's long-term survival.

Other actors also became involved in the mid-1970s. France-Ébauches hired Timex's R&D team and set up production of quartz movements. As for the Technical Centre of the French Watch Industry (Centre Technique de l'Industrie Horlogère, CETEHOR), it started manufacturing quartz movements with the help of independent companies.[45] However, this production was far from covering national needs. Above all, French watchmakers were unable to cope with Asian electronic watches. In 1978, Paul George, former director of research at Lip, stated in a confidential report that 'France is absent from the competition for the quartz watch'.[46]

The difficulties of the French watch industry then led to a double intervention by the state, at the industrial and commercial levels. In the industrial field, the government intervened through the Matra group, a state-owned enterprise

Figure 6.8 Charles Piaget, leader of the Lip workers, speaking in Besançon, August 1973.

active in aeronautics and defence. It bought the companies Jaz (1979), Jaeger (1979), and Yema (1982). In this context, it was looking for a partner to supply watch movements, as France-Ébauches was unable to meet all the demand, and approached Seiko. Technical cooperation between the two firms started in 1982, with Seiko providing watch movements and technical assistance in the organisation of assembly centres in France.[47] In the end, the privatisation of the Matra group, decided in 1987, led its president, Jean-Luc Lagardère, to get rid of an unprofitable watchmaking sector and to sell it to Seiko (1988).[48]

Finally, in the commercial field, in July 1981 the French Chamber of Watchmaking required state aid. It asked the authorities to introduce quotas for watches imported from Asia. The intervention was effective, and, in the same year, the European Economic Community (EEC) authorised such measures. For 1982 and 1983, France limited the annual import of quartz watches from Hong Kong to 4.4 million pieces. The authorities of the British colony intervened with the GATT (General Agreement on Tariffs and Trade), but without success. For the years 1984–1986, the French government, still supported by the EEC, again restricted the import of digital quartz watches: 4.4 million per year for Hong Kong, 815,000 for Japan, and about 1.5 million for other Asian countries.[49] However, these protectionist measures were short-lived and did not succeed in improving the competitiveness of French watch companies.

Conclusion

The quartz revolution led to a profound upheaval in the world watch industry. By making precision watches cheap and widely available, electronics technologies changed the conditions of competition. The transformation of the world watch industry between 1970 and 1985 had three main characteristics.

First, there was an abrupt end to the first phase of globalisation of this industrial sector, which was based on the relocation and outsourcing of low value-added activities to low-wage countries, notably Hong Kong. Roskopf mechanical watch manufacturers, in particular Timex and BFG, which were among the world's largest multinationals in this industry in the early 1970s, disappeared. They had been the actors who had helped to set up transnational organisations in the watch industry.

Second, electronics technology empowered Hong Kong watchmakers and enabled the emergence of new organisational models that differed from the large integrated multinational corporation. Entrepreneurs in the British colony moved from being subcontractors to key middlemen in new value chains (see next chapter), which integrated independent firms that were active in production in Hong Kong and distribution in the United States. Fossil was born in this context.

Third, the hierarchy between watchmaking nations was turned upside down, with the decline of Europe and the United States, the formidable growth of Japan and Hong Kong, and the rise of protectionist countries such as the Soviet Union and China. As a result, the nation remained an essential component of competition in the watch industry, despite the emergence of new transnational organisational models. In the mid-1980s, world watchmaking was based on nations as well as multinational enterprises. It was in the following decades that the transition from nation to enterprise as the basis of competition was completed, in the context of a second globalisation.

Notes

1. Donzé, *Du comptoir familial à la marque globale*, 218.
2. Landes, *Revolution in Time*, 364.
3. Georges Piotet, *Restructuration industrielle et corporatisme: le cas de l'horlogerie en Suisse, 1974–1987* (Lausanne: Imprivite SA, 1988); François Schaller, 'Les crises horlogères, y a-t-il une spécificité?', in *L'homme et le temps en Suisse de 1291 à 1991*, ed. Catherine Cardinal et al. (La Chaux-de-Fonds: IHT, 1991), 273–278; Thomas Perret, 'Un canton chahuté', in *Le Pays de Neuchâtel et son patrimoine horloger*, eds Laurent Tissot et al. (Chézard-Saint-Martin: La Chatière, 2008), 301–305; Hélène Pasquier, 'Une industrie remodelée', in *Le Pays de Neuchâtel et son patrimoine horloger*, eds Laurent Tissot et al. (Chézard-Saint-Martin: La Chatière, 2008), 307–315.
4. Pierre-Yves Donzé, 'La R&D dans l'horlogerie électronique suisse et japonaise de 1960 à 1980: une analyse comparative de Longines et de Seiko', *Le Mouvement Social*, vol. 258 (2017): 115.
5. Donzé, 'The hybrid production system'.

6 Statistics of the Swiss National Bank (www.snb.ch, accessed 7 July 2010); *Nihon chouki toukei souran* (Tokyo: Nihon tokei kyokai, 1988), vol. 18, p. 8.
7 *Kashio 15 nen shi* (Tokyo: Casio, 1972).
8 Between 1965 and 1970, the national production of electronic calculators increased from 4,000 to 1.5 million pieces, while the average value decreased fourfold. At the same time, the number of producers of calculators, rose from 5 to about 20. Casio's main competitor was Sharp. *Kashio 15 nen shi*, 3–4.
9 *Kokusai tokei tsushin* (1986), 345.
10 Ibid.
11 Archives of the Federation of the Swiss Watch Industry (AFHS), Biel, *Essay on the Seiko Group* (Biel: FH, 1980), 112.
12 Ibid., 107.
13 Ibid., 106.
14 Ibid., 115.
15 According to *Nihon tokei nenkan* (Tokyo: Sogocho, 1998 and 2000), 23.5% in 1998 and 24.2% in 2000.
16 *Tokei no honkon shijo chosa hokokusho*, 5.
17 *Hong Kong's Manufacturing Industries*.
18 Trueb, *The World of Watches*, 364.
19 *Tokei no honkon shijo chosa hokokusho*.
20 Ibid., 29.
21 *Seiko tokei no sengoshi*, 247.
22 *L'Impartial*, 2 February 2000.
23 *Statistique annuelle du commerce extérieur de la Suisse*, 1974–1983.
24 Convention patronale, *Recensement 2007*, 13.
25 Christoph Zürcher, 'Bulova Watch Company', in *Dictionnaire historique de la Suisse*, https://www.dhs.ch (accessed 15 February 2022).
26 Pasquier, *La 'recherche et développement' en horlogerie*.
27 Piguet, *La drôle de montre de Monsieur Roskopf*.
28 http://www.ronda.ch/fr/company/history/ (accessed 25 January 2012).
29 SSIH, Annual reports 1973–1980.
30 Richon, *Omega Saga*, 58–61.
31 JETRO Library, Osaka, Documentation on the Swiss watch industry.
32 ASUAG, annual reports, 1970–1979.
33 Estelle Fallet, *Tissot: 150 ans d'histoire* (Le Locle: Tissot, 2003), 185.
34 Hélène Pasquier, 'Swatch Group', in *Dictionnaire historique de la Suisse,* https://www.dhs.ch (accessed 25 June 2009).
35 Estelle Fallet, 'Nicolas Hayek', in *Dictionnaire historique de la Suisse*, https://www.dhs.ch (accessed 25 June 2009).
36 Pierre-Yves Donzé, *Histoire du Swatch Group* (Neuchâtel: Alphil 2012).
37 'Timex', in *International Directory of Company Histories*.
38 On the concept of technical choice applied to watchmaking, see Pasquier, *La 'recherche et développement' en horlogerie*.
39 'Bulova', in *International Directory of Company Histories* (Detroit: St James Press, 1996), 120–123.
40 *Moody's Industrial Manual*, 1977 and 1986.
41 Sauers, *Time for America*.
42 *Europa Star*, vol. 81 (1973): 238.
43 Osamu Shimizu, *Tokei* (Tokyo: Nihon Keizai Shimbun, 1991), 72.
44 Léon Vinzier, 'L'expérience de Lip', *Esprit*, vol. 439, no. 10 (1974): 470–480.

45 Archives Nationales, Paris, 19870344/23, Paul George, *Les industries horlogères et connexes et le Cetehor* (n.d.).
46 Ibid.
47 *Seiko tokei no sengoshi*, 298.
48 Hattori & Co. divested the Matra group in 2004.
49 Archives Nationales, Paris, 19910207/7, Hong Kong quota.

7

Reorganisation of global value chains after 1985

The ranking of the world's largest watchmaking firms, published regularly by the Zurich bank Vontobel since the beginning of the twenty-first century, includes companies whose presence may come as a surprise (see table 8.4, p. 172). In 2017, for example, a Greek company, Folli Follie, which specialised in the manufacture and distribution of entry-level jewellery watches, was ranked fifteenth in the world. Its turnover was then valued higher than that of Franck Muller or Richard Mille. How was a company headquartered in Athens and listed on the Greek stock exchange able to compete with prestigious Swiss watch brands? Obviously, it did not produce its watches at the foot of the Acropolis, but rather obtained its supplies from producers established in Asia. The transformations of the world watch industry since the second half of the 1980s have led to the emergence of new types of companies, embodied by the example of Folli Follie.

The quartz revolution changed the conditions of global competition. The ability to produce precise watches was no longer essential. The competitiveness of firms was rather based on the ability to sell watches. Marketing now prevailed over technology. But this did not mean that the productive stakes disappeared. The control of manufacturing costs remained essential because of the growing competition on a global scale. This factor has led to the concentration of world watch production in China since the 1990s. Chinese production rose from around 470 million watches in 1985 to more than 870 million in 1992, then to around 1.4 billion in the mid-2000s.[1]

Moreover, this transformation of the world watch industry took place in a new institutional context, characterised by increasing liberalisation, so that states appeared to be less and less important players. China's conversion to capitalism, the collapse of the Soviet Union, as well as the liberal turn of the European Union and Japan led to the emergence of a world in which the circulation of goods and capital was greatly facilitated. With a few exceptions, such as India, the nation no longer represented an adequate scale of analysis to consider the watch industry. It entered a second phase of globalisation.

This double dimension of global competition, commercial and industrial, in the context of a largely liberalised world market, led companies to adopt new organisational forms. Two major models emerged during the 1980s and continue to dominate the watch industry today: the large multinational enterprise and global value chains.

The large multinational enterprise has integrated and organised production and distribution on a global scale. It is a continuation of the model of the watchmaking multinationals of the first phase of globalisation, which based their international expansion on the relocation of low value-added productive activities to low-wage countries. However, since the 1980s, large globalised companies have also been investing in the extension of their distribution network in other countries. This model is essentially embodied by Swatch Group and Japanese watchmakers. Luxury industry conglomerates that have invested in Swiss watch companies, particularly LVMH, represent a new type of multinational watch company.

The real organisational innovation, however, is that of global value chains.[2] This concept, developed by management scholars in the 1990s, describes production and distribution networks that comprise a set of independent enterprises, established in distinct geographical locations and involved at particular stages in the design, manufacture, and sale of goods. Firms engaged in value chains are not mere subcontractors serving a client but companies specialising in particular activities for which they have competitive advantage. The challenge is no longer to control directly the entire production and sale of a product, but to coordinate a value chain for its benefit. The best-known example is undoubtedly that of the iPhone – designed in the United States and assembled in China by a Taiwanese company, it includes a broad range of components developed independently by electronics and materials companies based mainly in Japan, South Korea, North America, and Europe.[3] In the watch industry, this model is embodied by fashion watch companies such as the American group Fossil.

The new phase of globalisation experienced by the world watch industry makes it difficult to assess the worldwide production of watches after the mid-1980s. The circulation and re-exportation of watches throughout the world, as the example of Hong Kong illustrates below, no longer allows an estimate of the production of the main watchmaking nations. Such a figure anyway loses its meaning, as companies are largely globalised.

However, the trend in the value of exports by the main watchmaking countries highlights a number of characteristics of the world watch industry from the 1980s (see figure 7.1). Switzerland's historical domination was called into question between 1980 and 1985, when Japan and Hong Kong outstripped Switzerland in exports.

It should be noted, however, that Hong Kong's exports included complete Swiss watches which were re-exported to other Asian countries from the then British colony. These figures therefore do not accurately reflect the growth of the watch industry in this city. Furthermore, a quick reading of the comparative evolution of Swiss, Japanese, and Hong Kong watch exports between 1985 and 2010 gives the impression of a formidable growth of Swiss watchmaking, a significant expansion of Hong Kong watchmaking, and a slow but certain decline

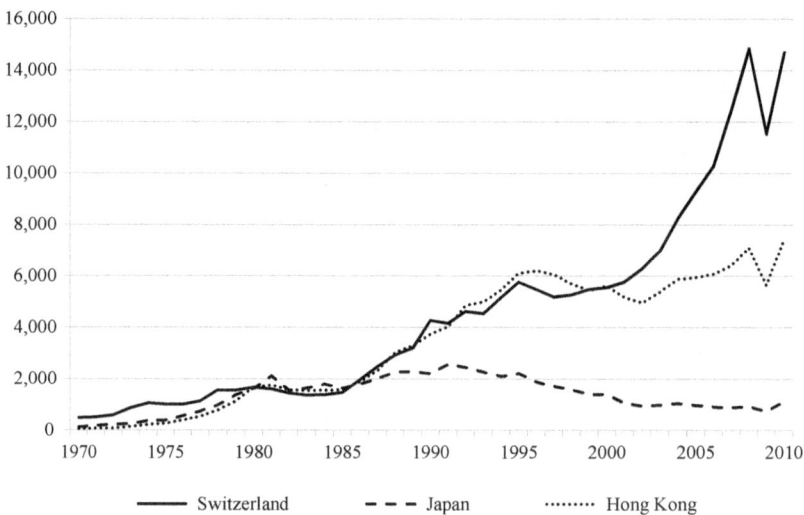

Figure 7.1 Value of watch exports by Switzerland, Japan, and Hong Kong, in millions of current US dollars, 1970–2010.

Sources: *Statistique annuelle du commerce extérieur de la Suisse* (Berne: Administration Fédérale des Douanes, 1970–2010); *Nihon gaikoku bokei nenpyo* (Tokyo: Ministry of Finance, 1970–2010); *Hong Kong Trade Statistics Export and Re-export* (Hong Kong: Census Department, 1970–2010). Currencies have been converted to US dollars on the basis of Lawrence H. Officer, 'Exchange rates between the United States dollar and forty-one currencies' (MeasuringWorth, 2019, https://www.measuringworth.com/datasets/exchangeglobal, accessed 15 February 2022).

of Japan. However, these national data give a very poor account of the state of global competition in the watch industry since the 1990s, precisely because of the globalisation of production systems. In the case of Switzerland, 'Swiss Made' legislation limited the scope for relocation. Swiss watchmakers export their watches from Switzerland, so the value of exports gives a fairly accurate reflection of the state of the industry in this country. The situation is different in the Far East. As Japanese watch companies relocated their production to Asia, particularly China, exports from Japan stagnated and then declined. This did not, however, reflect a decline in Japanese watch companies. As for Hong Kong, its exports experienced a sharp increase, even though watch production gradually disappeared from this city during the 1990s, to be transferred to China. It is essentially the re-export, worldwide, of watches manufactured in China by Chinese, Hong Kong, Japanese, and American companies, as well as Swiss watches, that explains Hong Kong's growing importance. Comparative foreign trade statistics now only very imperfectly express the real weight of industries rooted in national territories – although this is still the case for Switzerland. They reflect product flows generated by multinational companies and the global value chains on the basis of which the global watch industry is now largely organised. This transformation is the subject of this chapter.

The comeback of the Swiss watch industry

The development of the Swiss watch industry since the end of the 1980s has given rise to numerous academic works. Recent research in business history, anthropology, and economics has highlighted the profound transformation of the industrial organisation of the Swiss watch industry and its repositioning in the luxury market.[4] From the perspective of a global history of the watch industry, approached over a long period, three major elements must be examined: industrial reorganisation, the role of the Swatch, and repositioning on the luxury market.

The reorganisation of the industry

Controlling production costs was the major challenge faced by Swiss watch companies in the mid-1980s. To regain their competitiveness against Japanese watchmakers, they had to reorganise their production system. The rationalisation of Swiss watchmaking was characterised by a concentration of companies, the increased relocation of certain low value-added activities to Asia, and the standardisation of movement models. This could be observed both at the macroeconomic level and at the company level.

At the macroeconomic level, the census of the Convention patronale showed perfectly well that the return to growth after 1985 was not based on an increase in the number of firms but on an increase in the average number of employees per firm (see figure 7.2).

After the period 1970–1985, which saw a drastic reduction in the number of firms and employees, there was great stability in terms of companies: on average 585 for the whole period 1985–2013. As for the number of employees, it grew slowly over a period of 15 years, from 32,904 in 1985 to 37,334 in 2000, and accelerated sharply at the beginning of the twenty-first century. In 2013, it exceeded the 57,000 mark for the first time since 1975. However, the record figure of 1970 has never been reached again. This statistic therefore demonstrates that the renewed competitiveness of the Swiss watch industry was based on companies that were, on average, increasingly larger. The average number of employees per firm rose from 52 in 1985 to 65 in 2000 and 100 in 2013.

The need to control production costs also led to the transfer of the production of low value-added components to Asia. As seen in chapter 5, a first relocation movement, notably to Hong Kong, happened in the 1960s. It took on much greater proportions after the 1980s, leading to a genuine globalisation of the Swiss watch-production system. It mainly concerned watch covers, which are not affected by the Federal Ordinance on 'Swiss Made'. Figure 7.3 clearly shows that the proportion of Swiss watches fitted with foreign cases rose from less than 20% at the beginning of the 1990s to over 50% in 2000–2004 and to over 70% from 2005[5] onwards. Apart from Italy (16.8% of total case imports in 2010), where Swatch Group has a subsidiary active in the production of gold watch cases, the

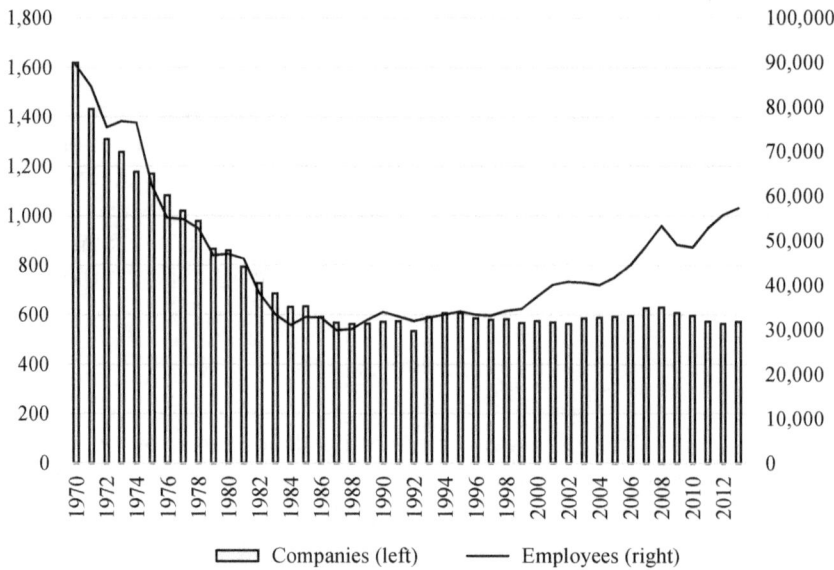

Figure 7.2 Number of companies and employees in the Swiss watch industry, 1970–2013.

Source: Convention patronale, *Recensement* 2007, 13 and *Recensement* 2018, 9.
Note: As of 2014, this statistic counts branches as full-fledged companies, which no longer allows a comparison with previous years.

main suppliers are in Asia, particularly China (40.8% of imports in 2010), Hong Kong (13.7%), and Thailand (7.6%).[6]

Bands and dials present a similar evolution. As the watchbands industry has almost disappeared from Switzerland following the liberalisation of the 1960s, there is a high degree of dependence on the outside world, including for metal bracelets. Between 2000 and 2010, Switzerland imported a total of 292 million bands, while the export volume of complete watches amounted to only 282 million pieces in the same period. For dials, only the weight is known, which makes the analysis of the development of Swiss dependence more approximate. Nevertheless, it should be noted that the average import of dials increased from 65.8 tonnes in 1996–2000 to 113.1 tonnes in 2010–2014. If we consider an average unit weight of 5 grams, this means that more than 20 million dials were imported each year from 2010 to 2014. Finally, the trade in watch-movement parts, precisely the target of 'Swiss Made', shows a development characterised by the growing importance of imports, mainly from Thailand. Whereas Switzerland was largely an exporting nation for movement parts in the mid-1990s, in 2006 it became an importing nation, and this trade deficit – or dependence on foreign countries – only grew until 2014, before declining somewhat.

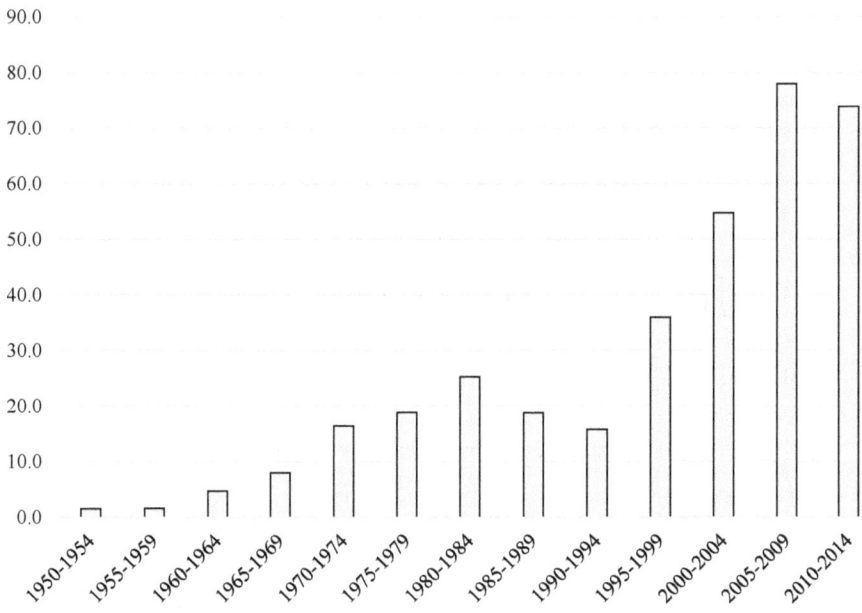

Figure 7.3 Proportion (%) of Swiss watches fitted with foreign cases, five-year average, 1950–2014.

Source: Author's estimates based on Swiss foreign trade statistics (Global Trade Atlas, https://www.gtis.com).

Note: Foreign cases are cases that have undergone at least one production operation abroad.

Rationalisation can also be observed at company level. The Swatch Group (SMH, until 1998), Switzerland's largest watch company, provides an excellent example of this. This company was founded in 1983 precisely with the aim of rationalising its production system, distribution, and brand portfolio. Its charismatic leader, Nicolas G. Hayek, had moreover long experience of reorganising companies and industrial sectors in difficulty when he entered the watch industry at over 50 years of age.[7] The 1980s were marked by an in-depth reorganisation of the company's production system, which had two main features. First, the development and manufacture of movements were centralised within the subsidiary ETA, which delivered the group's various brands. Consequently, the production of calibres at Omega and Longines was discontinued in 1985 and 1988, respectively. Second, ETA successively opened production subsidiaries in Thailand (1986), Malaysia (1991), and China (1996), helping to make the Swatch Group one of the world's largest producers of watch movements. In 2004, its production capacity amounted to around 130 million movements, of which around 100 million were produced in Asia.[8] This globalisation of the production system was reflected in a reduction in the proportion of employees in Switzerland. While the Swatch Group's workforce based in this country amounted to 80%

──── INTERVIEW ────

Nicolas Hayek: "We want to serve everyone in China with our products"

Nicolas Hayek, head of SMH, talks about the group's role in the development of China.

Exclusive Europa Star interview by Pascal Brandt

The progressive and promising opening of the Chinese market arouses the sharp interest of many investors and others involved in the Western economic and industrial world. The Swiss Company of Microelectronics and Horology (SMH), one of the three world giants of the watch and clock world with an annual output of 110 million units (including finished watches, movements, kits), is focusing its attention upon this market for all kinds of reasons including the fact that Hong Kong, that impressive and inevitable horological centre, will be reintegrating continental China in 1997. These factors have brought the SMH to start negotiations with the Shenzhen authorities in order to build there a first plant for the production and assembly of watch components. In the long run, the Swiss group's plant will also produce finished watches destined specifically for the Chinese market. There, they will be marketed probably under the Pacific brand. Nicolas Hayek, head of the SMH talks about the role that his group intends to play in the development of China.

Nicolas Hayek

Europa Star: *Why are you developing a product intended specifically for the Chinese market?*

Nicolas Hayek: It's important to make everything quite clear. The SMH is the only watch and clock multinational that is vertically integrated from the raw material until the finished watch. Only Seiko and Citizen in Japan have a comparable integration. We manufacture 95% of our products in Switzerland and we also export 95% of our output. This shows that we are very involved for the Swiss workplace. In our opinion, the brands are highly important. They must remain Swiss and benefit from the Swiss Made. The SMH occupies all the watch market sectors, with world known brands. We are the number 1 of the whole

Figure 7.4 Nicolas G. Hayek, 1994.

of the total in 1983–1985, this proportion fell to 71% in 1990 and 54% in 1998. This internationalisation was then based on Asian factories. The proportion of employees residing in Asia was 21% of the total in 1992 and 33% in 1998. The subsidiary ETA (Thailand) Co. Ltd employed nearly 3,000 people in 1994 – that is, 18% of the company's employees.[9] The Asian production centres were also restructured and concentrated in Thailand around 2005.

Finally, it should be emphasised that the reorganisation of Swatch Group alone embodied the national industrial transformation of Swiss watchmaking due to the weight of this company. Not only was Swatch Group the main employer in this industry (27.9% of Swiss watchmaking employment in 1985, 28.9% in 2000, 27.5% in 2010), but it had a *de facto* monopoly in the production of blanks and certain components of mechanical movements. It was also the leading manufacturer of quartz movements. The sale of timepieces outside the group accounted for more than 30% of turnover at the end of the 1990s.

The role of the Swatch

Developed since the end of the 1970s as a new type of watch to enable Swiss watch companies to compete with Japanese producers, the Swatch was launched on the market in 1983.[10] Conceived as a fashion item, this plastic quartz watch made entirely in Switzerland became increasingly popular around the world in the late 1980s. According to the 'Swatch legend', its success enabled the Swatch Group to invest in the acquisition and restructuring of other watch brands and to revive the entire Swiss watch industry. According to this legend, Hayek's launch of a cheap quartz watch, a product in which traditional watchmakers had not believed because of their conservative spirit, enabled the rescue and subsequent revival of the Swiss watch industry as a whole.

Due to the absence of data related to the various Swatch Group products, it is not possible to measure accurately the real impact of Swatch on the management of the company. However, Swiss foreign trade statistics do provide some valuable clues. They show the volume and value of exports of 'non-metallic watches'. Although this is not only the case for Swatch, these clearly occupy a prominent place, with the value of exports of this type of product showing strong growth after 1983, rising from 13.4 million francs in 1980 to 225.9 million in 1985 and a peak of 798.7 million in 1993, before falling sharply until 2000, and then stagnating at an average of 296.7 million in 2000–2009, the level of the second half of the 1980s (see figure 7.5).

These figures correspond only very imperfectly to the turnover of the Swatch. First of all, they include products of other brands, even if their share is probably very small due to a general trend towards the production of metal watches. Secondly, not all Swatches are included in these figures: watches sold on the Swiss market and Swatches of the metallic type are not included. Nevertheless, in the absence of any other data, it is interesting to relate the value of exports of non-metallic watches to the turnover of the Swatch Group.

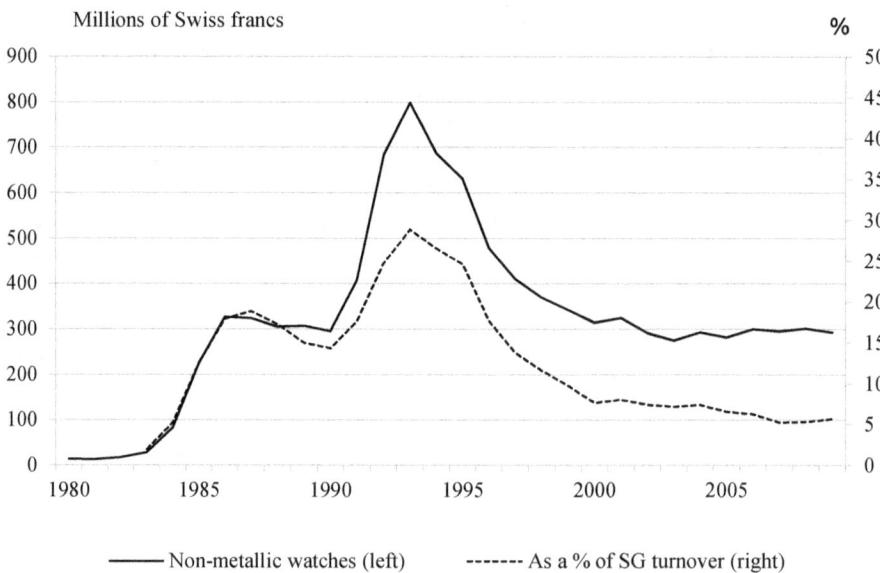

Figure 7.5 Value of Swiss exports of non-metallic watches (millions of francs), 1980–2009.

Sources: *Statistique annuelle du commerce extérieur de la Suisse* (Berne: Département Fédéral des Douanes, 1980–2009); Swatch Group, Annual reports 1983–2009.

This comparison highlights a dynamic within Swatch Group that is similar to the general trend. Despite the stagnation and then slight decline in the second half of the 1980s, exports of non-metallic watches represented an increasing share of Swatch Group turnover, but remained a minority. In the years 1985–1990, they averaged only 16% of turnover, then 22.8% in 1990–1995, peaking at 28.8% in 1993.

However, although figure 7.5 shows a decrease in the second half of the 1990s, it was not a decline of the Swatch. It concerned only non-metallic watches, whereas in 1994 Swatch launched a new collection, Irony, of metallic watches. The latter partly offset the sharp fall in sales of plastic watches, but growth did not continue. According to valuations by certain financial institutions, total sales of Swatch (plastic and metal) amounted to 640 million francs in 2006 (Helvea AG) and 710 million francs in 2010 (Vontobel). Since the mid-1990s, Swatch Group's growth has clearly been based on other brands in its portfolio – the luxury brands.

Although the Swatch undoubtedly had a large profit margin, which provided the company with part of the capital needed for its reorganisation, its importance did not derive solely from its financial impact, but rather from the marketing object it constituted. For the first time, Swatch Group managers demonstrated everything that could be done to promote and sell a watch: the Swatch became

THE SWATCH COLLECTION OF SUMMER 1986

This summer, the new Swatch models have adopted the sparkling colours of leisure fashions. New names such as "Calypso Beach", "Radar", "Rotor", "Vasily" and others dispute during these months of fun on the beach the prestige of a collection designed to please for one season but consisting of watches ready to show accurate time for many years.

After its triumphant debut on the major world markets, the Swatch is as young and dynamic as ever. It comes well ahead of the main body of Swiss or foreign manufacturers who, impressed by its success, have also started out on the perilous race waged by fancy watches against each other.

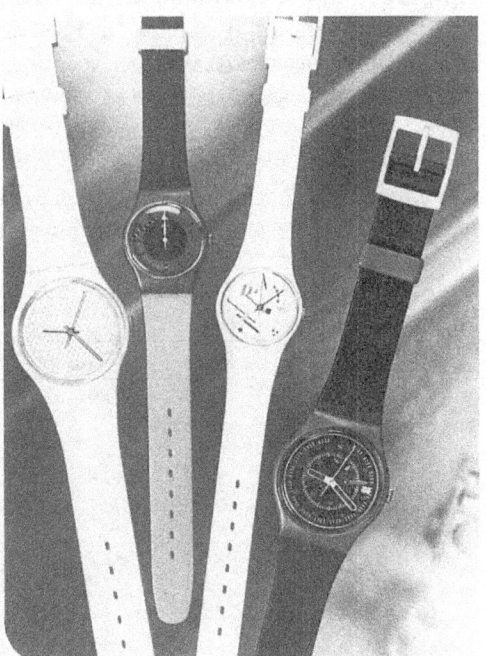

Figure 7.6 The Swatch summer collection, 1986.

the object of storytelling and major world events, and, above all, it was sold as a global brand – that is, a product that did not vary according to markets but was sold worldwide in the same way. Until the 1980s, Swiss watch brands were heterogeneous around the world. Their design, functions, price, communication, and image sometimes varied considerably from one country to another, so that we cannot speak of a 'global brand' for this period. The Swatch thus marks a real breakthrough in this field.

Repositioning in the luxury market

The transformation of Swiss watchmaking into a luxury industry is a phenomenon that had its origins in the early 1980s and took place in the second half of the 1990s. This change is in line with the marketing innovations brought about by the Swatch: the Swiss watch was no longer a utilitarian product aimed at telling the time, but a fashion accessory with a strong symbolic value. As in other sectors of the European luxury goods industry, the tradition of craftsmanship became, during the 1980s and 1990s, the core of the growth strategy of Swiss watch companies.

Foreign trade statistics perfectly express this transition at the macroeconomic level (see table 7.1). The 10 years of post-crisis recovery (1985–1995), marked by the success of the Swatch, saw strong growth in the volume (from 37.4 to 43.7 million pieces) and value (from 3.6 to 6.8 billion francs) of exports. In 1995, the switch to electronic watchmaking became apparent: quartz watches accounted for more than 90% of the volume of exports and 58.5% of their value. However, there was a new change of perspective after the 1990s. On the one hand, the volume of exports fell sharply, to around 30 million pieces after the mid-2000s. On the other hand, the value of exports was growing, reaching 15.3 billion Swiss francs in 2010. This meant that the average value of the watch rose sharply after

Table 7.1 Swiss watch exports, 1980–2010

	1980	1985	1990	1995	2000	2005	2010
Volume (millions of pieces)	47.1	37.4	41.6	43.7	35.9	29.9	31.9
Mechanical (%)	79.3	19.3	9.5	13.0	9.7	14.2	19.2
Quartz (%)	20.7	80.7	90.5	87.0	90.3	85.8	80.8
Value (millions of francs)	2,790.1	3,595.8	5,936.2	6,793.5	9,402.5	11,560.7	15,343.0
Mechanical (%)	68.4	43.4	41.5	47.3	47.5	62.2	71.9
Quartz (%)	31.6	56.6	58.5	52.7	52.5	37.8	28.1
Mean value, mechanical (A)	51.0	216.0	623.5	567.4	1,285.9	1,694.6	1,805.5
Average value, quartz (B)	90.3	67.5	92.2	94.2	152.2	170.6	167.3
A/B	0.6	3.2	6.8	6.0	8.4	9.9	10.8

Source: Federation of the Swiss Watch Industry (personal communication with author).

1995, reflecting its transformation into a luxury product. Moreover, the share of mechanical watches was increasing. In 2010, the latter generated 19.2% of the volume and 71.9% of the value of exports.

The repositioning in the luxury sector of the Swiss watch industry enabled Swiss watch manufacturers to change the competitive conditions on the world market. It was no longer just the control of production costs, and therefore the price of watches, that mattered, but the ability to add value to watches through new marketing strategies. Three main types of firms played an essential role in this process. First, new companies were created during the 1980s to produce high-quality mechanical watches and sell them as products of a long manufacturing tradition. These were usually small companies positioned in a niche market. One of the first and most important was Blancpain, which was re-launched in 1982 by Jean-Claude Biver. It experienced very strong growth and was acquired by the Swatch Group in 1992. Several independent designers also launched their own brands, such as Franck Muller (1991).[11] Second, the former luxury watch manufacturers, such as Audemars Piguet, Patek Philippe, and Vacheron Constantin, experienced great growth. These manufacturers were previously positioned in niche markets that were not very representative of the Swiss watch industry as a whole. Since the 1990s, they have become major players in the Swiss watchmaking renaissance.[12] For example, Patek Philippe increased production from 10,000 watches in 1980 to 65,000 in 2018, while having a tremendous price increase at the same time.[13] Whereas its turnover was only around 70 million francs in 1979, making it outside the top 10 Swiss watchmaking firms,[14] by 2017 it had become the seventh-largest watch company in the world, with an estimated turnover of more than 1.6 billion francs (see table 8.4, p. 172). Third, Rolex presents the case of a special company, which has built its success since the 1960s on a specific production system (mass production of high-precision mechanical watches) and precise and consistent marketing positioning – the brand expressing individual success.[15] It is one of the few Swiss watch companies that does not continue a tradition of craftsmanship and does not communicate its history. Rolex does not publish any financial information and cultivates a policy of absolute discretion with regard to the development of its business. However, this company did not experience any crises during the 1970s and 1980s. It established itself at that time as the world's leading watch brand while its competitors, such as Omega, were struggling to survive.

The success encountered by these luxury watch manufacturers led Swiss and foreign multinationals to buy up a large number of companies from the end of the 1990s, leading to significant industrial consolidation. Swatch Group played a pioneering role, with the takeover of Blancpain in 1992, followed by the application of a luxury strategy to its own brands, notably Omega and Longines. Jean-Claude Biver, the former chief executive officer of Blancpain, played a key role in the adoption of a new marketing strategy based on storytelling at Omega and the brand's move upmarket. Subsequently, Swatch Group successively bought Breguet (1999) and the Jaquet Droz brand (2000). Its main

150 The business of time

Figure 7.7 Advertisement for Omega, 1999.

current rival – Compagnie Financière Richemont, founded in 1988 in the canton of Zug to manage the foreign assets of South African multimillionaire Anton Rupert – has owned the Cartier, Piaget, and Baume & Mercier brands since its creation. It acquired, among others, Vacheron & Constantin (1997), IWC (2000), and Jaeger-LeCoultre (2000). As for the Paris-based luxury conglomerate LVMH, it invested in Swiss watchmaking in 1999 with the purchase of TAG Heuer, Zenith, and Ebel (the latter sold to the American group Movado in 2004), and took over Hublot in 2008.

These three examples of takeovers of Swiss luxury watch companies by large groups in the years 1997–2000 were followed by a multitude of smaller-scale acquisitions. Since 2000, many Swiss watch factories have been bought out by foreign companies, be they American, Chinese, French, or Japanese. For the Japanese, investment in companies established on Swiss territory provides access to a unique resource: the 'Swiss Made' watch – the expression of luxury in the watch industry.

The disappearance of the watch industry in France and its survival in Germany

Apart from in Switzerland, extremely few European watch companies managed to survive the 1980s. Labour costs were too high to maintain production centres in Europe that would produce anything other than luxury watches. The trajectories of the French and German watch industries highlight perfectly the stakes involved in the survival of firms.

In France, the takeover of the Matra group by Seiko in 1988 marked the failure of an industrial strategy based on state intervention and the protection of the EEC. The disappearance of the French watch industry, even though the luxury industry for other sectors flourished in this country, was also the result of the weakness of its companies, which were dependent on foreign technologies and positioned on the domestic market for cheap mass-produced watches. The lack of strong brands, which would have suggested the possibility of a repositioning on the luxury market, also led independent French designers to go to Switzerland to pursue their careers – and to benefit from the added value accorded to Swiss watches.

Richard Mille is undoubtedly the best example of this trajectory.[16] He began his career in a watch company in Besançon and then held a position as sales director in the Matra group for more than 10 years, until 1992. He then joined the Parisian jeweller Mauboussin, where he developed its watchmaking division. When he left this company in 1999, he decided to settle in Switzerland to launch his own brand. The collaboration with Swiss watchmakers, particularly Audemars Piguet, partly explains the location of his company, but the possibility of benefiting from the 'Swiss Made' label is certainly the main reason for his establishment on Swiss territory.

The repositioning in the luxury sector and the integration of the brands into a tradition of excellent craftsmanship also explain the continued production of watches in Germany. Junghans, the large company that traditionally dominated the watch industry in West Germany, experienced a significant decline during the 1980s. Its watch turnover fell from 320 million marks in 1981 to 140 million in 1988.[17] Despite investments in the modernisation of the production system and the introduction of quartz watches, the company was unable to survive in the context of a global market that had become extremely competitive. The company was gradually dismantled during the 1990s and the Junghans brand was sold in 2000 to Egana Goldpfeil, a mid-range fashion goods distribution company founded in Hong Kong in 1978 by a German entrepreneur and specialising in the licensed manufacture of accessories – including watches.[18]

It is essentially in East Germany, in the Glashütte region, that German watchmaking experienced a renaissance after the end of the communist regime. The public conglomerate GUB was bought in 1994 by two German businessmen. They renamed it Glashütter Uhrenbetriebe and launched mechanical watches presented as the heirs of a historical tradition, Glashütte being considered one of the cradles of German watchmaking.[19] The company was acquired by the Swatch Group in 2000. Furthermore, in 1990, a descendant of the Lange family, who owned the company A. Lange & Söhne before its nationalisation and integration into the GUB, recovered and relaunched this brand with the technical support of the Swiss manufacturer IWC, which in return obtained 10% of the capital of the German company. The latter was quickly integrated into Les Manufactures Horlogères (LMH), founded in 1991 when IWC and Jaeger-LeCoultre were bought out by the German financial group Mannesmann. The takeover of LMH by Richemont in 2000 led to the integration of Lange & Söhne into this Swiss-based group. Thus, since 2000, the two leading German watch companies that managed to survive the upheavals of the 1980s and 1990s have belonged to two of the world's leading luxury watch groups.

The relative decline of the Japanese watch industry

While Japan established itself as the world's leading watchmaking nation in the early 1980s, since the 1990s its watch companies have faced the same challenges as their European competitors.[20] The competitiveness of the world market and the continuing decline in production costs required a reaction from Seiko, Citizen, and Casio. However, unlike Swiss watchmakers, who adopted a semi-globalisation of their production system and a move upmarket towards luxury, Japanese manufacturers concentrated on increasing relocation to low-wage countries and pursuing technological innovation for their watches.

For all Japanese watch companies, the production statistics highlight the gradual transfer of manufacturing operations outside the Japanese archipelago (see figure 7.8). The share of production in foreign factories thus rose from 17.8% in 1995 to 24.2% in 2000 and to 45.8% in 2010. Seiko is an excellent illustration of this phenomenon. Since the late 1980s, this group has adopted a strategy of relocating its watch manufacturing activities to Asia, mainly China, in order to lower its production costs. On the one hand, the subsidiary of Seiko Instruments Inc. (SII) in Hong Kong, Precision Engineering Ltd (founded in 1968), has been subcontracting the assembly of electronic watches to a new company created in Guangzhou, Seiko Instruments (Whampoa) Factory, since 1988. A second company was opened in 1996 in Shenzhen (Sai Lai Factory), before all of SII's production on Chinese territory was reorganised at the end of the 2000s and centralised in a new factory in Guangzhou (2012). On the other hand, SII's Japanese headquarters also intervened directly and opened various subsidiaries in Thailand (1988), China (Dailan SII, 1989), Malaysia (1990), and South Korea (2004).

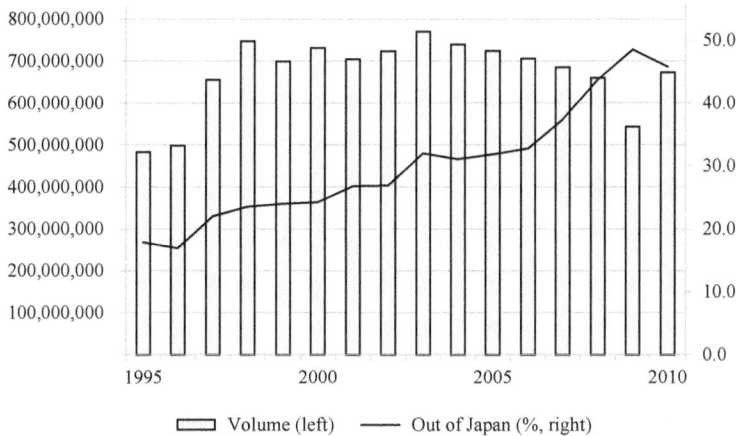

Figure 7.8 Global production of Japanese watch companies and proportion of production outside Japan, number of pieces (watches and movements) and %, 1995–2010.
Source: *Nihon no tokei sangyo tokei* (Tokyo: Nihon tokei kyokai, 1995–2010).

It should also be stressed that this relocation was accompanied by a very strong increase in production volumes: the total volume of watch movements produced by Japanese companies rose from 483 million pieces in 1995 to around 700 million between 1998 and 2010. The strategic objective of Japanese watchmakers was to dominate the world market by offering high-quality and extremely inexpensive movements.

Moreover, Japanese watch companies remained fundamentally high-tech. In line with the development of the quartz watch, they concentrated on the development of technical innovations that would improve the quality of watches in terms of precision and functions. The development of solar watches – that is, quartz watches without batteries – is an excellent example of this. This innovation gave rise to Citizen's Eco-Drive line (1995). The solar watch market was originally a speciality of this company: its watches with Eco-Drive movements sold in 2003 totalled 2.1 million pieces – that is, around one-third of the group's production.[21] However, this innovation is rapidly being incorporated into many models marketed by Citizen's competitors. As for Seiko, it has also embarked on the development of battery-free quartz watches. The technology used is that of quartz watches equipped with automatic rotor-winding systems, which provide the energy needed to generate electricity to power the quartz module. A first model was launched in 1988 with the Kinetic brand. Competition with Citizen led Seiko to develop this watch and to multiply the number of models (more than 90 in 1996),[22] until the launch of a fully hybrid watch, integrating elements of mechanical and quartz movements, called the Spring Drive (1999).[23]

The second new technology adopted by Japanese watch manufacturers was the radio-controlled watch. These are quartz watches equipped with modules

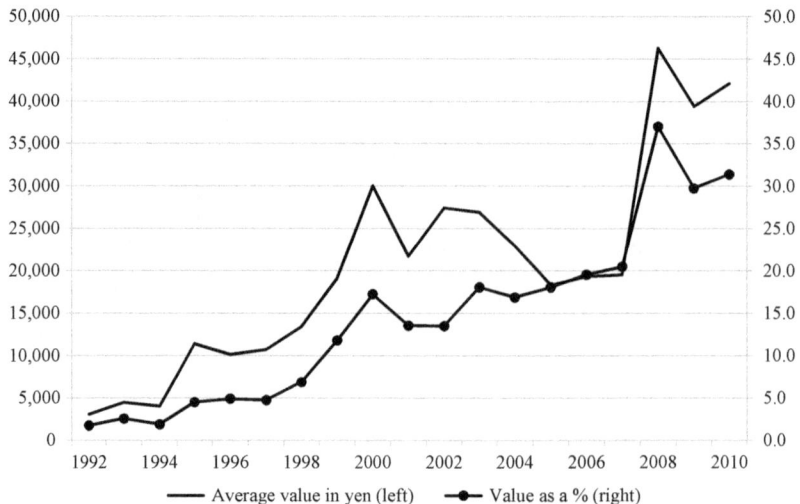

Figure 7.9 Shipments of Japanese mechanical watches in Japan, as % of total value and average value (in current yen), 1992–2010.

Source: *Nihon no tokei sangyo tokei* (Tokyo: Nihon tokei kyokai, 1992–2010).

that automatically receive a signal from atomic clocks, thus ensuring consistently high precision. The use of radio signals in several countries of the world (Japan, China, Germany, United States) allows a very wide use of these watches. Seiko is a promoter of this technology, integrated in 2005 and subsequently adopted by other Japanese manufacturers. In addition, some models combine solar and radio control technologies. In 2011, at the Basel Fair, Citizen presented a new model that was no longer controlled by radio antennas but by GPS satellites (Eco-Drive Satellite Wave), which made it possible to obtain the exact time anywhere in the world.

Beyond this obsessive quest for new products, it is worth highlighting here Seiko's strong comeback in the mechanical watch segment. The aim of this marketing strategy is clearly to move up the range and compete once again with Swiss watchmakers. The general production statistics of the Japanese watch industry, dominated by analogue quartz movements, do not underline an essential change which appeared at the end of the 1990s: the return of Seiko to top-of-the-range mechanical watches. Measured in terms of overall sales (in Japan and abroad), the share of mechanical watches (including movements) fell during the 1990s, from 10.9% of the total volume in 1992 to 4.5% in 2000, with an average of 4.4% in 2000–2010.[24] However, there has been a genuine return of mechanical watches to the Japanese market since 2000. The share of mechanical watches sold domestically by Japanese watch companies increased from 1.7% in 1992 to 17.2% in 2000 and 31.4% in 2010. This reflects the rebirth of quality mechanical watchmaking in Japan. The average value of the mechanical

Figure 7.10 Advertisement for Seiko, 2019.

watch sold in Japan in fact rose from 3,067 yen in 1992 to 30,024 yen in 2000 and 42,107 yen in 2010, while the average value of the mechanical watch sold abroad stagnated (2,197 yen in 1992; 2,698 yen in 2000; 4,135 yen in 2010).[25]

The key role of Hong Kong and China

Hong Kong and China have occupied an essential place in the global watch industry since the mid-1980s. Their functions are complementary but distinct. On the one hand, Hong Kong has developed from a production centre for cheap quartz watches for the world market to a specialised supplier of licensed watches for customers around the world, particularly fashion and accessory brands. Hong Kong entrepreneurs have established themselves as intermediaries between the world market and the Chinese production centres. On the other hand, China has become the main production centre for movements and watches in terms of volume. This boom is the result of investments and the relocation of factories by companies from Hong Kong, Japan, and Switzerland, as well as the development of local companies. However, Chinese manufacturers have only limited access to the world market for their own brands.

The repositioning of Hong Kong as an intermediary in global value chains

Hong Kong's watch industry, which freed itself from its historical dependence in the second half of the 1970s and prospered during the 1980s, entered a new phase in the 1990s with the growing transfer of its productive activities to neighbouring China. The new policy of relaxation of the Chinese authorities regarding foreign investment, adopted in 1992, encouraged many Hong Kong entrepreneurs to transfer their factories to the neighbouring country.[26] This transfer was also facilitated by the return of Hong Kong to China in 1997. While headquarters and marketing and design activities remained in the British colony, production centres were gradually relocated to the Shenzhen and Dongguan areas of Guangdong province. Hong Kong watchmakers also invested in Europe in order to internalise skills relating to the production of movements, such as Chung Nam Watch Co., which acquired the Swiss companies ISA, Technotime, and Roamer Watch (1994),[27] and Wellgain Precision Products Ltd, which bought half the capital of France Ébauches Microtechniques (2000).[28] As a result, domestic watch production in Hong Kong entered a phase of sharp decline: after peaking at 13.5 billion Hong Kong dollars in 1990, it fell to just 7.4 billion Hong Kong dollars in 1993.[29]

The evolution in the composition of Hong Kong's watch exports highlights the new function taken on by this city since the 1990s (see figure 7.11). Until 1985, the increase in exports was based essentially on the production and assembly of finished watches in the city's workshops. The proportion of re-exports (i.e. imported and directly exported watches), which was historically high due to Hong Kong's role as a trade hub in Asia (89.9% of total exports in 1960 and 86% in 1965), fell sharply between 1970 (50.8%) and 1985 (18.9%). However, during the second half of the 1980s, Hong Kong watch companies began to transfer their factories to China, leading to a decrease in direct exports and a sharp increase in re-exports (36.1% in 1990, 75.5% in 1995, and more than 90% since 2000). Moreover, while imported and re-exported watches were mainly Swiss and Japanese until the 1970s, re-exports since 1990 have mainly included watches produced in China, imported into Hong Kong, and shipped worldwide. Hong Kong imports of watches from China jumped from 49.9 million US dollars in 1980 to 885.5 million in 1990, 3.9 billion in 2000 and 7.4 billion US dollars in 2010.[30] These values represent 17.4% of re-exports in 1980 and more than 75% since 2000.

The repositioning of Hong Kong companies in global value chains, between Chinese suppliers and Western companies with which they sign licensing

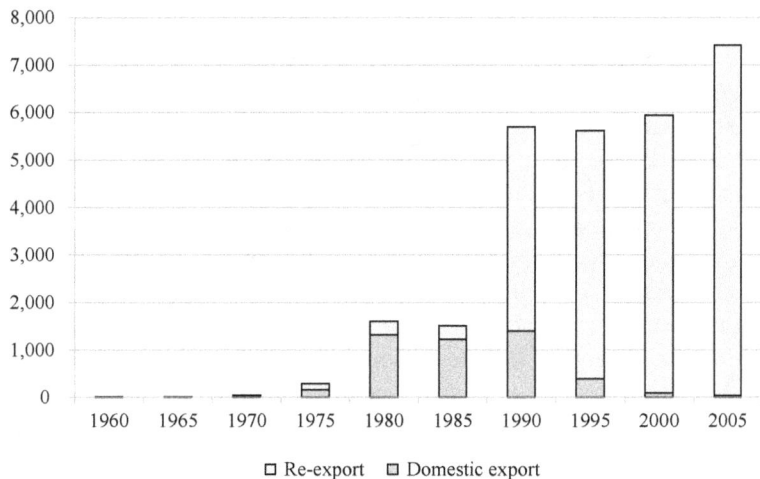

Figure 7.11 Composition of Hong Kong's watch exports (millions of US dollars), 1960–2010.

Source: *Hong Kong Trade Statistics Export and Re-export* (Hong Kong: Census Department, 1960–2005).

agreements, has had a strong impact on competitive conditions in Hong Kong. Some companies have been able to adapt their organisation and relocate their factories to China, following the example of Dailywin (1988), Crystal Electronic (1997), and Gordon C (1997).[31] Others have been unable to restructure and have disappeared, such as Betatronic (1990), Larnol Enterprises (1992), Beltime (1995), and Tinic Watch (2002). Several new entrepreneurs seized the opportunity of this change to enter the watch industry. This is notably the case of Renley Watch Manufacturing, a company founded in 1983 by Stanley Lau, headquartered in Hong Kong (150 employees in 2009) and with production subsidiaries in China (400 employees) and Switzerland (25 employees).[32] Entrepreneurs and firms from abroad have also established themselves in the city, such as the Swiss Jacques Froidevaux, who founded the company Jacques Farel Ltd (1984),[33] and the American group Fossil, which in 1992 bought a Hong Kong company to directly control its watch supply (see p. 160).

Finally, it should be noted that most Hong Kong watch companies have diversified their activities and have been engaged in the distribution as well as the retailing of Swiss and Japanese watches since the late 1980s. They have invested in building their own network of multi-brand boutiques throughout South-East Asia and have become important partners for watchmakers in other countries. It is also in this context that several of these Hong Kong distributors have acquired Swiss watch brands, such as Asia Commercial Holdings Ltd, which took over Juvenia in 1988, and Renley Watch, which acquired Le Phare Jean d'Eve and Sultana in 1991.[34]

China: the world's factory also for watchmaking

The relocation of Hong Kong factories to the Shenzhen region, the opening of production centres by Swiss and Japanese watch multinationals, and the rise of domestic companies made China the world's largest producer of watches by volume at the beginning of the twenty-first century. By 2015, apart from a few tens of millions of pieces produced in Europe and Japan, almost all of the world's production of complete watches (estimated at 1.4 billion pieces)[35] came from Chinese factories. Thirty years earlier, in 1984, China produced only 73 million watches (see table 7.1, p. 148). The main reason for this exceptional growth was the low wages (about 10 times lower than in Hong Kong in 2009),[36] which prompted many companies to invest in the country during the 1990s. Citizen and Swatch Group opened movement factories in China in 1995 and 1996, respectively – although the Swiss multinational divested around 2005 and concentrated its Asian production in Thailand.[37]

However, the main feature of the Chinese watch industry is the rise of dozens of independent private companies in Guangdong province, particularly in the city of Shenzhen. Some of them are the offspring of state-owned companies founded in the 1950s, such as Peacock and Tianjin Seagull, while others have been in existence since the mid-1980s, such as Ebohr, Rossini, and Fiyta. These companies have a very large production capacity and have also been engaged in a move upmarket for certain models since the 2000s.[38]

From the perspective of the global history of the watch industry, it is essentially the concentration of world production in China that remains the most remarkable phenomenon. Between 2000 and 2016, the country exported an average of 690 million complete watches per year, with the value rising from 941 million to 2.6 billion US dollars.[39] However, the position of Chinese companies changed during this period (see table 7.2). In 2000, the Chinese watch industry was still extremely dependent on external clients. More than 78% of its exports of complete watches were destined for the three countries that contained the headquarters of companies that had relocated their watch production to China – namely, Hong Kong, Japan, and the United States. The high volumes

Table 7.2 Main outlets for Chinese exports of complete watches, 2000 and 2015

	2000			2015		
	Volume (millions)	Average price (US dollars)	Market share (%)	Volume (millions)	Average price (US dollars)	Market share (%)
Hong Kong	434.8	0.9	47.2	254.2	6.0	36.5
USA	189.9	1.2	20.6	68.9	5.1	9.9
Japan	102.2	1.5	11.1	23.7	4.9	3.4
India	6.4	0.7	0.7	27.9	1.4	4.0
Total	921.7	1.0	100	696.9	4.2	100

Source: UN Comtrade database, https://comtrade.un.org/data (accessed 15 June 2019), codes 9101 and 9102.

clearly indicated a re-export to the whole world from these three centres. The situation was quite different in 2015, suggesting a growing empowerment of Chinese entrepreneurs. Although Hong Kong retained more than a third of exports, there was a greater dispersion of markets, which meant that Chinese entrepreneurs had better direct access to final markets. Thus, India had become a more important outlet than Japan, even though 15 years earlier this market had been almost negligible. In addition, the average value was much higher, which can probably be explained by the realisation of operations with higher added value directly in China.

A new business model at the heart of global value chains: fashion watch manufacturers

Although most of the world's watch production has gradually been transferred to China since the 1990s, this does not mean that all watches sold in the world are now Chinese-branded products. The fragmentation of the design–production–distribution–sales process between various independent companies established in separate territories – the so-called global value chains – now allows almost any company to have its own watches. The challenge is no longer to be able to produce them but to be able to sell them.

In this context, new entrants to the watchmaking market appeared during the 1980s and 1990s: fashion-brand companies. The fashion industry itself underwent a profound transformation during this period, marked in particular by the development of accessories, to improve its profitability. Like leather goods and cosmetics, watches became fashion accessories. This watch production was developed and distributed by new types of companies that benefit from licences issued by the big names in the world fashion industry. The American group Fossil is the best incarnation of this new business model.[40] Originally founded in Dallas in 1984 by brothers Tom and Kosta Kartsotis under the name Overseas Productions International, the company developed on the basis of a marketing project: the sale in the United States of watches produced in Hong Kong. It launched the Fossil brand two years later, for vintage-design watches embodying the image of 1950s America. Success was immediate, with sales rising from 2 million dollars in 1987 to more than 32 million in 1990. In 1993, the arrival of new investors allowed the company to continue expanding in two directions: diversification into fashion watches and the internalisation of distribution.

First of all, the strengthening of the positioning in fashion was based on a diversification of the Fossil brand towards accessories during the 1990s, before a clothing line was launched in 2000, followed by a shoe collection in 2008. However, watchmaking remained the core business (68.1% of sales in the 2000s and rising to 78% in 2014), thanks to the launch of a significant number of watches produced under licence for the big names in the global fashion business, such as Emporio Armani, DKNY, and Diesel. These initial contracts allowed Fossil to establish itself as a fashion-watch group, and to expand the licensing network with Michael Kors and Marc Jacobs (2004), Adidas (2005), and Karl Lagerfeld (2011). Finally, in 2012, Fossil took over Skagen Designs – itself a small firm founded in 1989 by Danish designers based in the United States and selling watches made in China under the Skagen Denmark brand since 1992.

Moreover, since the end of the 1990s, Fossil has been increasingly controlling the distribution of its products, in parallel with the internationalisation of its sales. In 1998, the first financial year for which there are detailed published data, Fossil was still heavily dependent on the American market (60.8% of turnover). The group then adopted a direct sales strategy through the establishment of a vast network of boutiques, the acquisition of distributors (notably in Taiwan and Sweden in 2005, and in Mexico in 2006), and the development of its website. The first Fossil shop opened in the United States in 1995 and the first abroad 10 years later. The total number of Fossil shops rose sharply, from 30 in 2000 to 245 in 2012. As a result, direct sales in shops and on the Internet represented a growing share of turnover (9% in 1999 and 25% in 2012). This boom in distribution around the world, based on the sale of fashion watches, led to a strong internationalisation of outlets. In 2008, the United States accounted for less than 50% of sales (see figure 7.12).

The strategic choice of selling watches under licence for the big names in fashion adopted during the 1990s enabled Fossil to expand dramatically. The company's total turnover rose from 161 million dollars in 1994 to a peak of more than 3.5 billion dollars 20 years later, which included 2.7 billion dollars in watch sales. Moreover, the growing internationalisation of business limited the impact of the financial crisis of 2008–2009. Although the arrival of Apple Watch in 2015 (see chapter 8) led to strong competition and a decline in business (see figure 7.12), Fossil established itself as one of the largest watchmaking groups in the world.

However, this boom was not only the result of a marketing strategy. The question of production remained essential and the supply of watches was a major issue for the Kartsotis brothers when they decided to embark on the design and sale of fashion watches. In 1992, they acquired a small watch company based in Hong Kong, which they renamed Fossil (East) Ltd. It was responsible for supplying the American headquarters with watches. They also acquired stakes in several companies based in Hong Kong, such as Amazing Time (60%), Pulse Time Center Company (60%), and Trylink International (51%). This presence in Hong Kong was a means of gaining access to watch and watch component producers based in China. Fossil's Chinese subcontractors totalled 38 watch manufacturers in 2000 and 44 in 2014.

In addition, in 2001 the American group founded a company in Switzerland, Swiss Technology Holding. It acquired the Zodiac brand, as well as three watch manufacturers: Montres Antima (watch assembly), Synergies Horlogères (watch design), and Méliga Habillement Horloger (components).[41] These acquisitions enabled Fossil to internalise a production capacity for 'Swiss Made' watches and to offer its clients in the fashion industry luxury collections. For example, in

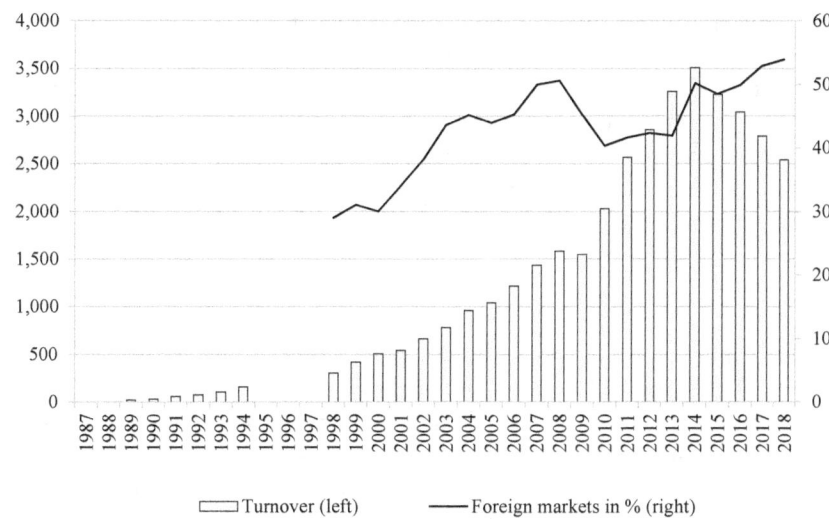

Figure 7.12 Fossil's turnover (millions of dollars) and share of foreign sales (%), 1987–2018.

Source: Fossil financial reports and 'Fossil', in *International Directory of Company Histories*, vol. 17 (Detroit: St James Press, 1997).
Note: No data for 1988 and 1995–1997.

2001 Fossil signed a contract with Burberry for the production of 'Swiss Made' watches. The American group also launched a 'Swiss Made' collection for Giorgio Armani in 2006, while Emporio Armani watches – the Italian designer's entry-level brand – are produced in China.

Fossil thus appears to be an exemplary case of a new type of company that emerged during the 1980s and 1990s thanks to the exploitation of new global value chains in the watch industry. The competitiveness of this firm does not lie in its control of the production apparatus, but in its ability to coordinate various activities (licences with fashion brands, watch design, production, distribution, sales) carried out by a number of legally independent and geographically distant companies. This model has been adopted by other companies, notably the American group Movado, as well as Folli Follie and Morellato & Sector, based in Greece and Italy, respectively.

The diverse fortunes of protectionist models

A watch industry emerged, and prospered, in new nations during the 1960s and 1970s, thanks to state protectionism. This was mainly the case in China, India, and Russia. The advent of quartz also initially strengthened these industries, all of which were highly centralised, because this technology facilitated the mass production of watches. However, the institutional and political changes of the 1980s and 1990s, mainly the end of the Cold War and the liberalisation of the global economy, led to an upheaval in the conditions of competition for these watch industries. While the Chinese experienced tremendous expansion due to the concentration of world watch production in that country and the dynamism of private enterprises (former privatised state-owned enterprises and new Chinese firms, as well as foreign-owned companies), watch manufacturing in Russia and India presented varying fortunes.

The end of the Russian watch industry

The watch industry in Russia collapsed after the end of communism and the break-up of the Soviet Union.[42] Between 1991 and 1999, total production of watches, clocks, and alarm clocks in the Republic of Russia fell from 61.1 million pieces to just 6.3 million. For watches alone, the production volume, which stood at 4.8 million pieces in 2000, fell to only 1.2 million in 2005 and 400,000 in 2008 (see figure 5.8, p. 110). Thus, although Russian and foreign investors have taken over some of the historic brands of the Soviet era, such as Poljot and Raketa, this is essentially a niche market for consumers nostalgic for the Soviet Union. Russian watch companies are no longer players who count on the world watch market. This rapid decline is the consequence of the opening of borders. Russian watchmakers have lost the market of the former communist countries, which was once their preserve and their main outlet. In 2000, Russian watch exports amounted to only 5.8 million US dollars and their leading market was Nigeria (24.1%), ahead of two former Soviet republics, Ukraine (17.2%) and Kazakhstan (13.8%). However, apart from these two countries neighbouring Russia, there is no marked presence of former Communist Bloc countries, especially eastern European countries, which have turned to Swiss and Chinese products. This detachment from the markets of the Cold War era was reinforced after 2000. Thus, in 2012, Russian watch exports, worth 5.9 million US dollars, went mainly to Switzerland (27.1%), Hong Kong (25.4%), and Germany (16.9%).[43] But above all, Russian consumers turned away from domestic products and the domestic market was now largely dominated by imported watches. The volume of imported watches in fact increased from 628,000 pieces in 2000, for a domestic production of 4.8 million watches, to 1.8 million pieces in 2010, while domestic production amounted to only 400,000 watches. The collapse of the domestic watch industry was therefore a direct consequence of its lack of competitiveness – and of the Russian consumer's preference for foreign products.

Thus Russia/the Soviet Union, one of the leading watchmaking nations in terms of production volume, had in less than 20 years become a country with practically no watch manufacturers on its territory. This collapse is the result of an industrial policy based on the development of a state-owned company in a context of political isolation and protectionism of the internal market, which lasted from the 1930s to 1991. This does not mean that protectionism in itself does not allow the emergence of globally competitive enterprises. The case of Japan, up to the 1960s, is precisely an example of an industry that managed to develop thanks to state protection. In that case, however, protectionism was intended to help domestic companies reach a technological and organisational level that made it possible for them to compete with Swiss and American companies. The Soviet authorities adopted a different policy, marked by the choice of isolation and the priority given to production volumes. The lack of marketing and design skills undoubtedly played a major role in the inability of Russian watchmakers to benefit from the opening of the borders after 1991.

Privatisation of watchmaking in India

Compared with Russia, India underwent a more measured transition from a public to a private model, while maintaining a protectionist policy that guaranteed local companies' dominance of the domestic market.[44] The state-owned conglomerate Hindustan Machine Tools (HMT), which started producing watches with the help of Citizen in the 1960s, entered a phase of decline during the 1980s, despite producing quartz watches since 1981. HMT is characterised by a lack of research activities, organisational difficulties, and interest in marketing and design issues, factors similar to those observed in the Soviet Union at the same time. However, the involvement of a private Indian company in the production of watches has allowed this industry to experience a different destiny from that of its Russian competitor.

In 1984, the Tata Group, one of the most powerful private industrial conglomerates in India, decided to invest in watchmaking, with the foundation of the joint venture Titan Industries, in collaboration with Tamil Nadu Industrial Development Corporation (TIDCO).[45] TIDCO hired engineers, technicians, and managers from HMT and set up its own watch production, with a special emphasis on design, advertising, and marketing. The first watches were launched on the market in 1986 and the Titan brand was registered the following year. After 1990, there was a slow decline in HMT's watch division, which, however, liquidated only in 2016, and a strong growth of Titan, which established itself as India's leading watchmaker. Titan also re-launched the Timex brand for the US market between 1992 and 1998, and in 2011 acquired the Swiss brand Favre-Leuba, historically strong in the Indian market. Its annual production rose from a volume of 2 million watches in 1990 to around 6 million in 2000 and 15 million in 2010. In addition, this impressive growth was accompanied by an increase in the supply of Chinese watches from Hong Kong, where an office was opened in 2007.[46] However, Titan's growth after 2000 was no longer based on watchmaking but on jewellery, an activity the Indian company embarked on in 1992 and one that has generated profits since 2000. The share of jewellery in Titan's turnover rose from 22.1% in 2000 to 53.4% in 2005 and 84.1% in 2018.

Titan thus has today a quasi-monopoly on the domestic market, thanks to the protectionism that continues to limit the presence of Swiss and Japanese competitors. On the other hand, it has difficulty in making a place for itself

THE DESIGN DEPARTMENT
It is logical to begin a visit to Titan's plant with the design department, where the team creates one new case every week, from scratch. On the basis of a sketch, the CAD station elaborates and controls the ensemble of the creative and industrial process: from the 3D model of the pieces, the plans and prototypes, to the conception and manufacture of the tools which will be necessary for its production. This system allows for a maximum of creative freedom and also provides a simulation of the industrial production process corresponding to the elaboration of each piece (i.e. the simulation of the electroerosion, the timing etc.). Thus, the design department is directly connected to the Tool Room and the production workshops. The standardisation of 80% of the pieces also adds to the flexibility of the designer's intervention.

THE TOOL ROOM
The Tool Room is a specialised workshop, producing tools, related to the manufacture of cases, bracelets and movements. The visitor is struck by the spacious and well lit workspace. High performance CAM and tool machines guarantee quality, precision and fine finishing of the surfaces, all important elements for the creation of the perfect tool, which will ultimately be at the base of the success of the production process.

Figure 7.13 Titan workshop, 1996: design department (top) and tool room.

on foreign markets – essentially the Middle East – even though Indian watch exports are generally on the rise. Their total value, which amounted to less than 1 million US dollars in 1988, rose from 2.5 million in 1990 to 46.3 million in 2010 and to a peak of 99.4 million US dollars in 2015, before declining slightly (94.3 million in 2018).[47] However, these figures remain very modest compared wotj the world market. In 2018, India was only twenty-seventh among the nations exporting complete watches (by value).

Conclusion

China's opening up and liberalisation policies – commonly referred to as neoliberalism – led to an upheaval in the global organisation of watch production in the 1980s and 1990s. Many industries that had retained a predominantly national character, thanks to state protection or their concentration on the domestic market, disappeared. This is particularly the case in the United States, France, and Russia. Of course, exceptions remain, as in India, but they owe their maintenance to a mixture of protectionism and the adoption of new managerial practices inspired by what can be observed elsewhere in the world (attention paid to design and marketing; use of global value chains). Generally speaking, the globalisation of the world watch industry developed dramatically during this period. This industry is now based on firms and no longer on nations. Multinational companies such as Swatch Group or Seiko, as well as smaller companies embedded in global production and distribution networks (such as Fossil), formed the new basis of the global watch industry at the beginning of the twenty-first century. The control of global value chains enabled these companies to strengthen or develop their competitiveness.

However, this globalisation does not mean that all territories are equal in the global competition. We are not witnessing the end of history as prophesied by Francis Fukuyama,[48] nor the flattening of the world as observed by Thomas L. Friedman,[49] but a re-composition of the conditions of competition. Although the world's leading watch companies have their headquarters in several Western and Asian countries, watch production has been concentrated mainly in two places: China for entry-level and mid-range products, due to extremely low wages; and Switzerland for high-end and luxury watches, due to an institutional innovation that guarantees the presence on Swiss territory of Swiss watch manufacturers ('Swiss Made' legislation), the latter embodying watchmaking luxury for consumers around the world.

Consumer behaviour and the very nature of watches have, moreover, undergone a profound transformation since the 1980s, accompanying the reorganisation of the global watch industry. The multiplication of electronic devices and the rise of mobile phones have made the watch as defined in the mid-nineteenth century obsolete. Accurate time is now within everyone's reach, and the precision of watches is no longer a competitive advantage for companies producing them. The watch has largely been transformed into a fashion accessory, whether it is cheap *fast fashion* produced between Hong Kong and China, or luxury fashion made in Swiss factories.

Notes

1 Estimates by the Federation of the Swiss Watch Industry (1985 and 1992), cited by Chiara Bentivogli, Hans H. Hinterhuber, and Sandro Trento, 'The watch industry: a strategic analysis', *International Review of Strategic Management*, vol. 5 (1994), 133–170;

estimates by the Japan Clock and Watch Association (2015), https://www.jcwa.or.jp/data/estimate.html (accessed 18 June 2019).
2. Jennifer Blair, 'Les cadres d'analyse des chaînes globales', *Revue française de gestion*, vol. 2 (2010): 103–119.
3. Seamus Grimes and Yutao Sun, 'China's evolving role in Apple's global value chain', *Area Development and Policy*, vol. 1, no. 1 (2016): 94–112.
4. Among the most recent works, see Donzé, *Histoire du Swatch Group*; Hugues Jeannerat and Olivier Crevoisier, 'Non-technological innovation and multi-local territorial knowledge dynamics in the Swiss watch industry', *International Journal of Innovation and Regional Development*, vol. 3, no.1 (2011): 26–44; Laurence Marti, *Le renouveau horloger. Contribution à une histoire récente de l'horlogerie suisse (1980–2015)* (Neuchâtel: Alphil, 2016); Hervé Munz, *La transmission en jeu: Apprendre, pratiquer, patrimonialiser l'horlogerie en Suisse* (Neuchâtel: Alphil, 2016).
5. Furthermore, it should be mentioned that these are not imported cases to be re-exported. In 2014, total Swiss exports of watch cases were worth 143.1 million francs, which represented only 20.7% of imports in that year (considering that all exports would in fact be re-exports).
6. UN Comtrade database, https://comtrade.un.org/data/ (accessed 15 June 2019).
7. Donzé, *Histoire du Swatch Group*.
8. Author's estimates based on Swatch Group, Annual report 2004.
9. Donzé, *Histoire du Swatch Group*, 53.
10. Gilles Garel and Elmar Mock, *La fabrique de l'innovation* (Paris: Dunod, 2012); Donzé, *Histoire de Swatch Group*, 39–43; Roland Carrera, *Swatchissimo, 1981–1991: l'extraordinaire aventure Swatch* (Geneva: Antiquorum, 1991); Allen Morrison and Cyril Bouquet, *Swatch and the Global Watch Industry* (Cambridge: Harvard Business School, Case Study, 1999).
11. Munz, *La transmission en jeu*.
12. Donzé, *L'invention du luxe*, 155–181.
13. Donzé, *Histoire de l'industrie horlogère suisse*, 175; *Bilan*, 27 September 2019.
14. *Suisu no kinzoku-sei tokei bando: shijo chousa* (Tokyo: JETRO, 1980).
15. Donzé, *Histoire de l'industrie horlogère suisse*, 174–176.
16. *Le Temps*, 20 January 2011.
17. Schmid, *Lexikon der Deutschen Uhrenindustrie*, 318.
18. Egana Goldpfeil, Annual report 2000.
19. Schmid, *Lexikon der Deutschen Uhrenindustrie*, 186, 190.
20. On the Japanese watch industry since 1990, see Pierre-Yves Donzé and David Borel, 'Technological innovation and brand management: the Japanese watch industry since the 1990s', *Journal of Asia-Pacific Business*, vol. 20, no. 2 (2019): 1–20.
21. Akira Takeishi, Kanayama Tadashi, and Mizuno Tatsuya, *Seiko Epson jidomaki kuotsu uochi no kaihatsu*, Working Paper 2–12 (Tokyo: Hitotsubashi University, 2005), 13.
22. *Nikkei Business*, 18 March 1996.
23. Takeishi et al., *Seiko Epson jidomaki kuotsu uochi no kaihatsu*.
24. *Nihon no tokei sangyo tokei*, 2010.
25. Ibid.
26. Suzanne Berger and Richard K. Lester (eds), *Made by Hong Kong* (Oxford: Oxford University Press, 1997).
27. Trueb, *The World of Watches*, 364.
28. *L'Impartial*, 14 March 2000.
29. *Hong Kong's Manufacturing Industries*.
30. *Hong Kong Trade Statistics Import* (Hong Kong: Census Department, 1980–2010).
31. Trueb, *The World of Watches*, 364–371.

32 *Hong Kong Manufacturing SMEs: Preparing for the Future: Watches and Clocks* (Hong Kong: Federation of Hong Kong Industries, 2010), 8.
33 Trueb, *The World of Watches*, 370.
34 Marti, *Le renouveau horloger*, 61.
35 Japan Clock and Watch Association, https://www.jcwa.or.jp/data/estimate.html (accessed 18 June 2019).
36 *Hong Kong Manufacturing SMEs*, 2.
37 Donzé, *Histoire du Swatch Group*, 54.
38 *Watches: China Sourcing Report* (Hong Kong: Global Sources, 2005).
39 UN Comtrade database.
40 Pierre-Yves Donzé, 'Fashion watches: The emergence of accessory makers as intermediaries in the fashion system', *International Journal of Fashion Studies*, vol. 4, no. 1 (2017): 69–85.
41 *L'Impartial*, 17 December 2001.
42 Donzé, 'Les relations horlogères entre la Suisse et la Russie.'
43 UN Comtrade database, Russian foreign trade statistics.
44 Chattopadhyay and Bhawsar, 'Effects of changing business environment on organization performance.'
45 See 'Our heritage' on the Titan Company website, https://www.titancompany.in/about-us/heritage (accessed 15 July 2019).
46 Titan Industries, Annual reports 1990–2018.
47 UN Comtrade database.
48 Francis Fukuyama, *The End of History and the Last Man* (New York: Free Press, 1992).
49 Thomas L. Friedman, *The World is Flat: Brief History of the Twenty-First Century* (New York: Farrar, Straus and Giroux, 2005).

8

Epilogue: the world watch industry in 2017

To conclude the vast saga analysing the evolution of the watch industry on a global scale to date, this final chapter draws up the current state of this industrial sector. While the previous chapter presented a dynamic perspective, stressing the nature of the changes that took place between the mid-1980s and 2010, this epilogue provides a snapshot that best describes the main characteristics of the global watch industry today.

The analysis focuses on the year 2017, which is the latest year for which complete data for all countries were available at the time of writing. Two main sources are used below: foreign trade statistics compiled by the United Nations (in its Comtrade database), and the ranking of the world's largest watch companies, based on estimates by Vontobel Bank. These sources offer a different and complementary view of the state of the world watch industry.

World watch exports

The figures for foreign trade in watches make it possible to distinguish between exports of complete watches and exports of components. This differentiation highlights the global division of labour.

For exports of complete watches, volume data are unfortunately not available for several countries, including China. Even a rough estimate of the quantities produced according to the main places of final assembly of watches is therefore illusory. Hence, it is necessary for us to confine ourselves to an analysis of complete watch exports in terms of value, which leads to a distorted vision of the industrial reality of world watchmaking due to the very high added value of Swiss watches. Table 8.1 presents the 10 largest watch-exporting countries. In total, world exports of complete watches amounted to 38.5 billion US dollars in 2017. This figure is clearly higher than the value of world production, as it includes the re-export of watches (watches imported and directly re-exported). This table emphasises two elements.

First, Switzerland has extremely strong dominance in the global market. Direct exports account for almost half of world exports. Switzerland is far above its competitors (Hong Kong with 14.7% and the others with less than 10%), especially since the latter are often places of re-export, especially of Swiss

Table 8.1 Top 10 exporters of complete watches in terms of value, 2017

Country	Value (billions of dollars)	% of total
Switzerland	19.1	49.7
Hong Kong	5.7	14.7
China	2.4	6.3
France	2.2	5.7
Germany	1.7	4.5
Singapore	1.3	3.5
United States	1.3	3.3
Britain	1.0	2.6
United Arab Emirates	0.7	1.9
Spain	0.4	1.1

Source: UN Comtrade database, https://comtrade.un.org/data/ (accessed 15 June 2019), codes 9101 and 9102.

watches, which reinforces the country's domination. Hong Kong, Singapore, and the United Arab Emirates are major commercial hubs on a regional scale (South-East Asia and the Middle East). As for the European countries present in this ranking, they no longer have a watch industry on their territory, with the exception of Germany. In total, only three of the 10 largest exporters of complete watches are watch manufacturers.

Second, world watch production is highly concentrated. If we add the figures for Switzerland and China, as well as those for Hong Kong (which re-exports mainly Swiss and Chinese watches), we obtain more than 70% of the world's watch exports. However, this does not mean that most of the world's complete watches are manufactured by Swiss and Chinese companies. Indeed, the absence of one major nation in world watchmaking history should be pointed out: Japan. Direct exports of complete watches from Japan represent only 0.5% of the world total. This is largely the result of the relocation of assembly plants of Japanese companies elsewhere in Asia, mainly to China. These companies then export their finished watches, sometimes via Hong Kong, all over the world, including Japan.

Let us now turn our attention to global exports of watch cases and movement components. In 2017, watch cases represented a trade of nearly 1.4 billion US dollars (see table 8.2). This production was highly concentrated in Asia, where China and Hong Kong accounted for 77.2% of total world exports, followed by Switzerland, France (where subcontractors to the Swiss watch industry are established), and other European and Asian countries of secondary importance. Cases were imported mainly by Switzerland (457.9 million US dollars), ahead of Hong Kong (330.6 million US dollars), and China (221.1 million US dollars). Thus, the top three case exporters were also their top three importers. This was due to a strong division of labour, with several million cases being produced transnationally each year between Switzerland and China (re-exported between the two countries according to the production process).[1]

Table 8.2 Top 10 exporters of watch cases in terms of value, 2017

Country	Value (millions of dollars)	% of total
Hong Kong	649.5	47.1
China	414.8	30.1
Switzerland	126.8	9.2
France	45.7	3.3
Malaysia	37.6	2.7
Singapore	36.9	2.7
Germany	17.0	1.2
Vietnam	10.3	0.8
Japan	9.4	0.7
Armenia	4.7	0.3

Source: UN Comtrade database, https://comtrade.un.org/data/ (accessed 15 June 2019), category 9111.

Exports of movement components (protected by 'Swiss Made' legislation) amounted to almost 2.7 billion US dollars, a much higher figure than that for cases (see table 8.3). Among the main exporters were again Switzerland, Hong Kong, and China (66.8% of the total). They were also the main importers (Switzerland, 365.3 million; Hong Kong, 347.4 million; China, 243.2 million). The trans-nationalisation of the production system observed for cases was also a feature of the production of movement components. The important position of Singapore, which acted as an intermediary between South-East Asian factories (mainly in Thailand and Malaysia) and watch producers based in China and Switzerland, should be highlighted here. As for the other nations, these are mainly producers of watch components, such as France, Malaysia, Japan, and Germany.

In conclusion, the foreign trade statistics for watches in 2017 show the concentration of the production of complete watches, in terms of value, in Switzerland and the globalisation of the production system. It should also be emphasised

Table 8.3 Top 10 exporters of movement components in terms of value, 2017

Country	Value (millions of US dollars)	% of total
Hong Kong	851.0	37.5
Switzerland	388.9	17.1
China	276.5	12.2
Singapore	265.5	11.7
France	130.6	5.8
Malaysia	120.5	5.3
Japan	82.5	3.6
Germany	32.0	1.4
The Netherlands	18.1	0.8
India	14.6	0.6

Source: UN Comtrade database, https://comtrade.un.org/data/ (accessed 15 June 2019), category 9114, including dials.

Epilogue: the world watch industry in 2017   171

Figure 8.1 ETA (Thailand) factory in Bangkok, December 2020.

that there is no distinction between a Swiss watch industry that is rooted in its productive territory, on the one hand, and the rest of the world's watch industry, which is organised on a global and transnational basis, on the other. The Swiss watch industry is part of a globalised production system, as shown by the ranking of the world's largest companies in 2017.

The world's largest watch companies

The ranking of the world's largest watch companies provides additional insight into foreign trade statistics on the state of the global watch industry. Table 8.4 lists the 25 largest companies in terms of watch turnover, according to estimates by Vontobel Bank. It shows five main characteristics.

First, the global watch industry is extremely concentrated. The three largest companies, all Swiss, dominate world watchmaking, accounting for almost half of global turnover (46.5%). The 10 largest companies have a combined share of 73.5%. Watchmaking is therefore a sector based on large companies. This book has highlighted the conditions for their emergence and globalisation after World War II.

Second, Swiss companies are in a prominent position. Eleven of the 25 largest companies are Swiss. In addition, most of the 14 companies headquartered outside Switzerland have production facilities and brands in Switzerland. These are foreign companies that have invested in Switzerland in order to provide 'Swiss Made' products. Among them, the strong presence of luxury goods companies is noteworthy, both conglomerates such as LVMH (which owns Hublot, Tag Heuer,

Table 8.4 The 25 largest watch companies in the world, 2017

Company	Country	Watch sales (millions of Swiss francs)	World market share (%)
Swatch Group	Switzerland	7,000	18.9
Rolex	Switzerland	5,200	14.1
Richemont	Switzerland	4,980	13.5
Fossil	United States	2,166	5.9
LVMH	France	1,971	5.3
Citizen	Japan	1,461	3.9
Patek Philippe	Switzerland	1,350	3.6
Seiko	Japan	1,232	3.3
Audemars Piguet	Switzerland	950	2.6
Casio	Japan	901	2.4
Movado	United States	559	1.5
Chopard	Switzerland	495	1.3
Breitling	Switzerland	430	1.2
Kering	France	400	1.1
Folli Follie	Greece	358	1.0
Citychamp	Hong Kong	325	0.9
Franck Muller	Switzerland	300	0.8
Richard Mille	Switzerland	260	0.7
Festina	Spain	200	0.5
Morellato	Italy	180	0.5
Hermès	France	176	0.5
Fiyta	China	143	0.4
Chanel	France	120	0.3
C. F. Bucherer	Switzerland	110	0.3
Raymond Weil	Switzerland	85	0.2

Source: *Vontobel Luxury Goods Shop* (Zurich: Vontobel Equity Research, 2018), 19.

and Zenith, among others) and Kering (Ulysse Nardin and Girard Perregaux) and independent companies such as Chanel and Hermès.

Third, Japanese watch manufacturers are among the 10 largest companies. Although Japan appears only discreetly in foreign trade statistics, its companies remain major players in the global watch industry. They produce mainly in Japan for the Japanese market and in China for the world market. Citizen, which has become the largest of them, also owns several companies in Switzerland (notably Frédérique Constant).

Fourth, this ranking includes several companies headquartered in non-watch-producing countries. Apart from the case of the French luxury goods companies mentioned above, these are firms that take advantage of the exploitation of new global value chains, such as Fossil (United States), Movado (United States), and Folli Follie (Greece). They source watches from foreign, mainly Chinese, suppliers and distribute them throughout the world.

Fifth, and finally, the very weak presence of Hong Kong and Chinese companies is remarkable, even though this region has seen the concentration of world watch production over the last 20 years or so. There are only two

Figure 8.2 Advertisement for Rolex, 2021.

companies – one of which, Citychamp, also owns Swiss brands (Corum, Eterna, and Ernest Borel) – that enable the region to appear in this ranking. This demonstrates the dependence of the Chinese watch industry on external firms for which it is a subcontractor.

The shock of Apple Watch

Finally, in the context of this analysis of the current world watch industry, a few words must be said about connected watches, particularly the Apple Watch, even if it is not possible today to assess accurately the impact of this new product. Still

Figure 8.3 Apple Watch.

discreet in 2010, connected watches (*smart wearable* or *smartwatches*) reached a market estimated at around 45 million pieces in 2018 and more than 60 million in 2019. The market is largely dominated by the Apple Watch, launched in 2015. Its production volumes rose from 13.6 million in 2015 (65% of all connected watches) to 22.5 million in 2018 (50%).[2]

In terms of volume, connected watches still have a relatively small impact on the global watch industry, with an estimated 1.4 billion pieces produced annually. However, the Apple Watch in particular has a direct influence on a specific market segment in which several of the world's largest watch companies are positioned: the mid-range segment. It is undoubtedly the competition from this new product that explains the decline of Fossil, particularly on the American market, since 2015 (see figure 7.12, p. 161). Furthermore, although it is not possible to measure exactly the impact of the Apple Watch on the Swiss watch industry as a whole, it must be noted that the start of the current period of decline in exports of watches worth 200–500 francs corresponds exactly to the launch of this connected watch, whose selling price is very similar. Clearly, this new product is having a negative impact on a very specific category of Swiss watches. On the other hand, it is not possible to observe any direct influence on the decline of watches worth less than 200 francs, which is part of a long-term trend. The impact of the Apple Watch on Swiss watchmaking should therefore not be overestimated, although it is real.

The world's leading watch companies are not standing idly by in the face of this threat. TAG Heuer, for example, in cooperation with Google and Intel, launched its own connected watch in 2017, allowing the other brands of the

LVMH group to do the same in the following years, while Citizen has internalised the skills relating to this new technology with the takeover of Frédérique Constant in 2016.[3] While it is too early to evaluate, even roughly, the real impact of Apple Watch on the evolution of the global watch industry, it is clearly a new competing product and a new technology that the old watch companies cannot ignore.

Notes

1 Marti, *Le renouveau horloger*.
2 *Vontobel Luxury Goods Shop* (Zurich: Vontobel, 2018); Business report by Strategy Analytics, https://news.strategyanalytics.com/press-release/devices/strategy-analytics-apple-watch-captures-half-18-million-global-smartwatch (accessed 29 August 2019).
3 *Le Temps*, 26 May 2016 and 14 March 2017.

Conclusion

The broad analysis of the historical development of the world watch industry from the mid-nineteenth century to the present day, carried out in this work, has been intended to highlight the general dynamics of this industry. The changes in competitive conditions and the transformation of the industrial organisation of the watch industry are mainly the result of the evolution of technological and institutional factors. They determine to a large extent the presence, in some countries, of large companies which dominate the industry. Four main phases can be highlighted.

First, from the beginning of the nineteenth century until around 1914, we can observe the birth and growth of a watch industry in several European countries and in the United States. In most cases, watch manufacturers concentrated on their domestic market, because either the latter was the largest in the world (the United States), or they sought – and largely obtained – protectionist support from the state (France), or companies were still too small to target the global market (Germany). The most remarkable development has been in American manufacturing. Watch companies took the model of the large vertically integrated company mainly because of the high cost of labour and the availability of capital. Capitalists invested in production technology and set up industrialised production. Industrialisation made it possible to lower the production costs of movements and to prevail over imported watches on the American market.

The two exceptions to this model of domestic market-centred development are Britain and Switzerland, although they followed fundamentally different trajectories. In the first case, British watchmakers had a weak position. Although they dominated the world market in the eighteenth century, they did not adopt new production techniques and faced the mass arrival of cheap foreign – mainly Swiss – products. The free trade paradigm of its economic policy did not allow Britain to benefit from the protectionist support of the state and British manufacturers disappeared at the beginning of the twentieth century. As for the Swiss watch industry, it perfectly embodies the model of small open economies developed by Peter Katzenstein.[1] The small size of the Swiss domestic market made it necessary to engage in foreign markets – and thus to adapt to the needs of a varied clientele – and to make companies highly competitive. Watchmaking in Switzerland was based both on a few large manufacturers who adopted a production mode inspired by the American mass-production system (mainly IWC, Longines, Omega, Tavannes Watch, and Zenith), and on cooperation between a few large industrial companies positioned upstream of the production process (manufacturers of blanks and certain components such as springs) and a multitude of assemblers of finished watches who ensured the flexibility of the offer. However, Swiss watchmakers concentrated on the export of watches. There was no direct investment abroad nor birth of multinational companies, in contrast to the other major Swiss industries of the same period (food, chemicals, machinery, textiles). This is one of the major specificities of the watch industry.

Second, the interwar period was a phase of consolidation of the competition between companies strongly rooted in national territories. Rising demand and the ability to mass-produce cheap products encouraged the rise of large companies, mainly in Germany and the United States, and the birth of a watch industry in Japan. The switch to wristwatches and the design of simple and inexpensive products for the working classes, such as Roskopf watches, led industrialists to invest in the mechanised manufacture of standardised goods – with quality and fancy watches being left to Swiss watchmakers and a few specialised factories, such as the one in Glashütte, Germany. In addition, these large companies benefited from customs protectionism, which boomed during this phase of de-globalisation, and sometimes set up cartels, as in Germany. This allowed them to grow in protected markets. Furthermore, as in other sectors of the manufacturing industry, Swiss watchmakers sought to overcome customs barriers by exporting watches as individual parts and assembling them on site (knockdown production). However, the negative effects of knockdown production on the Swiss economy, in terms of jobs (transferred elsewhere in the world) and the competitiveness of firms (assembly workshops giving rise to competing companies abroad), led the watchmaking and political elites to organise a cartel in the first part of the 1920s, supported by the state since the early 1930s. This intervention reinforced the concentration of the production of watch blanks and components within ASUAG (and its subsidiary Ebauches SA). It also put an end to the knockdown production and redeployment of Swiss watch companies on a global scale, so that before World War II, the world watch industry remained anchored in national territories for institutional reasons. This is also a specific feature of the watch industry, as most other sectors of activity saw multinational companies expand further during this period of protectionism.

Third, the 1950s and 1960s represented the period of first globalisation in the world watch industry. The factors in this change are both technological and institutional in nature. Indeed, the implementation of a system of mass production of standardised products in the world's major watch companies facilitated the relocation of assembly units around the world, as well as the subcontracting of the manufacture of simple technology components, such as watch cases, to countries with cheap labour (Hong Kong). Moreover, political change, with the increasing liberalisation of trade and investment, no longer allowed American, European, and Japanese watch companies to depend solely on their domestic market. They faced growing competition. The case of France, where a few large foreign companies have dominated national production since the 1960s, illustrates the failure of the protectionist model in this context. As for the Swiss authorities, they abolished the Watchmaking Statute and allowed Swiss companies to organise themselves freely from then on. The legislation on 'Swiss Made', adopted in 1971, however, put a limit on their internationalisation. It is therefore in this new institutional context that multinational companies dominating the watch industry began to emerge. A subcontracting industry has emerged in Hong Kong, but in a relationship of technological dependence on American, Japanese, and Swiss clients. Finally, the persistence of the protectionist model in the Soviet Union and in India, two countries that were experiencing strong growth in their watch industry, based on public companies that were developing on the fringes of the world market, should be emphasised.

Fourth, a period of second globalisation, which continues today, began in the 1980s. It was the consequence of a reorganisation of the structures of the world watch industry following a major technological innovation (the electronic watch) and the strengthening of trade liberalisation (China's conversion to capitalism). This transformation was based on an explosion in demand for watches, with world production rising from around 180 million pieces in 1970 to 600 million in 1984 and around 1.4 billion today. Two new organisational forms emerged: integrated multinational companies (Swatch Group, the major luxury conglomerates, and Japanese watchmakers) and global value chains (factories in China; coordination centres in Hong Kong; brand owners around the world). Mass production of watches is no longer the main source of competitiveness for watch companies. It is increasingly based on their ability to adopt marketing strategies on a global scale and to control their distribution system – with a strong trend after 2000 towards the verticalisation of sales networks. Moreover, despite the free movement of goods and capital, two countries are emerging as major production centres: Switzerland for luxury watches (thanks to the 'Swiss Made' legislation) and China for cheap watches (thanks to its low wages).

The persistence of productive activities in a country with high production costs at the beginning of the twenty-first century is not in itself original. It can be explained by the high added value of the activities carried out in Switzerland, as can be observed in other sectors featuring either luxury goods (French leather goods, Italian fashion, etc.) or high technology (aerospace, chemicals, pharmaceuticals, information technology, etc.). The specificity of the world watch industry, compared with other manufacturing industries, lies rather in the late nature of the globalisation process, due to the specific characteristics of the product (until the 1950s, watches were a high value-added and easily transportable product) and the existence of institutional factors (the Swiss watchmaking cartel and 'Swiss Made' law) which prevented the dominant companies from expanding on a global scale. This last characteristic became a major comparative advantage in the 1990s when the Swiss watch industry repositioned itself on the luxury market.

Figure C.4 Advertisement for Audemars Piguet, 2015.

The digital transition, which has been accelerating since 2010 with the launch of connected watches and the development of Internet distribution, is undoubtedly the next major step in the evolution of the global watch industry. The last decade has seen both the emergence of small independent brands that have grown rapidly thanks to social networks (Daniel Wellington) and the entry into the watch industry of the world's largest company (Apple). The big changes are yet to come, and the future is, as always, uncertain. However, it seems unlikely that the current hierarchy of the world's major watchmaking groups will remain unchanged in the medium term.

Note

1 Peter J. Katzenstein, *Small States in World Markets: Industrial Policy in Europe* (Ithaca: Cornell University Press, 1985).

Appendix. Estimates of world watch production

The figures for world watch production from 1790 to the present day presented in the various tables in this book are rough estimates which should be regarded as orders of magnitude that highlight the major trends in the development of the world watch industry over the long term. The absence of official data for most countries makes it impossible to arrive at precise figures. The following sources have been used to produce the estimates.

For the pre-statistical era (1790 and 1870), the estimates are extrapolations based on the following sources.

Switzerland

- Antony Babel, *Histoire corporative de l'horlogerie, de l'orfèvrerie, et des industries annexes* (Geneva: A. Jullien, 1916).
- Christophe Koller, *'De la lime à la machine'. L'industrialisation et l'État au pays de l'horlogerie: Contribution à l'histoire économique et sociale d'une région Suisse* (Courrendlin: CSE, 2003).
- Frédéric Scheurer, *Les crises de l'industrie horlogère dans le canton de Neuchâtel* (La Neuveville: Éd. Beerstecher, 1914), 135–142.

Britain

- Roy A. Church, 'Nineteenth-century clock technology in Britain, the United States, and Switzerland', *Economic History Review*, vol. 28, no. 4 (1975): 625.
- Amy K. Glasmeier, *Manufacturing Time: Global Competition in the Watch Industry, 1795–2000* (New York: Guilford Press, 2000).

France

- Marie-Agnès Dequidt, *Horlogers des lumières: temps et société à Paris au XVIIIe siècle* (Paris: CTHS, 2014).
- Jean-Luc Mayaud and Joelle Maüerhan. *Besançon horloger, 1793–1914* (Besançon: Musée du Temps, 1994), 64.

United States

- Michael C. Harrold, *American Watchmaking: A Technical History of the American Watch Industry, 1850–1930* (Columbia:NAWCC, 1984), 50.

'Other' and world

The category 'other' includes German production, estimated on the basis of:
- Peter Plassmeyer and Sibylle Gluch, eds, *Einfach – Vollkommen: Sachsens Weg in Die Internationale Uhrenwelt: Ferdinand Adolph Lange Zum 200. Geburtstag* (Dresden: Deutscher Kunstverlag, 2015).

Foreign trade figures have been available since the end of the nineteenth century, as well as production statistics for some countries. Estimates of world production made by the Swiss Chamber of Watchmaking (CSH), then the Federation of the Swiss Watch Industry (FHS), were used for the years 1937, 1950, 1970, and 1984. These figures are reproduced in:
- Jean-François Blanc,. 'Horlogerie: questions autour d'un redéploiement', in *La nouvelle Asie industrielle: Enjeux, stratégies et perspectives*, ed. Jean-Luc Maurer and Philippe Thierry Régnier (Paris: Presses Universitaires de France, 1989), 163–178.
- Davis S. Landes, *Revolution in Time: Clocks and the Making of the Modern World* (Cambridge: Belknap Press of Harvard University Press, 1983), 386.
- Hans Rieben, Madeleine Urech, and Charles Iffland, *L'Horlogerie et l'Europe* (Lausanne: Centre de recherches européennes, 1959).

However, for 1970, the figures for watch production in Hong Kong were added on the basis of official production statistics, as they were not included in the total of the FH estimates.

For the years 1890 and 1914, the figures quoted are extrapolations based on the following sources:

Switzerland

- Official figures from the *Statistique annuelle du commerce extérieur de la Suisse* (Berne: Direction Générale des Douanes) (volume of watches and movements), plus 5% for the domestic market.

Germany

- In the absence of official statistics on national production, German production is based on an extrapolation of average French and American production, these three countries being characterised by a watch industry oriented towards their own domestic market, in a relatively similar context of free trade. German per capita production was estimated as the average of the American (24 watches per 1,000 inhabitants in 1890 and 85 in 1914) and French (33 in 1890 and 48 in 1914) indices.

United States

- Michael C. Harrold, *American Watchmaking: A Technical History of the American Watch Industry, 1850–1930* (Columbia:NAWCC, 1984), 50.

France

- Claude Briselance, 'Les écoles d'horlogerie de Besançon: une contribution décisif au développement industriel local et régional (1793–1974)' (PhD diss., University of Lyon II, 2015), 300 and 342 (for 1914).
- Jean-Luc Mayaud and Joëlle Mauerhan, *Besançon horloger, 1793–1914* (Besançon: Musée du Temps, 1994), 64 (for 1890).

The production of gold and silver watches is known for Besançon. This figure is multiplied by three (same proportion as in Switzerland) to obtain the total number of Besançon watches, to which is added 10% for the estimate of the national total (proportion cited by Mayaud and Mauerhan).

Britain

- Roy A. Church, 'Nineteenth-century clock technology in Britain, the United States, and Switzerland', *Economic History Review*, vol. 28, no, 4 (1975): 625.
- Alun C. Davies, 'Time for a change? Technological persistence in the British watch industry', *Material Culture Review/Revue de la culture matérielle*, vol. 36, no. 1 (1992): 63 (for 1914).

Japan

- Ryuji Yamaguchi, 'History of the Japanese watch industry', *La Suisse horlogère*, vol. 40 (1970): 1536–1537.

'Other'

- Calculations based on the average percentage of the 1870s and 1937.

Bibliography

Archives

Archives Cantonales Jurassiennes (ACJ), Porrentruy

Fonds Péquignot, 100. Contract between the watchmaking organisations and Gruen Watch, 11 January 1943, and contract between the watchmaking organisations and Bulova Watch, 7 April 1948.

Fonds Péquignot, 122. Presentation by Karl Huber at a meeting of representatives of watchmaking organisations, 8 May 1959.

Archives Nationales, Paris

19870344/23. Paul George, *Les industries horlogères et connexes et le Cetehor* (n.d.).
19910207/2. Various documents on Timex, including Memorandum, 10 August 1979.
19910207/7. Hong Kong quota.
19910207/8. Statistics on the watch industry.
19870344/23. Paul George, *Les industries horlogères et connexes et le Cetehor* (n.d.).

Archives of the Federation of the Swiss Watch Industry (AFHS), Biel

Essay on the Seiko Group, Biel: FH, 1980.

Baker Library, Harvard University, Boston

MSS 598, American Waltham Watch, ZA-1.

Centre Jurassien d'Archives et de Recherches Économiques (CEJARE), Saint-Imier

Aubry Frères Papers, Francis Foëx. 'Histoire de la West End Watch Co.', unpublished manuscript, 1973.

JETRO Library, Osaka

Suisu no kinzoku-sei tokei bando: shijo chousa. Tokyo: JETRO, 1980.

Mémoires d'Ici, Saint-Imier (MDI)

Fonds de l'Ecole d'horlogerie de Saint-Imier.

Musée International d'Horlogerie (MIH), La Chaux-de-Fonds

Minutes of the meetings of the SIIJ, 30 June 1876.

Philadelphia City Archives

231.7. James D. McCabe, *The Illustrated History of the Centennial Exhibition*. Philadelphia: The National Publishing Co., n.d. 1877?

Seiko Museum, Tokyo

Hiaringu tokei gijutsushi shirizu, vols 1–33.

Swiss Federal Archives (SFA), Berne

E6.172, Letter from Consul Ritter to the Trade Division, 6 December 1895.
E6.178. Letter from the Neuchâtel Cantonal Chamber of Commerce, Industry and Labour to the Commerce Division, 16 April 1913.
E2200.10. Hong Kong. Letter from the Swiss Consulate to the DPF, 1950.
E2200.10. Hong Kong. Letter from Th. Von Mandach, lawyer for Shriro in Switzerland, to Péquignot, 15 September 1953.
E2200.10. Hong Kong. Letter from Consul General Mossaz to Trade Division, 10 March 1960.
E2200.10. Hong Kong. Agreement between the Federation of Swiss Watch Manufacturers and the Federation of Hong Kong Industries, 2 November 1966.
E2200.136. Letter from the delegations meeting to Péquignot, 11 April 1951.
E2200.174, 1968/3. Correspondence between the Swiss consulate in Shanghai and Swiss watch companies, 1953–1957.
E2200.174, 1971/46. Letter from Bernouilli to Bauer, 27 February 1958.
E2200.174, 1971/46. Letter from Shanghai Consulate to Beijing Embassy, 28 April 1958.
E2220.174, 1971/46. Report by Gilbert Étienne, 24 September 1958.
E2220.174, 1971/46. Translation of an article published in the newspaper *Sin Wen Jih Pao*, 2 January 1957.
E7004, 1967/12, 80. History of Gruen Watch Mfg., undated.
E7004, 1967/12, 80. Note from the Federal Department of Economic Affairs, 6 May 1958.
E7004, 1973/8. Band 37, Memorandum from six companies interested in producing in India to the DFEP, 5 October 1964.
E7004, 1973/8. Band 37, Note of 4 November 1964.
E7004, 1973/8. Band 37, Submission by six companies interested in producing in India to the DFEP, 5 October 1964.

Swiss Social Archive (SSA), Zurich

SMUV, 04–0063. Statistics on Roskopf watches.

Villingen-Schwenningen City Archive

VDU 4.9 / 864 industry report, Commerzbank/watch industry (April 1972): 20. Accessed 8 April 2019.

Published sources

Annual Survey of Manufactures. Washington, DC: US Census Bureau (1960–1990).
Archives de l'horlogerie. Berne: Office Polytechnique d'Édition et de Publicité, 1903.
ASUAG. Annual reports, 1970–1979.
Bilan, 2019.
'Bulova'. In *International Directory of Company Histories*, 120–123. Detroit: St James Press, 1996.
'Bulova Corporation'. In *International Directory of Company Histories*, 70–72. Detroit: St James Press, 2001.
Bureau of Foreign and Domestic Commerce, *Foreign Commerce and Navigation of the United States.* Washington, DC: US Department of Commerce, various years.
Bureau of the Census. *Biennial Census of Manufactures.* Washington, DC: US Department of Commerce, various years.
Convention patronale. *Recensement 2007.* La Chaux-de-Fonds: CPIH, 2008.
Convention patronale. *Recensement 2018.* La Chaux-de-Fonds: CPIH, 2019.
Credit Suisse Global Research. *Watch Industry: Prospects and Challenges.* Zurich: Credit Suisse, 2013.
Deutsche Uhrmacher Zeitung, 1923–1936.
Die Uhrmacher Woche, 1930.
'Distribution solennelle des récompenses aux ouvriers et apprentis'. *Revue Chronométrique*, vol. 9 (1876–1877): 221–232.
Documents statistiques réunis par l'administration des douanes sur le commerce de la France: années 1909, 1910 et 1911. Paris: Ministry of Finance, 1911.
Egana Goldpfeil. Annual report 2000.
Europa Star, vol. 81 (1973).
Feuille fédérale, Berne. 1848–1998.
Foreign Trade Statistics of the USSR [Внешние экономические связи СССР]. Moscow. Ministerstvo vneshneĭ torgovli, Planovo-ėkonomicheskoe, 1970 and 1980.
'Fossil'. In *International Directory of Company Histories, vol. 17. Detroit: St James Press, 1997.*
Hong Kong's Manufacturing Industries. Hong Kong: Hong Kong Government Industry Department, 1996.
Hong Kong Manufacturing SMEs: Preparing for the Future: Watches and Clocks. Hong Kong: Federation of Hong Kong Industries, 2010.
Hong Kong Trade Statistics Import. Hong Kong: Census Department, 1980–2010.
Hong Kong Trade Statistics Export and Re-export. Hong Kong: Census Department, 1960–1970, 1970–2010, 1960–2005, 1980–2010.
Indian Engineering Association. *Handbook of Statistics, 1970–1990 and Industrial and Economic Statistics Compendium.* Mumbai: All-India Manufacturers' Organization, 1967.
Industrial Commodity Statistics Yearbook. New York: United Nations, 1980–2008.
International Watch. November 2006, 187.
Japan Clock and Watch Association, 2015. Estimates. Accessed 18 June 2019. https://www.jcwa.or.jp/data/estimate.html.
Journal de Genève. 29 June 1873, 2 June 1877, 3 October 1927, 4 February 1949.
Journal suisse d'horlogerie (1930): 102–104.
Kaisha yoran. Tokyo: Daiamondo, 1971.
Kashio 15 nen shi. Tokyo: Casio, 1972.
Kikai tokei nenpo. Tokyo: MITI, 1960–1990.
Kokusai tokei tsushin. 1970–1986.

La Fédération horlogère suisse. 24 September 1893, 19 December 1914, 30 April 1930, 3 May 1930, 13 December 1930.
La Suisse horlogère et revue internationale d'horlogerie. December 1974–January 1975.
'Les concentrations dans l'industrie horlogère suisse'. *Annales Biennoises* (1971): 50.
L'Impartial. 11 February 1911, 4 March 1924, 17 April 1959, 19 October 1960, 16 November 1966, 25 August 1967, 3 June 1971, 17 August 1972, 25 February 1976, 2 February 2000, 14 March 2000, 17 December 2001.
L'Industrie de l'horlogerie. Paris:Banque de France, 1974.
Le Temps. 20 January 2011, 26 May 2016, 14 March 2017.
'Mayor Auguste'. *Actes de la Société Helvétique des Sciences Naturelles*, vol. 87 (1904): 61–69.
Mémoire sur les conditions actuelles d'importation de la petite horlogerie et la nécessité d'une tarification 'ad valorem'. Besançon: Le Fabricant Français, 1922.
Moody's Industrial Manual, 1929, 1939, 1948, 1962, 1973, 1977, and 1986.
Nestlé 150 Years: Nutrition. Health and Wellness, 1866–2016. Vevey: Nestlé, 2016.
Nihon chouki toukei souran. Tokyo: Nihon tokei kyokai, 1988.
Nihon gaikoku bokei nenpyo. Tokyo: Ministry of Finance, 1960–2010.
Nihon keizai shimbun, 19 June 1962.
Nihon no tokei sangyo tokei. Tokyo: Nihon tokei kyokai, 1995–2010.
Nihon tokei nenkan. Tokyo: Sogocho, 1998 and 2000.
Nikkei Business, 18 March 1996.
'Seiko gurupu no kaigai senryaku'. *Noryoku Kaihatsu Shirizu*, vol. 87 (1982): 14–15.
Seiko tokei no sengoshi. Tokyo: Seiko, 1996.
Société Générale de l'Horlogerie Suisse SA (ASUAG). *Historique publié à l'occasion de son vingt-cinquième anniversaire, 1931–1956.* Biel: Arts Graphiques SA, 1956.
SSIH. Annual reports 1973–1980.
Statistics of the Swiss National Bank. Accessed 7 July 2010. https://www.snb.ch.
Statistique annuelle du commerce extérieur de la Suisse. Berne: Direction Générale des Douanes (formerly the Administration or Département Fédérale des Douanes), various years.
Statistique mensuelle du commerce extérieur de la France. Paris: Ministère des Finances, various years.
Swatch Group. Annual reports 1983–2009.
'Timex'. In *International Directory of Company Histories*, 479–482. Detroit: St James Press, 1999.
Titan Industries. Annual reports 1990–2018.
Tokei no honkon shijo chosa hokokusho. Tokyo: Nihon kikai zushutsu kumiai, 1980.
UN Comtrade database. Accessed 15 June 2019. https://comtrade.un.org/data.
US Commodity Exports and Imports as Related to Output. Washington, DC: US Census Bureau, 1960–1970.
Vontobel Luxury Goods Shop. Zurich: Vontobel, 2018.
Watches: China Sourcing Report. Hong Kong: Global Sources, 2005.

Academic books and articles

Alft, E. C., and William H. Biska. *Elgin Time: A History of the Elgin National Watch Company, 1864–1968*. Elgin: Elgin Historical Society, 2003.

Babel, Antony. *Histoire corporative de l'horlogerie, de l'orfèvrerie, et des industries annexes*. Geneva: A. Jullien, 1916.

Béguelin, Sylvie. 'Naissance et développement de la montre-bracelet: histoire d'une conquête (1880–1950)'. *Chronometrophilia*, vol. 37 (1994): 33–43.

Bentivogli, Chiara, Hans H. Hinterhuber, and Sandro Trento. 'The watch industry: a strategic analysis'. *International Review of Strategic Management*, vol. 5 (1994): 133–170.

Berger, Suzanne, and Richard K. Lester, eds. *Made by Hong Kong*. Oxford: Oxford University Press, 1997.

Bergier, Jean-François. *Histoire économique de la Suisse*. Lausanne: Payot, 1983.

Blair, Jennifer. 'Les cadres d'analyse des chaînes globales'. *Revue française de gestion*, vol. 2 (2010): 103–119.

Blanc, Jean-François. *Suisse-Hong Kong: le défi horloger: innovation technologique et division internationale du travail*. Lausanne: Éditions d'En bas, 1988.

Blanc, Jean-François. 'Horlogerie: questions autour d'un redéploiement'. In *La nouvelle Asie industrielle: Enjeux, stratégies et perspectives*, edited by Jean-Luc Maurer and Philippe Thierry Régnier. Paris: Presses Universitaires de France, 1989.

Blanchard, Philippe. *L'établissage: étude historique d'un système de production horloger en Suisse (1750–1950)*. Chézard-Saint-Martin: La Chatière, 2011.

Bodenmann, Laurence, ed. *Philadelphia 1876: le défi américain en horlogerie*. La Chaux-de-Fonds: Musée International d'Horlogerie, 2011.

Boillat, Johann. *Les véritables maîtres du temps: le cartel horloger suisse (1919–1941)*. Neuchâtel: Alphil, 2013.

Bolli, Jean-Jacques. *L'aspect horloger des relations commerciales américano-suisses de 1929 à 1950*. La Chaux-de-Fonds: La Suisse horlogère, 1956.

Borer, Harry. '1878–1978. Centenaire de la manufacture des montres Rolex SA, Bienne'. *Neues Bieler Jahrbuch* (1979): 101–109.

Bouquet, Cyril. 'Swatch and the global watch industry'. In *Cases in the Environment of Business: International Perspectives*, edited by David W. Conklin, 50–69. Thousand Oaks: Sage, 2006.

Briselance, Claude. 'Les écoles d'horlogerie de Besançon: une contribution décisif au développement industriel local et régional (1793–1974)'. PhD diss., University of Lyon II, 2015.

Burton, M. Diane, and Tom Nicholas, 'Prizes, patents and the search for longitude'. *Explorations in Economic History*, vol. 64 (2017): 21–36.

Carrera, Roland. *Swatchissimo, 1981–1991: l'extraordinaire aventure Swatch*. Geneva: Antiquorum, 1991.

Carstensen, Fred V. *American Enterprise in Foreign Markets: Studies of Singer and International Harvester in Imperial Russia*. Chapel Hill: University of North Carolina Press, 1984.

Chandler, Alfred D. *Strategy and Structure: Chapters in the History of the Industrial Enterprise*. Cambridge: MIT Press, 1962.

Chattopadhyay, Utpal, and Pragya Bhawsar. 'Effects of changing business environment on organization performance: the case of HMT Watches Ltd'. *South Asian Journal of Business and Management Cases*, vol. 6, no. 1 (2017): 36–46.

Church, Roy A. 'Nineteenth-century clock technology in Britain, the United States, and Switzerland'. *Economic History Review*, vol. 28, no. 4 (1975): 616–630.

Cimoli, Mario, Giovanni Dosi, and Joseph E. Stiglitz, eds. *Industrial Policy and Development: The Political Economy of Capabilities Accumulation*. New York: Oxford University Press, 2009.

Clarke, Roger A., and Dubravko J. I. Matko. *Soviet Economic Facts, 1917–1981*. New York: St Martin's Press, 1983.

Daclin, Pierre. *La crise des années 30 à Besançon*. Besançon: Belles Lettres, 1968.

David, Jacques. *Rapport à la Société intercantonale des industries du Jura sur la fabrication de l'horlogerie aux États-Unis*, 1876 [Report to the SIIJ on the manufacture of watches in the United States; unpublished at the time but facsimile published by Longines, Saint-Imier, 1992].Davies, Alun C. 'Time for a change? Technological persistence in the British watch industry'. *Material Culture Review/Revue de la culture matérielle*, vol. 36, no. 1 (1992): 57–64.

de Coulon, Philippe. *Les ébauches: deux siècles d'histoire horlogère*. Neuchâtel: La Baconnière, 1951.

Dequidt, Marie-Agnès. *Horlogers des Lumières: Temps et société à Paris au XVIIIe siècle*. Paris: CTHS, 2014.

Donat, André. 'L'industrie horlogère russe'. *Production Horlogère Française*, vol. 12 (1958): 2.

Donzé, Pierre-Yves. 'Des montres et des pétrodollars: la politique commerciale d'une PME horlogère suisse. Aubry Frères SA, 1917–1993'. *Revue Suisse d'Histoire* (2004): 384–409.

Donzé, Pierre-Yves. 'Les industriels horlogers du Locle (1850–1920), un cas représentatif de la diversité du patronat de l'Arc jurassien'. In *Les systèmes productifs dans l'Arc jurassien. Acteurs, pratiques et territoires (xixe–xxe siècles)*, edited by Jean-Claude Daumas. Besançon, 61–82. Besançon: Maison des Sciences de l'Homme, 2005.

Donzé, Pierre-Yves. *Les patrons horlogers de La Chaux-de-Fonds: social dynamics of an industrial elite (1840–1920)*. Neuchâtel: Alphil, 2007.

Donzé, Pierre-Yves. *Histoire de l'industrie horlogère suisse de Jacques David à Nicolas Hayek (1850–2000)*. Neuchâtel: Alphil, 2009.

Donzé, Pierre-Yves. 'Le district industriel horloger suisse de la cartellisation à la globalisation: L'exemple de l'industrie de la boîte de montres au cours du xxe siècle'. In *Histoires de territoires. Les territoires industriels en question, xviiie–xxe siècles*, edited by Laurent Tissot et al. Neuchâtel: Alphil, 2010.

Donzé, Pierre-Yves. 'The Department for Arms Production of the University of Tokyo and the beginnings of the Japanese precision machine industry (1930–1960)'. *Osaka Economic Papers*, vol. 61, no. 1 (2011): 37–59.

Donzé, Pierre-Yves. 'The hybrid production system and the birth of the Japanese specialized industry: watch production at Hattori & Co. (1900–1960)'. *Enterprise and Society*, vol. 12, no. 2 (2011): 356–397.

Donzé, Pierre-Yves. *Du comptoir familial à la marque globale: Longines*. Saint-Imier: Éditions des Longines, 2012.

Donzé, Pierre-Yves. *Histoire du Swatch Group*. Neuchâtel: Alphil, 2012.

Donzé, Pierre-Yves. 'Les relations horlogères entre la Suisse et la Russie au cours du 20e siècle'. *Revue économique et sociale*, vol. 72 (2014): 15–25.

Donzé, Pierre-Yves. *'Rattraper et dépasser la Suisse': histoire de l'industrie horlogère japonaise, 1850 à nos jours*. Neuchâtel: Alphil, 2014.

Donzé, Pierre-Yves. 'Les origines militaires du 'miracle économique' japonais: l'essor technologique de Canon et de Seiko des années 1930 aux années 1960'. *Entreprises et Histoire*, vol. 85 (2016): 12–25.

Donzé, Pierre-Yves. 'Fashion watches: the emergence of accessory makers as intermediaries in the fashion system'. *International Journal of Fashion Studies*, vol. 4, no. 1 (2017): 69–85.

Donzé, Pierre-Yves. 'La R&D dans l'horlogerie électronique suisse et japonaise de 1960 à 1980: une analyse comparative de Longines et de Seiko'. *Le Mouvement Social*, vol. 258 (2017): 109–122.

Donzé, Pierre-Yves. *L'invention du luxe: histoire de l'horlogerie à Genève de 1815 à nos jours.* Neuchâtel: Alphil, 2017.

Donzé, Pierre-Yves. 'Swiss Made but global: from technology to fashion in the watch industry, 1950–2010'. In *Industries and Global Competition: Business Beyond Borders*, edited by Bram Bowens, Pierre-Yves Donzé, and Takafumi Kurosawa, 195–214. New York: Routledge, 2017.

Donzé, Pierre-Yves. 'National labels and the competitiveness of European industries: the example of the 'Swiss Made' Law since 1950'. *European Review of History*, vol. 26, no. 5 (2019): 855–870.

Donzé, Pierre-Yves, and David Borel. 'Technological innovation and brand management: the Japanese watch industry since the 1990s'. *Journal of Asia-Pacific Business,* vol. 20, no. 2 (2019): 1–20.

Donzé, Pierre-Yves, and Shigehiro Nishimura, eds. *Organizing Global Technology Flows: Institutions, Actors, and Processes.* New York: Routledge, 2014.

Dreyfus, V. *La défense d'une industrie nationale: la fabrique d'horlogerie de Besançon.* Besançon: Imprimerie Millot Frères et Cie, 1890.

Edgerton, David. *The Shock of the Old: Technology and Global History Since 1900.* London: Profile Books, 2006.

Fallet, Estelle. 'Nicolas Hayek'. In *Dictionnaire historique de la Suisse.* Accessed 25 June 2009. https://www.dhs.ch.

Fallet, Estelle. *Tissot: 150 ans d'histoire.* Le Locle: Tissot SA, 2003.

Friedman, Thomas L. *The World Is Flat: Brief History of the Twenty-First Century.* New York: Farrar, Straus and Giroux, 2005.

Fukuyama, Francis. *The End of History and the Last Man.* New York: Free Press, 1992.

Gagnebin-Diacon, Christine. *La fabrique et le village: la Tavannes Watch Co (1890–1918).* Porrentruy: Cercle d'Études Historiques de la Société Jurassienne d'Émulation, 1996.

Garavini, Giuliano. *After empires: European integration, decolonization, and the challenge from the global south 1957–1986.* Oxford: Oxford University Press, 2012.

Garel, Gilles, and Elmar Mock. *La fabrique de l'innovation.* Paris: Dunod, 2012.

Gern, Philippe, and Silvia Arlettaz. *Relations franco-suisses: la confrontation de deux politiques économiques.* Geneva: Georg, 1992.

Gerschenkron, Alexander. *Economic Backwardness in Historical Perspective: A Book of Essays.* Cambridge: Belknap Press, 1962.

Gilberti, Bruno. *Designing the Centennial: A History of the 1876 International Exhibition in Philadelphia.* Lexington: University Press of Kentucky, 2015.

Glasmeier, Amy K. *Manufacturing Time: Global Competition in the Watch Industry, 1795–2000.* New York: Guilford Press, 2000.

Grimes, Seamus, and Yutao Sun. 'China's evolving role in Apple's global value chain'. *Area Development and Policy*, vol. 1, no. 1 (2016): 94–112.

Harrold, Michael C. *American Watchmaking: A Technical History of the American Watch Industry, 1850–1930.* Columbia: NAWCC, 1984.

Henry-Bédat, Jacqueline. *Une région, une passion: l'horlogerie: une entreprise: Longines.* Saint-Imier: Compagnie des Montres Longines, 1992.

Higgins, David M. *Brands, Geographical Origin, and the Global Economy: A History from the Nineteenth Century to the Present.* Cambridge: Cambridge University Press, 2018.

Hilaire-Pérez, Liliane. *La pièce et le geste: artisans, marchands et savoir technique à Londres au xviiie siècle.* Paris: Albin Michel, 2013.

Hirano, Mitsuo. *Seikosha Shiwa.* Tokyo: Seiko, 1968.

Hoke, Donald R. *Ingenious Yankees: The Rise of the American System of Manufactures in the Private Sector.* New York: Columbia University Press, 1990.

Hounshell, David A. *From the American System to Mass Production 1800–1932: The Development of Manufacturing Technology in the United States*. Baltimore: Johns Hopkins University Press, 1985.

Humair, Cédric. *Développement économique et État central (1815–1914): un siècle de politique douanière suisse au service des élites*. Berne: Lang, 2004.

Jeannerat, Hugues, and Olivier Crevoisier. 'Non-technological innovation and multi-local territorial knowledge dynamics in the Swiss watch industry'. *International Journal of Innovation and Regional Development*, vol. 3, no.1 (2011): 26–44.

Johnson, Chalmers. *MITI and the Japanese Miracle: The Growth of Industrial Policy, 1925–1975*. Stanford: Stanford University Press, 1982.

Jones, Geoffrey. *Multinationals and Global Capitalism: From the Nineteenth to the Twenty-First Century*. New York: Oxford University Press, 2005.

Judet, Pierre. *Horlogeries et horlogers du Faucigny (1849–1934): Les métamorphoses d'une identité sociale et politique*. Grenoble: Presses Universitaires de Grenoble, 2004.

Karsten, Luchien. *Globalization and Time*. New York: Routledge, 2013.

Katzenstein, Peter J. *Small States in World Markets: Industrial Policy in Europe*. Ithaca: Cornell University Press, 1985.

Kipping, Matthias, Takafumi Kurosawa, and Eleanor Westney, eds. *Oxford Handbook of Industry Dynamics*. New York: Oxford University Press, forthcoming.

Knickerbocker, F. *Note on the Watch Industries in Switzerland, Japan, and the United States*. Boston: Harvard Business School, 1974.

Knobel, Joëlle. 'Une manufacture d'horlogerie biennoise: la Société Louis Brandt & Frère (Omega), 1895–1935'. Master diss., University of Neuchâtel, 1997.

Koller, Christophe. *'De la lime à la machine'. L'industrialisation et l'État au pays de l'horlogerie: Contribution à l'histoire économique et sociale d'une région suisse*. Courrendlin: CSE, 2003.

Kurosawa, Takafumi. 'Industry history: its concepts and methods'. In *Industries and Global Competition: A History of Business beyond Borders*, edited by Bram Bouwens, Pierre-Yves Donzé, and Takafumi Kurosawa. New York: Routledge, 2017.

Kwolek-Folland, Angel. *Incorporating Women: A History of Women and Business in the United States*. New York: Twayne Publishers, 1998.

Lachat, Stéphanie, *Les pionnières du temps: vies professionnelles et familiales des ouvrières de l'industrie horlogère suisse (1870–1970)*. Neuchâtel: Alphil, 2014.

Lamard, Pierre. *Histoire d'un capital familial au xixe siècle: le capital Japy (1777–1910)*. Montbéliard: Société Belfortaine d'Émulation, 1988.

Landes, David S. *Revolution in Time: Clocks and the Making of the Modern World*. Cambridge: Belknap Press of Harvard University Press, 2nd end 2000, 1st edn 1983.

Linder, Patrick. *Au cœur d'une vocation industrielle: les mouvements de montre de la maison Longines: (1832–2007): tradition, savoir-faire, innovation*. Saint-Imier: Édition des Longines, 2007.

Linder, Patrick. *De l'atelier à l'usine: l'horlogerie à Saint-Imier (1865–1918). Histoire d'un district industriel. Organisation et technologie: un système en mutation*. Neuchâtel: Alphil, 2008.

Maddison, Angus. *The World Economy*. Paris: OECD, 2006.

Marti, Laurence. *Une région au rythme du temps: Histoire socio-économique du Vallon de Saint-Imier et environs, 1700–2007*. Saint-Imier: Édition des Longines, 2007.

Marti, Laurence. *Le renouveau horloger: Contribution à une histoire récente de l'horlogerie suisse (1980–2015)*. Neuchâtel: Alphil, 2016.

Mayaud, Jean-Luc, and Joëlle Mauerhan. *Besançon horloger, 1793–1914*. Besançon: Musée du Temps, 1994.

McCabe, James D. *The Illustrated History of the Centennial Exhibition*. Philadelphia: National Publishing Co., n.d. (1877?).

McCrossen, Alexis. *Marking Modern Times: A History of Clocks, Watches, and Other Timekeepers in American Life.* Chicago: University of Chicago Press, 2013.

Moore, Charles W. *Timing a Century: History of the Waltham Watch Company.* Cambridge: Harvard University Press, 1945.

Morri, Ryoji. *19 seiki doitsu no chiiki sangyo fukko: kindaika no naka no byutenberuku shoeigyo.* Kyoto: Kyoto University Press, 2013.

Morrison Allen, and Cyril Bouquet. *Swatch and the Global Watch Industry*, Case Study. Cambridge: Harvard Business School, 1999.

Motomochi, Kinuyuki. 'Soren no tokei kogyo ni tsuite'. *Nihon tokei gakkaishi,* vol. 4 (1957): 49–54.

Moutet, Aimée. *Les logiques de l'entreprise: la rationalisation dans l'industrie française dans l'entre-deux-guerre.* Paris: Éditions EHESS, 1997.

Munz, Hervé. *La transmission en jeu: Apprendre, pratiquer, patrimonialiser l'horlogerie en Suisse.* Neuchâtel: Alphil, 2016.

Nonada, Ikujio, and Hirotaka Takeuchi Nonaka. *The Knowledge-Creating Company: How Japanese Companies Create the Dynamics of Innovation.* Oxford: Oxford University Press, 1995.

Officer, Lawrence H. 'Exchange rates between the United States dollar and forty-one currencies'. MeasuringWorth, 2019. Accessed 15 February 2022. https://www.measuringworth.com/datasets/exchangeglobal.

Ogle, Vanessa. *The Global Transformation of Time, 1870–1950.* Cambridge: Harvard University Press, 2015.

Oxtoby, F.-E. 'The role of political factors in the Virgin Islands watch industry'. *Geographical Review,* vol. 60, no. 4 (1970): 463–474 .

Pasquier, Hélène. *La 'recherche et développement' en horlogerie: acteurs, stratégies et choix technologiques dans l'arc jurassien suisse (1900–1970).* Neuchâtel: Alphil, 2008.

Pasquier, Hélène. 'Une industrie remodelée'. In *Le Pays de Neuchâtel et son patrimoine horloger,* edited by Laurent Tissot et al., 307–315. Chézard-Saint-Martin: La Chatière, 2008.

Pasquier, Hélène. 'Swatch Group'. In *Dictionnaire historique de la Suisse.* Accessed 25 June 2009. https://www.dhs.ch.

Penrose, Edith. *The Theory of the Growth of the Firm.* New York: John Wiley and Sons, 1959.

Perrenoud, Marc. 'Mouvements migratoires et mouvement ouvrier neuchâtelois dans les années 1930'. *Revue d'Histoire Neuchâteloise,* no. 1–2 (2001): 37–54.

Perret, Thomas. 'Un canton chahuté'. In *Le Pays de Neuchâtel et son patrimoine horloger,* edited by Laurent Tissot et al., 301–305. Chézard-Saint-Martin: La Chatière, 2008.

Petiteau, Natalie. *L'horlogerie des Bourgeois conquérants: histoire des établissements Bourgeois de Damprichard, Doubs: 1780–1939.* Besançon: Les Belles Lettres, Université de Besançon, 1994.

Piguet, Jean-Michel, ed. *Le drôle de montre de Monsieur Roskopf.* Neuchâtel: Alphil, 2013.

Piotet, Georges. *Restructuration industrielle et corporatisme: le cas de l'horlogerie en Suisse, 1974–1987.* Lausanne: Imprivite SA, 1988.

Plassmeyer, Peter, and Sibylle Gluch, eds. *Einfach – Vollkommen: Sachsens Weg in Die Internationale Uhrenwelt: Ferdinand Adolph Lange Zum 200. Geburtstag.* Dresden: Deutscher Kunstverlag, 2015.

Platt, John G. *Lancashire Watch Company History and Watches.* Chester: Inbeat Publications, 2016.

Porter, Michael E. *Competitive Strategy: Techniques for Analyzing Industries and Competitors.* New York: Free Press, 1980.

Richon, Marco. *Omega Saga.* Biel: Fondation Adrien Brandt Pour le Patrimoine Omega, 1998.

Rieben, Hans, Madeleine Urech, and Charles Iffland. *L'Horlogerie et l'Europe*. Lausanne: Centre de Recherches Européennes, 1959.
Romy, Bernard. *Le meunier, l'horloger et l'électricien: les usiniers de la Suze, 1750–1950*. Biel: Intervalles, 2008.
Sauers, Don. *Time for America: Hamilton Watch, 1892–1992*. Lititz: Sutter House, 1992.
Schaller, François. 'Les crises horlogères, y a-t-il une spécificité?' In *L'homme et le temps en Suisse de 1291 à 1991*, edited by Catherine Cardinal et al., 273–278. La Chaux-de-Fonds: IHT, 1991.
Scheurer, Frédéric. *Les crises de l'industrie horlogère dans le canton de Neuchâtel*. La Neuveville: Éd. Beerstecher, 1914.
Schmid, Hans-Heinrich. *Lexikon der Deutschen Uhrenindustrie 1850–1980*. Nuremberg: German Society for Chronometrie 2017.
Schröter, Harm. 'Cartels'. In *Dictionnaire historique de la Suisse*. Accessed 15 June 2009. https://www.dhs.ch.
Shafaeddin, Mehdi. *How Did Developed Countries Industrialize? The History of Trade and Industrial Policy: The Cases of Great Britain and the USA*. Geneva: United Nations Conference on Trade and Development, 1998.
Shimizu, Osamu. *Tokei*. Tokyo: Nihon Keizai Shimbun, 1991.
Siegenthaler, H.-J., and H. Ritzmann-Blickenstorfer, *Historische Statistik der Schweiz*. Zurich: Chronos, 1996.
Silvia, Robert. 'Édouard Bovet-dit-de-Chine, négociant en horlogerie (1797–1849)'. In *Biographies Neuchâteloises*, vol. 2, 48–55, edited by Michel Schlup. Hauterive: G. Attinger, 1998.
Speckhart, Gustav. *Peter Henlein der Erfinder der Taschenuhr: fachgeschichtliche Abhandlung*. Nuremberg: Verl. J. L. Engraving, 1890.
Studer, Roman. 'When did the Swiss get so rich? Comparing living standards in Switzerland and Europe, 1800–1913'. *Journal of European Economic History*, vol. 37, no. 2 (2008): 405–452.
Takeishi, Akira, Kanayama Tadashi, and Mizuno Tatsuya. *Seiko Epson jidomaki kuotsu uochi no kaihatsu*. Working Paper 2-12. Tokyo: Hitotsubashi University, 2005.
Thrift, Nigel. 'The making of a capitalist time consciousness'. In *The Sociology of Time*, edited by J. Hassard, 105–129. London: Palgrave Macmillan, 1990.
Trincano, Louis. *L'industrie horlogère française*. Besançon: Chambre Intersyndicale des Fabricants d'Horlogerie de l'Est, 1927.
Trueb, Lucien F. *The World of Watches: History, Technology, Industry*. New York: Ebner Publishing International, 2005.
Uchida, Hoshimi. *Tokei kogyo no hattatsu*. Tokyo: Seiko Institute of Horology, 1985.
Uchida, Hoshimi. *Evolution of Seiko, 1892–1923*. Tokyo: Hattori Seiko, 2000.
Veyrassat, Béatrice. 'Manufacturing flexibility in nineteenth-century Switzerland: social and institutional foundations of decline and revival in calico-printing and watchmaking'. In *World of Possibilities: Flexibility and Mass Production in Western Industrialization*, edited by Charles Sabel and Jonathan Zeitlin, 188–238. Cambridge: Cambridge University Press, 1997.
Veyrassat, Béatrice. 'Sortir des montagnes horlogères: les faiseurs de globalisation (1750-years 1830/1840)'. In *Unternehmen, Handelshäuser und Wirtschaftsmigration im neuzeutlichen Alpenraum*, edited by Marie-Claude Schöpfer, Markus Stoffel, and Françoise Vannotti, 257–279. Brig: Rotten Verlag, 2014.
Vinzier, Léon. 'L'expérience de Lip'. *Esprit*, vol. 439, no. 10 (1974): 470–480.
Watson, James C. *American Watches: An Extract from the Report on Horology at the International Exhibition at Philadelphia in 1876*. New York: Robbins & Appleton, 1877.

Wilkins, Mira, and Ernest Frank Hill. *American Business Abroad: Ford on Six Continents.* Detroit: Wayne State University Press, 1964.

Yamaguchi, Ryuji. 'History of the Japanese watch industry'. *La Suisse horlogère*, vol. 40 (1970): 1536–1537.

Yang, Yuming. 'L'industrie horlogère suisse et ses relations avec la Chine de 1949 à 1982'. PhD diss., Geneva: Graduate Institute of International Studies, 1984.

Zürcher, Christoph. 'Bulova Watch Company'. In *Dictionnaire historique de la Suisse.* Accessed 15 February 2022. https://www.dhs.ch.

Index

Accutron, 95
Adidas, 160
Aetos Group, 91–92
Allgemeine Schweizerische Uhrenindustrie AG (ASUAG), 70–73, 80, 83, 88–90, 92, 98, 114, 128–130, 133, 177
American Watch Company, 12, 20–23, 26–32, 35–36, 38–39, 42–44, 52–55, 61, 63, 77, 79–80, 91–92, 94
Anglo-American Watch Company, 39
Ansonia Watch Co., 82
Apple, 4, 160, 173–175, 179
Armani, 159, 161
Asia Commercial Holdings Ltd, 157
Asian Swiss Industrial Company, 107, 125
Aubry Frères SA, 93
Audemars Piguet, 149, 151, 172

Badollet & Cie, 36
Ball & Co., 55
Bauer, Gérard, 87, 111
Baume Bros., 12
Baumgartner Frères Granges (BFG), 107, 128, 135
Beaucourt, 16, 41, 57–58
Benguerel & Humbert, 16
Benrus Watch, 80
Berthoud, Ferdinand, 18
Besançon, 8, 18–19, 39–41, 56–58, 74–76, 96, 98, 113, 132, 134, 151
Biel/Bienne, 34, 55, 58–59, 65, 92, 105, 112, 126
Birmingham, 10, 28, 39
Biver, Jean-Claude, 149
Blancpain, 92, 149
Borel & Courvoisier, 29, 31, 93, 173
Bovet, Edouard, 8, 18
Brandt, Louis & Fils *see* Omega

Breguet, Abraham-Louis, 18, 149
Breitling, 172
Bretton Woods, 121, 127
Britain, 9–13, 19, 22–23, 26–28, 35, 38–39, 43–44, 48, 50, 53, 57, 63, 76, 110, 130, 169, 176
British Horological Institute, 12, 38–39
Brown Boveri Co. (BBC), 125
Bucherer, C. F., 172
Buhré, Paul, 52
Bulova, Joseph, 48, 55
Bulova (company), 48, 55, 63, 80, 84, 88, 94–97, 106, 126, 130–131
Büren Watch AG, 97

Casio, 121–122, 152, 172
Cassardes Watch Co., 62
Centre Électronique Horloger (CEH), 119
Chandler, Alfred D., 2
Chanel, 172
Chaux-de-Fonds, La, 14–16, 22, 32–34, 36, 58, 111
China, 1, 3, 8, 10, 28, 50, 67, 88–89, 104–105, 109–114, 118–119, 135, 138–140, 142–143, 152, 154–161, 165, 168–170, 172, 178
Chopard, 172
Chronos Holding SA, 92
Chung Nam Watch Co., 156
Citizen Watch1, 61–62, 81–82, 88, 97, 101–104, 106, 108, 113, 119, 122, 125, 152–154, 158, 163, 172, 175
Citychamp, 172–173
Clockmakers' Company, 10
Compagnie Européenne d'Horlogerie, 133
Compagnie Financière Richemont *see* Richemont
Courvoisier, Louis, 14
Coventry, 10

David, Jacques, 26, 29, 31–33, 35
Dennison, Aaron L., 20, 28, 39
Diesel, 159
DKNY, 159
dollar watches, 53, 63
Dreyfus, Victor, 40
DuBois, Moïse, 10
Dueber-Hampden Watch Co., 82
Durowe AG, 99–100

East India Company8, 10
Ébauches SA, 70–71, 73, 80, 89, 99–100, 107, 131, 177
Ebohr, 158
Economic Swiss Time Holding, 92, 128–129
Egana Goldpfeil, 151
Eguet, 16
Elgin, 20–21, 27–28, 39, 55, 63
European Economic Community (EEC), 99, 132, 134, 151

Fabriques d'assortiments réunies SA, 71
Fabriques de balanciers réunies SA, 71
Fabrique suisse de ressorts d'horlogerie SA, 112
Fairchild, 125, 130–131
Favre-Jacot, Georges & Cie *see* Zenith
Favre-Leuba, 93, 113, 163
Favre-Perret, Édouard, 28
Festina, 172
Fiyta, 158, 172
Folli Follie, 138, 161, 172
Fontainemelon, 16, 34, 70
Fossil, 132, 135, 139, 157, 159–161, 165, 172, 174
France, 1, 3–5, 8–10, 16–19, 21–23, 27, 35, 38, 43, 47–48, 50, 56–58, 63, 65–67, 71, 74, 76–77, 84, 88–89, 94, 96–99, 101, 104, 110, 113, 118–119, 132–134, 151, 156, 165, 169–170, 172, 176, 178
France-Ébauches, 133–134
Francillon, Ernest, 15, 26, 29, 35–36
Frédérique Constant, 172, 175
Furtwangen, 22

GATT (General Agreement on Tariffs and Trade), 134
Gebrüder Junghans *see* Junghans (company)
General Electric, 51, 131

General Motors (GM), 2
General Watch Co., 91–92, 129
Geneva, 13, 16, 18–19, 33, 36, 43, 55, 82
Germany, 10, 21–22, 26–27, 38, 42, 44, 48, 50, 56, 58, 61, 65–67, 69, 71, 73, 76–77, 83–84, 88–89, 94, 96, 99–101, 110–111, 113, 118–119, 132, 151–152, 154, 162, 169–170, 176–177
Gerschenkron, Alexander, 3
Gilman & Co., 104, 122
Glashütte, 21–22, 42, 99, 152, 177
Glashütter Uhrentriebe (GUB), 101, 132, 152
global value chain, 138–140
Golay-Buchel & Cie, 112
Google, 174
Greenwich Mean Team (GMT), 47
Gregorian calendar, 47
Grenchen, 34, 112, 128
Gribi, Théodore, 29, 31–32
Gruen Watch, 80

Haller, Thomas AG, 42, 58, 76
Hamburg-Amerikanische Uhrenfabrik AG, 76
Hamilton, Alexander, 2
Hamilton Watch, 53–55, 78–79, 88, 95, 97, 130–131
Harrison, John, 10
Hatot, 76
Hattori, Kintaro, 60–63
Hattori & Co. *see* Seiko
Hayek, Nayla, 6
Hayek, Nicolas, 2, 129–130, 143–145
Henlein, Peter, 21
Hermès, 172
Heuer-Léonidas *see* TAG Heuer
Hindustan Machine Tools (HMT), 113, 163
Hitachi, 125
Hong Kong, 5, 87–88, 91, 94, 96, 104–109, 114, 118–119, 121–122, 124–125, 128, 131–132, 134–135, 139–142, 151–152, 155–160, 162–163, 165, 168–170, 172, 177–178
Hong Kong & Kowloon Clock & Watch Trade Merchants Association, 106
Huguenin, A. Fils, 97

Indo-French Time Industries Private Ltd, 113
Ingersoll & Bro., 53
Ingold, Pierre Frédéric, 12

Intel, 174
International Watch Company (IWC), 34, 49, 150, 152, 177
Intersil, 119, 125, 131
ISA, 156

Jacobs, Marc, 160
Jaeger, 134
Jaeger-Lecoultre, 93, 150, 152
Japan, 1–6, 28, 31, 48, 50, 52, 57, 59–63, 65–67, 69, 81–84, 88–89, 92–97, 101–114, 118–122, 124–126, 130–131, 134–135, 138–141, 145, 151–159, 162–163, 169–170, 172, 177–178
Japan Pocket Watch Manufacturing, 60
Japy, Émile, 41
Japy, Frédéric, 16, 18
Japy (company), 16, 19, 34, 40–42, 57–58, 75–76
Jaz, 134
Jeanneret-Gris, Jean-Jacques, 16
Junghans, Charles, 59
Junghans, Oskar, 58
Junghans (company), 22, 42, 58–59, 63, 76–77, 84, 88, 99, 101, 132, 151
Juvenia, 157

Kartsotis, Tom and Kosta, 159–160
Kasper & Co., 113
Kelton, 98
Kering, 172
Kienzle, 58, 76, 99, 101
Knockdown production, 49–52, 55, 60, 62–63, 65, 69, 72–73, 77, 80, 82–84, 99, 177
Kors, Michael, 160

Lacher & Co. AG, 99
Lagardère, Jean-Luc, 134
Lagerfeld, Karl, 160
Lancashire, 10, 39
Lancashire Watch Company, 39
Lange, Ferdinand Adolph, 21
Lange & Söhne, 21–22, 42, 59, 101, 152
Langendorf Watch Co., 92
Lévy Frères, 76
Lindt & Sprüngli, 2
Lip, 75, 98, 132–134
Lipmann, 75–76
List, Friedrich, 2

Locle, Le, 6, 10, 14–17, 33, 43, 58, 61, 112
London, 8, 10–13, 18, 28, 38, 43–44
Longines, 15, 26, 29, 32, 34, 36, 47, 49, 52, 72, 821, 91–92, 118, 131, 143, 149, 177
Longines-Wittnauer, 80
LVMH, 1, 139, 150, 171–172, 175

Magniac & Co., 8
Malaysia, 122, 143, 152, 170
Massachusetts, 20, 30, 77
Matra group, 122, 133–134, 151
Matsumoto, Dai, 102
Mauboussin, 151
Mayor, Auguste, 17
Mégevand, Laurent, 18
Merchandise Marks Act, 12
Mido, 82, 91
Mille, Richard, 138, 151, 172
Moët & Chandon Louis Vuitton *see* LVMH
Morellato, 161, 172
Moser, 52
Motorola, 125
Movado, 90, 150, 161, 172
Muller, Franck, 138, 149, 172
Müller, Guido, 65

Nardin, 81, 172
National Association of Jobbers in American Watches, 28
National Watch Company, 20, 27, 39, 53, 55, 95
Neuchâtel, 8, 16–18, 29, 34, 42, 52, 58, 62, 71, 94, 126
New Light Watch Co., 112
New York, 10, 20, 48, 53, 55, 82
Nuremberg, 21

Omega, 34, 36–37, 49, 52, 91–92, 113, 128, 143, 149–150, 177
Osaka Watch, 60–61

Paris, 18, 41, 150–151
Patek, Philippe & Cie, 43, 55, 149, 172
Peacock, 158
Perrelet, Abraham Louis, 16
Pforzheim, 77, 96, 99, 113
Philadelphia, 17, 28–30, 32, 35
Poljot, 162
Porter, Michael, 2
Prescot, 39

Raketa, 162
Rayville SA Montres Blancpain *see* Blancpain
Renley Watch Manufacturing, 157
Richemont, 1, 150, 152, 172
Ricoh Watch, 97, 131
Roamer Watch, 156
Rolex, 1, 69, 102, 105, 149, 172–173
Ronda, 107, 128
Roskopf watches, 15, 69, 88, 92, 96, 98, 102, 127–130, 135, 177
Rossini, 158
Russia, 31, 38, 52, 82–83, 110–112, 161–163, 165

Saint-Imier, 14–16, 26, 31, 49
Saint-Petersburg, 52
Samsung, 118, 122
Sandoz & Cie, 42
Saphir, 93
Schmid, Rodolphe, 61–63, 71, 81–82
Seiko, 4, 60, 81, 92, 94, 101–104, 108, 118–119, 121–123, 134, 151–155, 165, 172
Sherman Antitrust Act (1890), 28, 53
Shriro, 105–107
Siemens & Beckman, 125
Skagen Designs, 160
Smoot–Hawley Tariff Act (1930), 65, 79
Société anonyme des Spiraux français, 75
Société des fabriques de spiraux réunies SA, 71
Société des Garde-Temps, 91–92
Société générale des Monteurs de boites, 76
Société Intercantonale des Industries du Jura, 29, 31, 35
Société Suisse de Microélectronique et d'Horlogerie (SMH) *see* Swatch Group
Société Suisse pour L'industrie Horlogère SA (SSIH), 88, 91–92, 13, 128–130
Soviet Union, 1, 3, 5, 82–83, 87–89, 101, 109–112, 114, 118–119, 135, 138, 162–163, 178
Smartwatch, 173–175
Springfield Watch, 31
Stelux, 125
Swatch, 145–148
Swatch Group, 1–2, 6, 98, 126, 130, 139, 141, 143, 145–149, 152, 158, 165, 172, 178
Swikong Manufacturing, 107

Swiss Ebauches Production (Sepro) Ltd, 107
Swiss Federation of Watch Manufacturers Associations (FH), 62, 70–71, 73, 80, 87, 107, 111
Swiss Made law, 91, 107, 140–142, 151, 160–161, 165, 170–171, 178
Swiss Plating Co., 107
Swiss Time Hong Kong, 107
Swiss Watch Case Centre, 107
Switzerland, 1–3, 5–6, 8–10, 13–23, 26–27, 31–32, 37, 39–40, 43–44, 47–53, 55–58, 60–63, 65–66, 70, 72–75, 77–84, 87–88, 90–91, 94–99, 101, 105–109, 111–114, 118–121, 126–130, 132, 139–151, 156–157, 160, 162, 165, 168–172, 176, 178
Synchron SA, 92–93

TAG Heuer, 127, 150, 171, 174
Takano, 97
Tata Group, 163
Tavannes Watch, 34, 36, 49, 51, 82, 177
Technotime, 156
Texas Instruments, 130–131
Thailand, 1, 128, 142–143, 145, 152, 158, 170–171
Thiel, Gebrüder, 42
Thong Sia, 104
Thuringia, 42
Tianjin Seagull, 158
Tiffany, 55
Timex, 88, 92, 94, 96, 98–99, 107, 114, 130, 132–133, 135, 163
Tissot, Ch. & Fils, 52, 91–92, 113
Tissot, Marie, 6
Titan Industries, 163–164
Tokyo, 60, 62, 81, 102, 121
Toyota, 2
Trincano, Louis, 74–75
Truman, 77

Union des Branches Annexes de l'Horlogerie (UBAH) *see* Union of Watch-Related Branches
Union of Soviet Socialist Republics (USSR) *see* Soviet Union
Union of Watch-Related Branches (UBAH), 70–71, 80, 87, 89
United Kingdom *see* Britain
United States Time Co. *see* Timex
USSR *see* Soviet Union

Vacheron & Constantin
Vallée de Joux, 13
Vereinigte Freiburger Uhrenfabrik AG, 76–77
Virgin Islands, 95, 107
Volkswagen, 2
Vulliamy & Son, 12

Waltham, 12, 20–21, 26–28, 39, 42, 77
Waltham Watch Company *see* American Watch Company
Watchmaking Conventions, 70–73, 77, 80, 82
Watchmaking Statute, 66, 73, 83–84, 87, 90, 127, 178
Waterbury Clock Co., 53
Weil, Raymond, 172
Wristwatch, 6, 62, 67–69, 75, 79, 81, 83, 99, 177

Yema, 134
Yokohama, 59, 62, 71, 81

Zenith, 34, 49, 52, 76, 150, 172, 177
Zurich, 13, 129–130, 138

EU authorised representative for GPSR:
Easy Access System Europe, Mustamäe tee 50,
10621 Tallinn, Estonia
gpsr.requests@easproject.com